Choreographing Empathy

"This is an urgently needed book – as the question of choreographing behavior enters into realms outside of the aesthetic domains of theatrical dance, Susan Foster writes a thoroughly compelling argument."
André Lepecki, *New York University, USA*

"May well prove to be one of Susan Foster's most important works."
Ramsay Burt, *De Montford University, UK*

What do we feel when we watch dancing? Do we "dance along" inwardly? Do we sense what the dancer's body is feeling? Do we imagine what it might feel like to perform those same moves? If we do, how do these responses influence how we experience dancing and how we derive significance from it?

Choreographing Empathy challenges the idea of a direct psychophysical connection between the body of a dancer and that of their observer. In this groundbreaking investigation, Susan Foster argues that the connection is in fact highly mediated and influenced by ever-changing sociocultural mores. Foster examines the relationships among three central components in the experience of watching a dance – the choreography, the kinesthetic sensations it puts forward, and the empathetic connection that it proposes to viewers. Tracing the changing definitions of choreography, kinesthesia, and empathy from the 1700s to the present day, she shows how the observation, study, and discussion of dance have changed over time. Understanding this development is key to understanding corporeality and its involvement in the body politic.

Susan Leigh Foster, choreographer and scholar, is Distinguished Professor in the Department of World Arts and Cultures at UCLA, USA. She is the author of *Reading Dancing: Bodies and Subjects in contemporary American Dance; Choreography and Narrative: Ballet's Staging of Story and Desire*; and *Dances that Describe Themselves: The Improvised Choreography of Richard Bull*, and editor of *Choreographing History; Corporealities*; and *Worlding Dance*.

Choreographing Empathy
Kinesthesia in Performance

Susan Leigh Foster

Routledge
Taylor & Francis Group

LONDON AND NEW YORK

First published 2011 by Routledge
2 Park Square, Milton Park, Abingdon, Oxon OX14 4RN

Simultaneously published in the USA and Canada
By Routledge
711 Third Avenue, New York, NY 10017

Routledge is an imprint of the Taylor & Francis Group, an informa business

Choreographing Empathy: Kinesthesia in Performance
© 2011 Susan Leigh Foster

The right of Susan Leigh Foster to be identified as author of this work has been asserted by her in accordance with sections 77 and 78 of the Copyright, Designs and Patents Act 1988.

Typeset in Sabon by Saxon Graphics Ltd
Printed & bound in Great Britain by the MPG Books Group

British Library Cataloguing in Publication Data
A catalogue record for this book is available from the British Library

Library of Congress Cataloging in Publication Data
Foster, Susan Leigh.
Choreographing empathy : kinesthesia in performance / Susan Leigh Foster.
p. cm.
Includes bibliographical references and index.
1. Choreography. 2. Movement, Aesthetics of. I. Title.
GV1782.5.F67 2010
792.8'2--dc22
2010016753

ISBN13: 978-0-415-59655-8 hbk
ISBN13: 978-0-415-59656-5 pbk
ISBN13: 978-0-203-84070-2 ebk

Table of Contents

List of Illustrations

Acknowledgments

Over a late night aquavit, Lena Hammergren tactfully urged me to put down the flag of choreography I had been carrying, and to focus on choreography as an intertextual problem rather than a universal solution. For that suggestion and all the many delightful conversations we have had, I thank her. Ever excited to think about the connections between performance and writing, Joe Roach asked me if I might find a possible structure for this book in one of the dances I had made. I am immensely grateful to him for that suggestion as well as for the close readings and many thoughtful responses he offered to the work in progress.

George Haggerty, Sharon Salinger, and Carroll Smith-Rosenberg all fortified my knowledge of eighteenth century history in crucial ways, and I thank them for their generous assistance. Kenneth Olwig graciously entered into a lengthy email correspondence with me, a complete stranger, and provided helpful comments and suggestions. Donald Moyer's understanding of yoga has given me much greater insight into the protean nature of physicality and its relationship to language, and his teaching is a constant inspiration. Hayden White and Margaret Brose gave me invaluable insights into the project's theory and structure. A day does not go by without my thinking of them.

I am indebted to my colleagues in the *Worlding Dance* project, Jacqueline Shea Murphy, Lena Hammergren, Anthea Kraut, Priya Srinivasan, Ananya Chatterjea, Yutian Wong, and Marta Savigliano, for their conversation and insights. Thanks also to the members of the International Federation for Theater Research Working Group in Choreography and Corporeality and to David Roman, Susan Manning, Tommy DeFrantz, and Randy Martin for their comments and support. Tanya Lukin Linklater, Lea Anderson, Andrew Simonet, Pichet Klunchun, and KATHY all provided documentation of their work and generously corresponded with me about it.

Acknowledgments

I extend special thanks to the staff of UCLA's excellent libraries, who have been immensely resourceful and always ready to help. I received outstanding research and editorial assistance from Harmony Bench, and also from Cristina Rosa, Angeline Shaka, and Ana Paula Höfling, and I thank Dean Christopher Waterman for funding their work. I also thank the wonderful graduate students at UCLA, both in the MFA and PhD programs, who have cheered the project on, and engaged in critical discussions of its development. And thanks to my marvelous colleagues in Dance at UCLA who have shared with me their immense talent, humor, and devotion to dancing.

Finally, I thank my dearest Sue-Ellen, dance partner for all these years, who has always known how to read my kinesthesia.

Portions of this book were first published in the following essays, and I thank the Presses for permission to reproduce them here:

"Watching *Woman and Water*," *Theater Survey* 51, no. 1 (2010): 121–25.
"'Throwing Like a Girl?' Gender in a Transnational World," in *Contemporary Choreography: A Critical Reader*, ed. Jo Butterworth and Lisbeth Wildschut, London: Routledge, 2009, 52–64.
"Choreographies and Choreographers," in *Worlding Dance*, ed. Susan Leigh Foster, London: Palgrave Macmillan, 2009, 98–118.
"Movement's Contagion: The Kinesthetic Impact of Performance," in *Cambridge Companion to Performance Studies*, ed. Tracy C. Davis, Cambridge, England: Cambridge University Press, 2008, 46–59.
"The Earth Twice Shaken Wonderfully," *Assaph, Studies in Theatre*, Special Issue no. 21 (2007): 151–70.
"Kinesthetic Empathies and the Politics of Compassion," in *Critical Theory and Performance*, ed. Janelle Reinelt and Joseph Roach, 2d ed., Ann Arbor: University of Michigan Press, 2007.
"Choreographing Empathy," *Topoi: An International Review of Philosophy* 24, no. 1 (2005): 81–91.

Introducing Choreographing Empathy

What do we feel when we watch dancing? Do we "dance along" even without moving overtly? Do we sense what the dancer's body is feeling? Do we imagine ourselves performing those same moves? Launching buoyantly into the air? Rolling with increasing speed across the floor? Balancing on our toes? Undulating the spine? Floating? Diving? Bursting? Or pausing in stillness? Do we sway to the rhythm of the motion we see? Do we strain forward, lift upwards, or retreat backwards in response to different motions? Might we even feel our muscles stretching or straining? Our skin rushing past air or sliding across the ground? A shortness of breath? The damp from perspiration? Do we feel fear, witnessing the precariousness of the dancer's next step? Delight in its expansiveness? Anxiety from its contortedness? And to the extent that we feel any of these things, in what ways do these responses form part of or otherwise influence how we experience dancing and how we derive significance from it?

Choreographing Empathy responds to these questions by examining various claims that have been made concerning the sense of immediate and unmitigated contact between dancer and viewer. Early twentieth century dance theorist John Martin argued for a vital rapport between dancer and viewer and an equally basic connection between movement and emotion. Dance, he explained, conveys meaning because viewers, even though sitting in their seats, feel the movements and consequently the emotions of the dancer. Now at the beginning of the twenty-first century neurophysiologists are likewise claiming an intrinsic connectivity between dancer and viewer based on the discovery of mirror neurons – synaptic connections in the cortex that fire both when one sees an action and when one does that action. Although both claims argue for a fundamental physical connection between dancer and viewer, they differ markedly in their underlying presumptions about the nature of subjecthood and the way that perception takes place. Martin believed in an autonomous inner self that, impressed upon by its witnessing of the dance, responded with its unique interpretation of the dance's expression. Neuroscientists, in contrast, propose that selfhood is continually reforming as part of the ongoing process of perceiving the dance.

This study foregrounds the differences in claims such as Martin's and those of contemporary neuroscience in order to challenge the assumptions of a natural or spontaneous connection between the dancing body and the viewer's body. It seeks to demonstrate that what is often experienced as unmediated is, in fact, carefully constructed. The dancer's performance draws upon and engages with prevailing senses of the body and of subjectivity in a given historical moment. Likewise, the viewer's rapport is shaped by common and prevailing senses of the body and of subjectivity in a given social moment as well as by the unique circumstances of watching a particular dance. And these experiences of body and self have changed radically over time. In order to launch an inquiry into how dance summons its viewers into an empathic relationship with it, I have undertaken a genealogical analysis of three related terms: "choreography," "kinesthesia," and "empathy." I argue that any notion of choreography contains, embodied within it, a kinesthesis, a designated way of experiencing physicality and movement that, in turn, summons other bodies into a specific way of feeling towards it. To "choreograph empathy" thus entails the construction and cultivation of a specific physicality whose kinesthetic experience guides our perception of and connection to what another is feeling.

What is choreography?

The term "choreography" currently enjoys widespread use as referent for a structuring of movement, not necessarily the movement of human beings. Choreography can stipulate both the kinds of actions performed and their sequence or progression. Not exclusively authored by a single individual, choreography varies considerably in terms of how specific and detailed its plan of activity is. Sometimes designating minute aspects of movement, or alternatively, sketching out the broad contours of action within which variation might occur, choreography constitutes a plan or score according to which movement unfolds. Buildings choreograph space and people's movement through them; cameras choreograph cinematic action; birds perform intricate choreographies; and combat is choreographed. Multiprotein complexes choreograph DNA repair; sales representatives in call centers engage in improvisational choreography; families undergoing therapy participate in choreography; web services choreograph interfaces; and even existence is choreographed.[1]

Dances also evince or articulate a choreography, and some artists who make dances call themselves choreographers. Dance scholars have also implemented the term in a range of debates concerning dance's meaning in relation to society and politics. They have theorized the ephemerality of performance in relation to the documentation and analysis of it, and they have examined how choreography operates in relation to the construction of agency. They ask where might agency be located when dances are authorless? And, depending upon the specificity of the choreography, to what extent do dancers exert agency in their individual performances of it? They have also considered the relationship of choreography to issues of ownership in dance and how choreography has participated in arguments concerning access to copyright.

Sometimes choreography is construed as being in opposition to improvised or spontaneous elements in the dance performance. At other times, it is interpreted as a score or set of principles that guide spontaneous invention. In her study of contact improvisation, *Sharing the Dance*, Cynthia Novack observed that the modern dance tradition out of which contact improvisation emerged typically posed an opposition between choreography and improvisation, envisioning improvisation as a creative method that could be implemented in support of choreography as the making of a dance. Contact improvisors, in contrast, eschewed choreography as the formal and crafted shaping of movement for presentation to viewers, preferring instead to focus intensively on the moving point of contact between two bodies and the concomitant and unpredictable unfolding of movement produced by that focus. Sensitive to their pursuit of an informal, spontaneous and open-ended exploration of movement possibilities, Novack identified the central and underlying precepts governing the generation of movement in contact improvisation – sensing with the skin, using 360 degree space, going with the momentum, etc. – as forming a style of moving.[2] She posited that the practice of these precepts generated meaning that permeated the individual and social lives of the dancers. Thus, "Going with the flow" was a value to be embraced in dance and in everyday life.

Novack argued persuasively for dance as a site capable of producing, and not just reflecting, key cultural values and concerns, including notions of gender, class, and race. Along similar lines, Randy Martin, Mark Franko, and Thomas DeFrantz have challenged the notion that choreography operates only in an aesthetic register separated from social or political realms of experience. Martin has identified choreography's capacity to summon together bodies whose exuberant expenditure of effort defies traditional economic theories and offers, instead, a new vision of what political mobilization might be.[3] He has also examined the ideological effects of specific choreographic structures.[4] Aligning dance with labor, Franko imbues choreography with the ability to organize "the physical potentials and limitations of the human body's movement," and, consequently, to represent the social and political consequences of a given action.[5] DeFrantz locates choreography at a nexus of physical and representational events that includes the arrangement of motion, formulations of gender and sexuality, beauty and class mobility, and also an "unusual nodule of everyday American politics . . ."[6] All three scholars envision dance movement and its organization as containing and purveying a politics.

Rather than defining choreography in terms of its capacity to formulate guidelines for action, André Lepecki explores its function as, what he calls, an "apparatus of capture."[7] Similar to the arguments made by Peggy Phelan concerning the ephemerality of performance, Lepecki locates the dance in an always vanishing present and charges choreography with the role of pinning the dance down. It thereby performs reductively to designate and stand in for only a residue of the actual dancing. At the same time, it opens up the potential to celebrate the dance's vitality as an effect of its liveness or presence. As Diana Taylor points out, however, this approach forecloses consideration of the ways that performance endures in cultural and individual imaginaries and how, as a result, aspects of its form persist in time. By bringing into liveness various values and what she calls "scenarios" that render visible power relations, any performance creates a trace whose ideological impact can be examined and evaluated.[8]

In a series of publications engaging with the term, I have proposed that "choreography" can productively be conceptualized as a theorization of identity – corporeal, individual, and social. Working to contest the reception of dance as the presentation of a kind of spectacle without a history or methodology for engaging with the physical, I initially envisioned choreography as the hypothetical setting forth of what the body is and what it can be based on the decisions made in rehearsal and in performance about its identity. Each moment of watching a dance can be read as the product of choices, inherited, invented, or selected, about what kinds of bodies and subjects are being constructed and what kinds of arguments about these bodies and subjects are being put forth. These decisions, made collectively or individually, spontaneously or in advance of dancing, constitute a kind of record of action that is durable and makes possible both the repetition of a dance and analysis of it.

Approaching choreography as this kind of theorizing about what a body can be and do makes evident the ways in which dance articulates with social, aesthetic, and political values. Expanding choreography to include what Novack identified as movement style, I argued, like her, that the implementation of choices both produces and reflects these values.

Subsequently, I argued for the further expansion of choreography to encompass a consideration of all manner of human movement including the operations of gender in constructing masculine and feminine roles and the guidelines according to which protestors have conducted nonviolent direct action.[9] Proposing a dialectical tension between choreography and performance, I emphasized the ways that choreography presents a structuring of deep and enduring cultural values that replicates similar sets of values elaborated in other cultural practices whereas performance emphasizes the idiosyncratic interpretation of those values. Not a permanent, structural engagement with representation, but rather a slowly changing constellation of representational conventions, choreography, more than any performance, is what resonates with other systems of representation that together constitute the cultural moment within which all bodies circulate. Both choreography and performance change over time; both select from and move into action certain semantic systems, and as such, they derive their meaning from a specific historical and cultural moment. And both offer potential for agency to be constructed via every body's specific engagement with the parameters governing the realization of each dance.

Pointing to the claims for universality inherent in my arguments, Marta Savigliano and Jens Giersdorf have both questioned the viability of choreography as a rubric within which to contemplate not only all kinds of dances but also the larger choreographies of social action of which they are a part. Savigliano reflects on the two sets of archives within which documentation on dance has been collected – the arts archives that emphasize aesthetic features and the ethnographic archives that probe dance's social function.[10] She sees "choreography" as a term implemented as a means of suturing together these two domains of knowledge production. In the process of unifying the social and the aesthetic, however, the use of choreography threatens to erase the histories of violence to dances and dancers that are embodied in each archive's distinctive formation. Giersdorf likewise questions the potential loss of specificity that such a definition of choreography entails, noting that it could become an unmarked strategy within transnational academic and artistic exchange that would work complicit with other forces in globalization to erase difference.[11] Anthea Kraut compounds these reservations about the utility of the term by excavating choreography's role in excluding certain kinds of dance practices, often improvised or occurring in popular rather than elite venues, from the various canons of dance history.[12]

In response to these reflections on the term "choreography" and also to the emerging demands of the new global stage, this book conducts a genealogical inquiry into the term "choreography." Observing the accommodations, sometimes uneasy, that the world's dancers are making to the global stage, given its demands for distinctive blends of tradition suffused with experimentation, and generalized spectacle embedded with local detail, I determined to excavate histories of the term and its usage that undoubtedly bear down on our contemporary moment. Noting my own students' hesitations to identify a choreography as separate from a performance and from a history of practicing a given form of dance, I have endeavored to decenter choreography from functioning as an explanatory rubric, and instead, to highlight the dilemmas that the term embodies.

Thus Chapter 1 surveys various iterations of the term beginning with its neologization in the eighteenth century as the practice of recording dances on paper through the use of a taxonomic system of symbols. I examine the assumptions underlying the notations, and discuss the consequences of breaking movement down into principles of action that locate dance within a blank geometrized space where the floorpath of the dancer can be tracked and recorded. Assessing the impact of these early dance notations on the development of dance technique, dance authorship, and the autonomy of dance as an art form, I show how the notation helped to partition dance-making from learning to dance and teaching dances. I then analyze the reemergence of choreography at the beginning of the twentieth century as the individual act of creating a dance, focusing on pedagogies of dance composition and charting the development of choreography from the act of expressing deeply felt emotions at the beginning of the century to the current practice of facilitating a collaborative encounter among dancers, directors, and artists in allied mediums. Throughout, I consider how choreography, whether as notation or as composition, functions to privilege certain kinds of dancing while rejecting or repressing others.

What is kinesthesia?

Especially when compared with the widespread application of the term "choreography," remarkably little use of the term "kinesthesia" has been made in scholarly or public domains. Often derided or dismissed within the academy, kinesthesia and the information it might provide have typically been received with skepticism at best. Pervasive mistrust of the body and the classification of its information as either sexual, unknowable, or indecipherable, have resulted in a paucity of activities that promote awareness of the body's position and motion, or the degree of tension in its muscles. The term has been sporadically referenced and investigated in medicine and neurobiology, and more consistently in kinesiology textbooks and dance pedagogy, but otherwise rarely appears in discourse.

Kinesthesia was coined in 1880, in response to a growing body of research establishing the existence of nerve sensors in the muscles and joints that provide awareness of the body's positions and movements. The meaning of the term has been expanded, abandoned, and revised several times over the course of the twentieth century. At the beginning of the twentieth century, kinesthesia was largely replaced in neurological investigations by the concept of proprioception, naming a more focused system of spinal-level neural arcs that continually adjust for the body's changing relationship to gravity. At mid-century it was revived by perceptual psychologist James J. Gibson, who envisioned kinesthesia as a perceptual system that synthesized information about joint positioning, muscular exertion, and orientation within space and with respect to gravity. Gibson further posited that kinesthesia assisted in integrating sensory information from all other systems. More recently it has been taken up in the work of neurobiologists exploring how the brain senses bodily movement.

If physiological inquiries into kinesthesia have been somewhat sporadic, dance pedagogy and criticism have consistently cultivated understanding of the existence and importance of kinesthetic awareness. John Martin based his entire theory of how dance communicates upon the assertion that viewers actively partake in the same kinesthetic experience as the dancers they are watching onstage:

> When we see a human body moving, we see movement which is potentially produced by any human body, and therefore by our own . . . through kinesthetic sympathy we actually reproduce it vicariously in our present muscular experience and awaken such associational connotations as might have been ours if the original movement had been of our own making.[13]

Working to validate and champion the new modern dance, he further argued that kinesthetic experience was intrinsically connected to emotional experience. Noting the new cultivation of movement's rhythm and tensility pursued by early modern dancers such as Isadora Duncan, Mary Wigman and Martha Graham, Susan Manning and Dee Reynolds have examined these artists' elaboration of kinesthesia as a central component of modernism.[14]

Focusing more on the ability of the dance researcher to perceive her own kinesthetic experience along with that of others, Diedre Sklar argues for kinesthetic analysis as a crucial methodology in understanding cultural distinctiveness not only in dance but also in all aspects of daily life.[15] For Sklar kinesthetic analysis entails attending to the qualitative dimensions of movement, the kind of flow, tension, and timing of any given action as well as the ways in which any person's movement interacts and interrelates with objects, events, and other people. Deepening Bourdieu's concept of the habitus by taking the example of religious worship and examining in detail the kinds of movement patterns practiced at specific events, Sklar, like Bourdieu, imbues these patterns with symbolic meaning. Taken together, these patterns constitute a way of knowing in a given cultural context, a form of embodied knowledge in which "are stored intertwined corporeal, emotional, and conceptual memories."[16]

Similarly, Randy Martin posits the existence of a social kinesthetic, a set of movement attributes or traits that make evident the "deeper affinities between movement and culture."[17] Where Sklar considers in detail how movement repertoires engage with religious and gendered symbolic systems, Martin emphasizes the politics implicit in a given kinesthesis. He posits a connection between a decolonized worldview and a preference for decentered movement, and points to the range of contemporary practices including capoiera, contact improvisation, and hip-hop that celebrate an off-balance and risk-oriented investigation of the body's capacities for movement. That bodies might develop such diverse movement practices that nonetheless share common preferences for moving illustrates a crucial feature of diversity in today's globalized world.

Like Sklar and Martin, Lena Hammergren focuses on the connection between kinesthetic experience and cultural values. Unlike them, she utilizes the kinesthetic as a framework for organizing aspects of physical experience that would help the historian reconstruct performance and value systems from an earlier time.[18] Remodeling Walter Benjamin's concept of the flâneur with its emphasis on visual information, Hammergren introduces the flâneuse as a figure whose kinesthetic engagement with her surroundings in terms of touch, smell, and physical action, amplifies the historian's access to the past. Hammergren sends her flâneuse on a hypothetical stroll around the 1930 Stockholm Exposition, where she is able to synthesize information from multiple documents and sources that all provide clues to the kinesthetic experience of engaging with the vision of modernity promulgated by the exposition's architecture, dining, and entertainment offerings. By noting the feel of doorknobs, the smell of flowers or rye bread, and the spectacles of social dancing and gymnastic exercises, the flâneuse registers a different story about the event and its historical moment.

This study also focuses on the experience of kinesthesia in past moments and on how that experience might have changed over time. Although the term "kinesthesia" was invented only at the end of the nineteenth century, Chapter 2, aligned with the history of choreography presented in Chapter 1, first examines early eighteenth-century practices of bodily disciplining in order to establish general features of physicality that indicate how people might have experienced the body and movement. In so doing, it historicizes the invention of the term while also asserting the enduring yet specific nature of kinesthetic experience. Considering the assumptions about the nature of the body implicit in a wide variety of sources, including cartography, medicine, courtesy and conduct literature, and physical education, it endeavors to ascertain standards of physicality in a given historical moment and from these to infer a normative experience of kinesthesia. Dancing, I argue, developed alongside these other practices, both drawing upon and producing a kinesthetic experience similar to the one yielded up in these other activities. Yet dancing also foregrounded the production of kinesthetic experience, making it an important source for how the body and its movement are experienced in a given historical moment.

The chapter tracks the transformation of the Galenic conception of the body as a sack of sloshing humours into a physicality displaying an erect posture and acquiring the ability to maintain an awareness of its own movements through space. It demonstrates that choreography was only one of many practices that encouraged this awareness of one's body, configured almost as a vertical silhouette located on a blank horizontal grid. I then show how the body assumed an increasingly volumetric and dynamic forcefulness over the course of the nineteenth century, and how its musculature, itself a concept only invented in the late nineteenth century, came to play an increasingly important role in self-presentation. By the early twentieth century, the body was no longer experienced as a mechanics of pulleys and levers, but instead, as a tensile and momentum-driven force that alternately exerts and relaxes in relation to gravity. At mid-century the body transformed yet again into a vehicle for exploring consciousness and its many modalities. James Gibson drew upon this experience of physicality in his pioneering work in perception. Mirror neuron theorists, in turn, draw upon Gibson's work as precursor to their own interpretation of mirror neuron functions, yet they also envision the body as a network. I associate their neurological inquiries with new disorienting and orienting practices such as the cellphone and GPS navigation systems, all of which are helping to produce a new kind of kinesthetic experience as well as a new awareness of that experience.

What is empathy?

Invented in the same decade as the term "kinesthesia," "empathy" was coined by German aestheticians seeking to describe and analyze in depth the act of viewing painting and sculpture. Calling the experience Einfühlung, they posited a kind of physical connection between viewer and art in which the viewer's own body would move into and inhabit the various features of the artwork. When the term first came into English language usage at the beginning of the twentieth century, it likewise connoted a strong physical responsiveness to both people and objects. Over the course of the twentieth century, however, the term, like "kinesthesia," changed substantially, eventually residing within the domain of psychology where it has been investigated largely as an emotional, and not physical experience. Sklar, for example, calling for recognition of the fact that empathy entails a kinesthetic level of recognition, names her own technique for observing the actions of others a practice of "kinesthetic empathy."[19] The fact that the experience of empathy needs to be qualified with the adjective "kinesthetic" belies the pervasive assumption that emotional and physical experiences are separate.

In keeping with the original usage of the term, Chapter 3 explores how empathy has been variously conceptualized in relation to physical experience. In tandem with the genealogies of choreography and kinesthesia, it first looks to the antecedents of empathy proposed in the early eighteenth century in theories of sympathy such as those of Bernard Lamy, Abbé DuBos, and David Hume and the refinements to these made by Adam Smith. During the eighteenth century, sympathy was most often theorized as a form of fellow-feeling, the product of "delicate nerve fibers" reacting to the sorrow or joy of another. Both the individual's expression and demeanor, and also the entire scene affecting the object of one's sympathy needed to be evaluated in order for a sympathetic reaction to occur. When empathy was neologized in the 1880s, it functioned quite differently, as a process in which one's entire physicality comes to inhabit the other. Early twentieth century theories, such as those of Vernon Lee and John Martin, included a strong kinesthetic component in which the observer's sense of their own physicality plays a central role. Seen from this perspective, the term "empathy" was invented not to express a new capacity for fellow-feeling, but to register a changing sense of physicality that, in turn, influenced how one felt another's feelings. As the body acquired a musculature and transformed into a volumetric and dynamic organism, the entire project of inhabiting another's situation or feelings likewise changed. Instead of casting one's self into the position of the other, it became necessary to project one's three-dimensional structure into the energy and action of the other. Although empathy was subsequently taken up in psychotherapies, where it became associated with emotional reactions, its kinesthetic dimension has more recently been reintegrated in the neuroscientific investigations of mirror neurons.

Alongside this tracking of the concept of empathy, the chapter poses the question of the power relations inherent between those who feel and those who feel for or with them. Although a large number of scholarly works examine empathy as an aesthetic and social theory, little of it places this work within the context of Britain's discovery of the new world and subsequent colonial expansion. The history of sympathy and then empathy when placed in parallel with the history of colonization helps to explain how the British evaluated and responded to the foreigners whom they encountered in North America, Asia, and the Pacific. Sympathy and empathy each served to establish the grounds on which one human being could be seen as differing from another. Like the term "choreography," they were mobilized, in part, to rationalize operations of exclusion and othering.

Correspondances

The structure of this book is modeled after an evening-length dance I choreographed in 1979 entitled *Correspondances*. In that work I dance and talk about the dancing, recording my voice and the sounds of the dancing, for about 15 minutes. Then, the recording is played back while I dance and talk again, this time about a different aspect of dancing. The process is repeated a third and fourth time, with the commentary moving from the structure of the choreography to the movement vocabulary to the style of motion, culminating in a fourth segment, where I "write a letter" to a dear friend about the ways dance can mean. One of the delights in performing this semi-improvised work was to leave silences for subsequent dialogues among the voices, and to ask questions that I might then answer when the tracks were replayed. Since some of the commentary was humorous, audience members sometimes laughed, and that response was also recorded and played back. The piece constituted a kind of meditation on different ways that one can think about dancing and also on a different experience of time in which past and present coexist and reverberate with one another.

In patterning this book after *Correspondances*, I have written the first three chapters, on choreography, kinesthesia, and empathy respectively, trying to achieve equivalent lengths for each of their sections and for the lengths of the chapters as a whole so that they could well be placed on a single page in columns side by side. Like the letter I write to my friend, the fourth chapter, offers an overview of the previous three, examining the ways that choreography, kinesthesia, and empathy work together, using as examples performances by artists from diverse backgrounds – Tanya Lukin-Linklater, Rimini Protokoll, Headlong Dance Theater, Jérôme Bel, Pichet Klunchun, Lea Anderson, and KATHY. I gravitated towards this organization for the book in order to foreground the partial nature of genealogical inquiry. Rather than strive for a comprehensive account of all three terms, as if that could exist, what I hope to provoke is an awareness of how productive it might be to consider these terms or similar ones alongside each other, whatever the frame, or specificity of a given inquiry.

Just as *Correspondances* created a co-presence of different moments in the dance, each of the first three chapters offers a non-chronological account, beginning in the present, moving to around 1700, then to earlier meanings of the terms, before considering more recent practices. Focusing largely on English language implementations of the terms, this inquiry examines moments where there is a density or concentration of usage. As a result, the analysis considers British uses of dance notation in the eighteenth century, U.S. uses of choreography as the art of making dances in the early twentieth century, and a more international discourse around the terms in the late twentieth and twenty-first centuries. It also moves from a consideration of ballet and aristocratic social dance practices in the eighteenth century to modern dance in the early twentieth century, where, I would argue, the most urgent discourses around choreography and kinesthesia developed. Often, I look to dance pedagogy, rather than to individual artists, in order to illustrate more fully how the terms themselves were comprehended and implemented.

One of the principle goals of this project is to demonstrate how dance practices have been aligned with rather than isolated from other forms of cultural and knowledge production, including anatomy and medicine, cartography, etiquette and social comportment, and physical education.[20] Approaching these various practices as forms of physicalized discourse, I analyze how they each contributed to the formation of a specific experience of the body and of subjecthood. Emphasizing the congruencies among these practices rather than their differences, I show how they function collectively to establish a specific conception of the body and its parts and to organize protocols for shaping and fashioning the body and training its movements. This disciplining of the body produces a distinctive kinesthetic sense of the body, and it is this experience of the body, its movement, and its location that, in turn, sets the limits and conditions within which an empathetic connection to another can emerge.

A second goal has been to examine dance in relation to the history of inquiries into sympathy/empathy. Both concert and social dance forms call out to their viewers to be received and interpreted in specific ways, and this rhetoric of address to their audience has changed over time. Theories of sympathy/empathy also analyze the empathetic encounter as if it were a performance, staging the moment of connection by describing the positions, movements, and feelings of all those involved. Again focusing on congruencies, I show how dance's manner of address has changed in tandem with the theories of sympathy/ empathy and how each discourse, one danced and the other written, can illuminate the workings of the other.

Choreography, kinesthesia, and empathy function together to construct corporeality in a given historical and cultural moment. By looking at them alongside one another over time, it is possible to argue for the existence of corporeal epistemes that participate in the production of knowledge and the structuring of power. In analyzing the contours of each of these epistemes, certain themes emerged as productive frameworks for illuminating their ideological operations and efficacy. Land or ground became a central concept that helped to elucidate how dance notation functioned and also how kinesthesia has been variously conceptualized. In many ways equivalent to the body, land, especially in its transformation into property, has been parsed and parceled using strategies very similar to those implemented for disciplining the body. Gender has also functioned as a critical analytic frame for understanding how corporeality has changed time. Not only do dancers perform specific constructions of gender, and various bodily practices cultivate specifically gendered identities, but the very notion of choreography itself has been variously gendered over time. The notion of economy has also served to illustrate important connections between dance and other forms of cultural production. Dance, as Franko, Martin, and

Savigliano have all demonstrated, is a process through which wealth can be acquired, negotiated, and dispensed. And finally, the world's dances have posed an enduring question concerning how English language meanings of choreography, kinesthesia, and empathy have been mobilized to encounter them. I hope to show that a critical assessment of the underlying assumptions used to rationalize aesthetic and emotional understanding of dancing is essential to establishing a more egalitarian dialogue among and about dances worldwide.

Although partial and one of many narratives that might be told about how bodies feel and how they feel about each other, the ecological and political crises of our times call out for synthesizing perspectives on our situation, and I hope that this book offers one such perspective. Postcolonial and gender studies have provided invaluable techniques for historicizing and particularizing experience, yet they must continue to grapple with the nature and constitution of what is shared or communal within experience. In order not to risk excessive focus on the individual, they must continue to ask: Is there something we could call women's experience? Or, can the subaltern speak? And these debates recur in theories of dance history and dance spectatorship: how and what do viewers feel watching a dancer execute a particularly demanding or spectacular movement such as those performed by the rope dancers of the eighteenth century? How and what can scholars claim about what viewers might have felt watching another body performing in some past moment and/or distant place? These epistemological dilemmas lie at the center of dance studies, but they have equal relevance for the humanities more generally. For example, human rights discourses, especially in this moment of transnational and global consolidation, implement arguments in favor of partiality and universality of experience both to justify and contest the workings of power. Are there any frameworks within which to affirm the located and partial understanding yielded up in the empathetic moment of witnessing another body? Are there ways in which a shared physical semiosis might enable bodies, in all their historical and cultural specificity, to commune with one another? Are there techniques of knowledge production that invite us to imagine the other without presuming knowledge of the other? *Choreographing Empathy* does not provide answers to these questions, but instead offers a way of reflecting on them.

1 Choreography

In the last year I have seen the word "choreography" used in our local newspaper, the *Los Angeles Times*, to describe troop movements in the war in Iraq, the motions of dog whisperer Cesar Millan, the management of discussion at board meetings, and even the coordination of traffic lights for commuter flow – all these applications of the term in addition to the patterning of movement observed in a dance. This variety of usages suggests that choreography has come to refer to a plan or orchestration of bodies in motion. And in this refined definition, the plan is distinguished from its implementation and from the skills necessary for its execution. Choreography would seem to apply to the structuring of movement in highly diverse occasions, yet always where some kind of order is desired to regulate that movement.

At the same time that the term is proliferating beyond the context of dance, it is also being ignored or suppressed within certain dance events. In their first seasons, two recent and highly popular TV shows that feature dance, *So You Think You Can Dance* and *Dancing With the Stars*, consistently refrained from addressing the creative process of selecting and sequencing the movement that was performed. Although the young artists who auditioned for *So You Think You Can Dance* devised their own original dance in order to be eligible, once they were accepted onto the show, they were placed in technique classes for weeks and judged, not on the basis of their compositional skills, but instead on their abilities to "take class" – that is, to faithfully copy what another body was doing and then perform that movement fully. Over subsequent seasons, more emphasis has been placed on the choreographers who provide the audition pieces, however, their work is championed as exemplary of a particular tradition of dancing – jive, contemporary, or jazz, among others – and the emphasis of the competition has remained on the execution of that tradition. Similarly, the "trainer-partners" on *Dancing With the Stars* who make up the routines that make the stars look good in performance are only credited with being excellent dancers and partners. Why ignore or suppress their labor? Both programs seem to promote a pure or natural performance, achieved by hard work at disciplining the body but not at crafting its motions. Is this a function of their reluctance to imagine that one's identity can be and is shaped through the moves one makes? Or does it follow from the distinctions to which they may be conforming between dance as "art," emphasizing composition and creativity, and dance as "social" or "popular" pastime?

The *Oxford English Dictionary* offers two definitions for the word "choreography": the first, a simple assertion, informs us that choreography is "the art of dancing"; and the second, marked as an obsolete usage, refers to choreography as "the art of writing dances on paper." The first definition identifies all aspects of dance as choreographic, whether the process of teaching someone how to dance, the act of learning to dance, the event of performing a dance, or the labor of creating a dance. The second definition, used perhaps for the last time by Rudolph Laban in his *Choreutics* (1966), specifies choreographers as those who endeavor to notate the spatial and rhythmic properties of movement through the use of abstract symbols. Neither definition seems to convey its current usage as the act of arranging patterns of movement.

This chapter traces the various meanings and usages of choreography since its first widespread implementation in the early eighteenth century. It examines how the practice of choreography, just as in the TV shows' or newspaper's versions of the term, has served to validate some forms of dancing while excluding others. In its eighteenth century meaning as the art of notating dances, choreography provided the basis upon which the separation of making, performing, and learning dance took place. It likewise set forth criteria for technical skill and virtuosity in dancing. And it established the means through which dances from around the world could be categorized. Falling out of use in the nineteenth century, choreography reemerged in the early twentieth century as the process of individual expression through movement. Since that time the notion of choreography has been challenged, expanded and transformed, its meanings proliferating even as it continues to instantiate typologies of dance with distinctive artistic and social merit.

The word "choreography" derives from two Greek words, *choreia*, the synthesis of dance, rhythm, and vocal harmony manifest in the Greek chorus; and graph, the act of writing.[1] The first uses of the term, however, are intertwined with two other Greek roots, *orches*, the place between the stage and the audience where the chorus performed, and *chora*, a more general notion of space, sometimes used in reference to a countryside or region. Where *choreia* describes a process of integrating movement, rhythm, and voice, both *orches* and *chora* name places. Four of the earliest efforts to notate dances draw upon these three Greek roots: Thoinot Arbeau's treatise on dancing, sword play, and drumming, *Orchésographie* (1589); Raoul Auger Feuillet's *Chorégraphie* (1700); Weaver's translation of Feuillet, *Orchesography* (1706); and John Essex's application of Feuillet's system to English country dances, *For the Further Improvement of Dancing, A Treatise of Chorography* (1710).

Both *orches* and *choreia* had long been associated with dance. The Dutch classicist Johannes Meursius, who inventoried every reference to dance in ancient Greek texts, published his findings under the title *Orchestra* in 1618.[2] Choreography itself, however, has had a shorter life in the English language. It was first used at the end of the eighteenth century to refer back to the practice of notating dances, instigated at the beginning of that century when Feuillet's *Chorégraphie* was first translated by Weaver. In contrast, chorography, Essex's subtitle for his adaptation of Feuillet notation, signaled his effort to neologize a new English word, or else to indicate a connection between the newly invented notation and the well-known sub-discipline of geography known as chorography. Concentrating on the study of a region or landscape, chorography developed intensively in England during the sixteenth and seventeenth centuries as a practice of mapping and also describing and analyzing a locale's terrain and inhabitants. Perhaps Essex, who would have known this meaning of the term, hoped to suggest an analogy between traditional chorographies and his notation which focused on the routes taken by dancers in a variety of line dances performed by multiple couples.

Although we cannot know what motivated each of the authors to name their treatises as they did, the proliferation of titles, all referencing the same project, signals a complex relationship between process and place, a relationship that was then translated into a written document. Choreography thus began its life as the act of reconciling movement, place, and printed symbol. The project of translating from moving bodies to words and symbols was embraced by all these authors as both imminently achievable and a hallmark of progress. They saw no opposition between the written and the live, nor did they lament the potential loss of some aspect of movement that might not be documentable. (This sentimental notion of documentation emerges more in the nineteenth and twentieth centuries.) Instead, the first choreographers presumed that their contributions to documenting dance would better preserve it for subsequent generations and, in addition, improve the status of dance.[3] What exactly did they document and how did their efforts work to construct a relationship between movement and its surroundings?

Inventories and taxonomies

Sometime in the 1670s, Louis XIV ordered principal Dancing Master Pierre Beauchamps to "discover the means of making the art of dance comprehensible on paper." According to Beauchamps he set about to apply "himself to shaping and disposing characters and notes in the form of tablature in order to represent the steps of the dances and ballets performed before the king and at the Opera" in such a way that the dances could be learned "without need of personal instruction."[4] Along with Beauchamps's system, at least three other distinctive notation systems emerged in response to Louis's mandate, yet Feuillet's collection from 1700 utilizing Beauchamps' system predominated, becoming so popular that new collections of dances in notated form were distributed annually through the 1730s, and Feuillet notation, as it came to be called, was widely adopted in England and throughout northern Europe.

These collections of notated dances documented a small number of theatrical dances, mostly solos, as well as a variety of dances to be taught and then performed at aristocratic balls and other social gatherings. They fortified teachers with new material with which to instruct their students and alerted practitioners to some of the latest fashions in the art of dancing. They did not thoroughly detail dancing on any of the various stages, whether the elite, licensed productions of the Opera or the experiments with pantomime at the fair theaters.[5] Nor did they document the kind of aesthetic traffic in styles and vocabularies proliferated by itinerant companies of dancers who traveled back and forth across the continent and to England. Nonetheless, this regularization of dances so that they might travel and be reproduced "without the aid of personal instruction" profoundly influenced both the conceptualization of dancing and the categorization of diverse dances.

Feuillet's system first posited the existence of a small number of essential elements from which dancing was composed: "Positions, Steps, Sinkings, Risings, Springings, Capers, Fallings, Slidings, Turnings of the Body, Cadence or Time, Figures, etc."[6] The system then integrated these elements into a single planimetric representation of the dancing body that highlighted its directionality, the path it took through space,

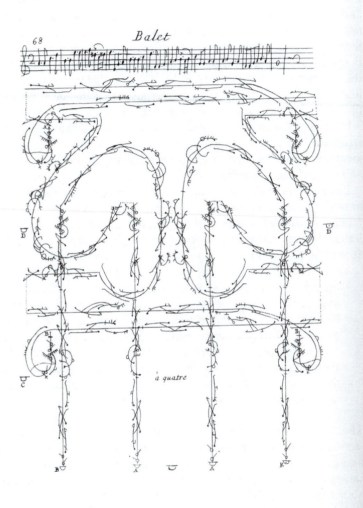

Figure 1.1 This excerpt from a "Balet for Nine Dancers," collected in Raoul Auger Feuillet's *Recueil de Danse* (1703) shows the symmetrical and interweaving patterns of dancers' floorpaths as they progress across the room. Courtesy of University of California, Los Angeles, Performing Arts Special Collections Library

and the motions of the feet and legs. Sinking, rising and springing were measured in terms of the body's vertical positioning, whereas sliding and turning marked its horizontal progress through space. A single line notating the dancer's path was embellished on either side by characters indicating the position and action of the feet – the direction in which they extend, their height, on the ground, on half point, or jumping in the air, and their interactivity in beating, paralleling, or turning. The line marking the body's path through space also referenced the vertical placement of the body since it suggested the basis for one leg or the other to gesticulate on either side of a continuous and stable skeletal structure. Thus the graphing of motion summoned the body into and located it within a geometrically defined grid stipulating both horizontal and vertical positionings.[7]

Prior efforts at documenting dances did not systematize movement in this way. Instead, they listed the sequence of steps with occasional references to spatial path and facings for each dancer. For example, Italian Dancing Master Fabritio Caroso's explanation of the Laura Suave (Gentle Lady) in 1581 included this description:

> the gentleman does a symmetrical variation . . . [of] two limping hops with the left foot raised and the right limping, two fast half Reverences . . . two falling jumps, one foot under with the left and a cadence with the left forward; repeat beginning with the right. The lady does two doubles in French style . . . two double scurrying sequences together, turning first to the left and then to the right in the shape of an S; and approaching each other, they take customary hands.[8]

The "reverences," "falling jumps," and "doubles" referred to here were standard steps in the sixteenth century court dance repertoire.[9] A major innovation of Dancing Master Thoinot Arbeau, who first made the effort to notate these dances in 1589, consisted in substituting abbreviations for the names of the steps.

Arbeau's *Orchesography* was organized around a dialogue between instructor and student who, together, produce the classifications and descriptions of specific dances. Although the ostensible aim of the manuscript was to record dances so that "posterity" would not "remain ignorant of all these new dances," Arbeau could not escape entirely from the physical interactivity of dancing and learning to dance.[10] As his eager student Capriol sought guidance in one dance after another, asking questions about one aspect of the movement and then another, Arbeau was prompted to reveal how the dances were each related one to another, and hence, to specify an order in which to learn them. For each dance Arbeau recounted a brief history and a general sense of the function and feeling of the dance, whether solemn, lively, sedate, or gay. He then identified a basic set of steps and placed these alongside the musical accompaniment in order to indicate their sequence and timing. He also accompanied this notation with a narrative of the experience of performing each particular dance that indicated changes in direction from one step to the next, engagement with one's partner, and a suggested path for the dancers to take through the room.

For example, in describing La Volta Arbeau began by asking Capriol to place himself,

> hypothetically, facing me with *pieds joints*. For the first step, make a rather short *pied en l'air* while springing on to your left foot and at the same time turning your left shoulder towards me. Then take a rather long second step with your right foot, without springing, and in so doing, turn you back to me.[11]

Arbeau continued his narration by examining the relationship of the partners in this dance that is full of turns:

> he who dances the lavolta must regard himself as the centre of a circle and draw the damsel as near to him as possible when he wishes to turn . . . To bring her nearer to you proceed as follows:
> Make your *révéverance* . . . and before you begin turning take a few steps around the room, by way of preparation . . . When you wish to turn release the damsel's left hand and throw your left arm around her, grasping and holding her firmly by the waist above the right hip with your left hand. At the same moment place your right hand below her busk to help her to leap when you push her forward with your left thigh. She, for her part, will place her right hand on your back or collar and her left hand on her thigh to hold her petticoat and dress in place, lest the swirling air should catch them and reveal her chemise or bare thigh.[12]

Although La Volta required far more detailed descriptions of the partnering than many of the other dances, Arbeau's narrative nonetheless presents the categories that he found it necessary to discuss in order to comprehensively account for any dance: the steps, their size, their timing and sequence (indicated through their placement alongside the musical notation), the location of the dancers in space, their protocols

zardez & intereſſez. Ie vous en ay deſia dit mon opinion.

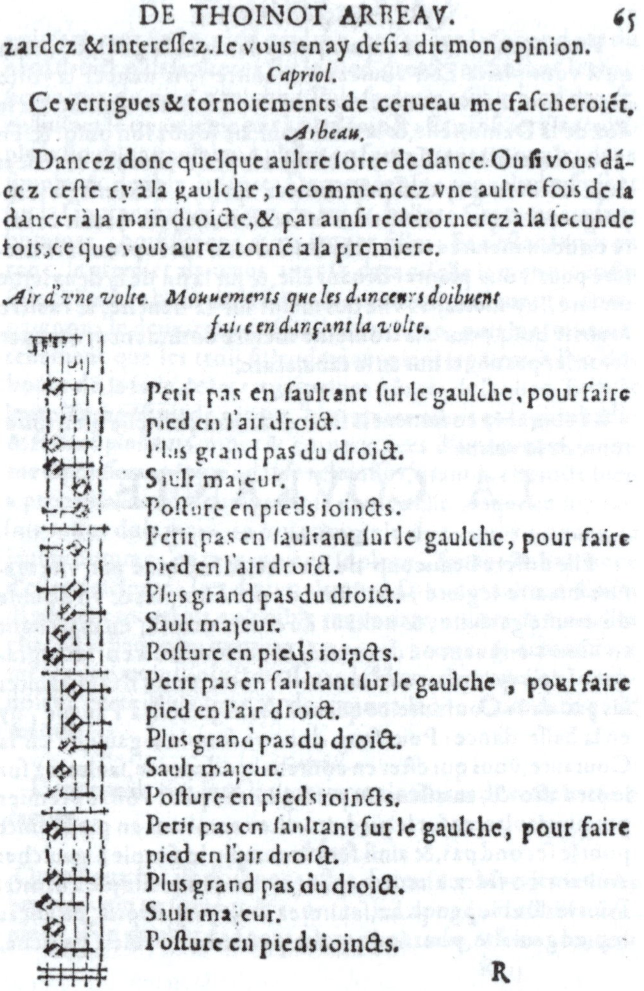

Capriol.

Ce vertigues & tornoiements de cerueau me faſcheroiét.

Arbeau.

Dancez donc quelque aultre ſorte de dance. Ou ſi vous dá-
cez ceſte cy à la gaulche, recommencez vne aultre fois de la
dancer à la main droicte, & par ainſi redetornerez à la ſecunde
fois, ce que vous aurez torné a la premiere.

*Air d'vne volte. Mouvements que les danceurs doibuent
faire en dançant la volte.*

Petit pas en ſaultant ſur le gaulche, pour faire
pied en l'air droict.

Plus grand pas du droict.

Sault maieur.

Poſture en pieds ioincts.

Petit pas en ſaultant ſur le gaulche, pour faire
pied en l'air droict.

Plus grand pas du droict.

Sault maieur.

Poſture en pieds ioincts.

Petit pas en ſaultant ſur le gaulche, pour faire
pied en l'air droict.

Plus grand pas du droict.

Sault maieur.

Poſture en pieds ioincts.

Petit pas en ſaultant ſur le gaulche, pour faire
pied en l'air droict.

Plus grand pas du droict.

Sault maieur.

Poſture en pieds ioincts.

R

Figure 1.2 In this description of La Volta, Arbeau concludes his narrative account of the dance with a step-by-step set of directions, aligned with the melody of the music.

From: Thoinot Arbeau. *Orchésographie: traité en forme de dialogue par lequel toutes personnes peuvent facilement apprendre et pratiquer l'honnê exercice des danses.* Dominique Guéniot, éditeur. Facsimilie. 1988 of touch, and in some cases, the dancers' experience of it. (In the case of La Volta, its performance frequently made one quite dizzy.)

Feuillet's system differed markedly from these earlier attempts to record dances because it broke steps, such as a skip, a turn, or a triplet, down into constituent parts, posited as universal actions. Whereas the "reverance" or "double" in Caroso's description named a step that could be sequenced in different orders or performed at different speeds, the "sinking," "rising," and "springing" actions in Feuillet notation denoted properties or characteristics of a given step.[13] In addition to these basic actions, movements that served as adornments, such as beats, circulars, or changes of orientation, were identified as such and could be appended to different steps. The result was a system that suggested an infinitely variable compendium of possibilities.[14] Arbeau had anticipated these new foundational principles by specifying some of the positions to which the body should return between movements, however Feuillet's analysis detailed an entirely new level of specificity, all organized around horizontal and vertical axes. Because these characteristics were imbued with universal status as actions occurring within vertical or horizontal dimensions of space, they served as tools for analyzing any and all dances.[15]

Feuillet notation thus conformed to research being conducted in other fields of inquiry within the Royal academies, each of which was being asked to establish the basic precepts and norms of its discipline. For example, botanist Joseph Pitton de Tournefort created one of the first universal systems of plant classification in 1694 based on the shape of a plant's flower.[16] Like Tournefort's taxonomy, Feuillet notation asserted that a small number of seemingly neutral motions or aspects of the body subtended all dance movements. These could be varied and recombined in an infinite number of ways to produce any and all dances. To secure the neutrality of these motions, Feuillet notation used symbols that appeared to reference basic and universal aspects of the body such as its upright carriage and the support of that carriage provided by two semi-autonomous feet.[17] The symbols used in Feuillet notation also signified underlying principles of movement that referred only to its direction, timing, and the spatial orientation of the body performing it.[18] Movement was reduced to a set of possibilities to elevate and lower, to trace a semi-circle or line, etc.

Implementing these geometric laws of movement, the cultural specificities of particular dances were smoothed out or erased. As Jean Noël Laurenti explains:

> The French dancing masters had to unify a vocabulary of steps with diverse origins, from the provinces or from abroad: to

Figure 1.3 In this image from Kellom Tomlinson's collection of notated dances, the solitary male figure stands, secure and self-possessed, at the center of space with a variety of options for moving all laid out around him.

Kellom Tomlinson. *The art of dancing explained by reading and figures: whereby the manner of performing the steps is made easy by a new and familiar method: being the original work/first design'd in the year 1724, and now published by Kellom Tomlinson, dancing master.* London. The second edition. 1744. Book 1, plate III

Courtesy of The William Andrews Clark Memorial Library, University of California, Los Angeles discover what this vast repertoire had in common, it was necessary to first distinguish all the constituent parts. This would permit the use of the same signs (in different sequence of course) to note down a minuet or passepied, originally from the west of France, as well as a gavot or a rigadoon, imported from the southeast, or a "Spanish-style" sarabande or chaconne.[19]

Such a system allowed instructors to master various regional styles and assimilate them into a single repertoire. What had been a region's indigenous production was transformed into stylistic features of a single repertoire that set one dance apart from another. Cultural and historical specificities of particular dances were homogenized by a system that implemented absolute conceptions of space and of time. Perhaps for the first time, dance was asserted to be a universal language.

Not only did Feuillet notation propose clear underlying principles that governed each movement, but it also taught the body a new locatedness in space. As part of the instructions for learning to read the notation, Feuillet discussed the relationship of the aspiring dancer to the page on which the notation was printed, even detailing how to hold the book while learning the dance:

> You must observe always to hold the upper end of the Book against the upper end of the Room, and whether the Dance have any Turning in it or not, you must carefully avoid removing the Book from the Situation above demonstrated . . . for Example, in a quarter Turn to the Right, you must put your left Hand to the farther part of the Book, and your Right to the nearest. Your Hands being thus prepared, in turning your quarter Turn, bring your left Hand in to you, whilst your right removes from you; so that both Hands will by this means be equally advanc'd before you, holding the Book by the same places before-mentinon'd, and you will find, that in turning a quarter round, the Book will still remain in its former Situation.[20]

These instructions suggest that the body's ability to remain oriented with respect to the fixed horizontal planes of floor and paper could not be assumed. In order to keep the page aligned with the front of the room, Feuillet explained to the reader holding the notation how to adjust the hands in order to perform a quarter turn. He found it necessary to provide these meticulous instructions so that dancers could maintain a kind of "true north" even as their bodies wound along a circuitous path.[21]

Feuillet notation thus taught dancers to maintain a single directional orientation and also to cultivate a bird's eye view of their own path while at the same time, regularizing each step. The effect of Feuillet's notation on various dance forms was not unlike that of Tournefort's and subsequently Linnaeus's taxonomies for classifying the world of plants. Paul Carter argues that Linnaeus's taxonomic system extracted each object of scrutiny from its ecology,

> its historical and geographical surroundings. In this process it loses all power to signify beyond itself, to suggest lines of development or the subtler influences of climate, ground and aspect. In short, its ecology, its existence in a given, living space is lost in the moment of scientific discovery.[22]

Feuillet's notation similarly erased the locality of dance steps in order to place all dancing on the plane of pure geometry where each dance's specificities could be compared and evaluated. Performing this evaluation, dancers disciplined by the notation enjoyed a consolidated and singular perspective onto the world from which to track their own progress in relation to others.

This kind of conceptualization of a pure space, capable of being organized only according to abstract and geometric principles, intimated a profound reorganization of corporeality. It not only supported the notion of a centrality that extends itself outwards in space towards a periphery, but it also reinforced a bodily experience of having a center that extends into and moves through an unmarked space.[23] The act of moving through such a pure space was characterized as value-free, and any labor entailed in traversing this space went unregistered. Within such a space, neutral bodily features and motions, such as those identified in Feuillet notation, operated to confirm the existence of an absolute set of laws to which all bodies should conform. The notation bound the dancing to the ground on which it occurred, not to its indigenous location, but rather to an abstract and unmarked ground.

Traveling and disseminating

Feuillet's system migrated to England with remarkable alacrity. At the encouragement of his patron, the renowned dancer and Court Dancing Master Mr. Isaac, Weaver began to study and apply Feuillet's system soon after it was published. As early as 1703 Weaver began notating Isaac's dances, and followed his translation of Feuillet with a collection

Figure 1.4 In this imaginary visit by Louis XIV to the Royal Academy of Science, he seems to be surveying the homologous investigations of structure evident in the skeleton hanging on the wall, the globe positioned at his feet, and even the garden seen through the window.

Claude Perrault, *Mémoires pour servir à l'histoire naturelle des animaux*. Paris: De l'Imprimerie royale .1676. Engraving by Sebastien LeClerc, Frontispiece.

Courtesy of University of California, Los Angeles, Special Collections Library of Isaac's work published in the same year. Several translations and amended versions of Feuillet's system appeared soon thereafter: P. Siris in 1706; John Essex, in1710; and E. Pemberton in 1711.[24] All these publications were made possible through the donations of subscribers who patronized the Dancing Masters, and their numbers grew consistently from Weaver's translation which listed thirty-one contributors to Tomlinson's *The Art of Dancing* (1735) which boasted 169 supporters. Like their French counterparts, a substantial number of English Dancing Masters worked with notation and found it useful for transmitting the latest dances and consolidating an English style.[25]

As the English Dancing Masters clearly apprehended, the advantages of the system seemed to lie not only in its capacity to collect and store diverse dances, but also to record and transport new ones. It enabled the dissemination of the latest and most fashionable urban and court innovations, while at the same time securing the value of those who could read and teach the collections.[26] Especially valuable for provincial instructors, these collections set forth a basic rubric for the teaching of dance – a set of fundamental positions and steps for the student to practice. Like books of fashion plates depicting the latest sartorial inventions, they also celebrated the most recent vogue in dancing. This motion from the urban centers to the periphery helped to consolidate recent efforts across the continent to build the nation state. Securing the dominance of urban over rural aesthetics, it reinforced class-based hierarchies while at the same time transforming regional distinctiveness into genre or style.

During Arbeau's time, notation was construed as preserving dances and guiding instruction, but dancing still required personal interaction. As documented in Arbeau's dialogue with his eager student, knowledge about dancing was co-produced by the two people who cogitated on a given subject. Among the upper classes, even dancing itself was largely envisioned as a practice of incurring mutual indebtedness. Whether a slow bassadanza, or a livelier balli, all dances involved a careful self-presentation, an assessment of others, and a judicious intermingling of performers. Reigning the body in, and then calibrating its position and distance in relation to others, each dancer should evidence the ability continually to readjust one's location in relation to all the other bodies moving through the space. Courtiers deciphered the proximity between bodies, how close someone was sitting or standing to someone else, as a sign of their relative status and as an appropriate performance of gendered identity.[27]

In this ongoing flux of bodies mutually readjusting and reassessing their relationships to one another based on each body's most recent movements, pathways through the space were not defined against a stable and constant plane. Instead, the room itself had to be read and reread based on the progress of each dancer. Only through this ability to self-accommodate to a changing spatial flux could dancers participate effectively in the civil intercourse of dancing, scrutinizing one another's bearing and comportment. As Arbeau described it, dance was a form of mute rhetoric that allowed dancers to persuade viewers of their nobility, spiritedness, modesty, and grace. Far from being ornamental, their decorousness offered evidence of their morality. In this way dancing seamlessly attached to quotidian interaction as an extension of the ongoing project of fashioning oneself in manner and measure, while at the same time, scanning others for any lapses or ruptures in their composure. Caroso identified this back and forth display of identity as a "pedalogue," or foot conversation.[28]

Mark Franko argues that in its eloquence, the dancing body served as a means of acquiring both social and political capital.[29] As all bodies continually recalibrated their manner and measure in response to one another, they built up a framework of mutual indebtedness. Sir Thomas Elyot, remarking on the advantages of learning to dance as part of the education necessary to govern responsibly, put it this way: "In every of the said dances, there was a concinnity (fitness) of moving the foot and body, expressing some pleasant and profitable affects or motions of the mind."[30] Needing both to profit and to please, dancers performed proof of their goodness that yielded the profit of power over others.[31] As men asserted their fierce courage and women displayed mild and timorous meekness, the dance bound each couple into a felicitous and morally upright union. Both within and among all couples, the ongoing indebtedness to one another augmented with each successive movement performed. Arbeau's inventory of the means through which this negotiation of the civil took place thus constituted a certification of that accumulation and the resulting moral wealth of its practitioners. Dancing served as a tool for upward mobility, and eager students paid for lessons to improve their grace, agility, and mannerly comportment. Skill at dancing demonstrated men's worthiness as potential administrators and governors and women's suitability as their spouses.[32]

With the introduction of Feuillet notation, it became possible for dancers to participate in an entirely new economy, one in which they purchased the collections of dances and then modeled the latest fashion. Rather than a mutual indebtedness, incurred through the "pedalogue" performed in every dance, dancing became a display of virtuosity and social standing, but also a sign of access to novelty. Male and female dancers no longer embodied the moral attributes appropriate to their distinctive roles in society as in Elyot's time. Instead, the notation cast male and female bodies onto the same plane where their performances differed in amount or degree but not in essence. The strength displayed by the male dancer in the height of his jumps or the number of beats and the delicacy evident in the female dancer's turns did not give proof of their moral character, but rather demonstrated their facility at executing their roles.

Feuillet notation empowered "choreographers," those with the ability to read and write the dances, to participate centrally in the circulation and sale of dances to students eager to master the latest trends in physical accomplishment. Dances became authored for the first time. They moved from city to country across regional and national boundaries, entering a new economy of self-fashioning based on hierarchies of sophistication, urbanity, and inventiveness. Like the sphere of exchange shared by botanists who had begun to inventory and evaluate the world's plants based on a shared system of taxonomic naming and classification, the ephemeral dance could be collected and sold, secured by the permanence of its representation in symbols.[33]

Dance's new economy was based in the same assumptions of value and worth that launched the new national economy based on the issuing of bank notes, a kind of paper money. John Law, who proposed the adoption of paper money in 1709, argued that coinage or goods, much like Arbeau's steps, could become devalued according to demand and availability. Paper money, in contrast, secured a universal system of constants that could effectively respond to the urgent vicissitudes of a world trade with a vastly expanded credit market. Law advocated issuing paper money that was secured and backed by land, the only absolute constant whose value never decreased:

> The Paper Money Propos'd is equal to its self; but to continue equal to such a Quantity of any other Goods, is to have a Quality that no Goods can have: For that depends on the Changes in these other Goods. It has a better and more certain Value than Silver Money, and all the other Qualities necessary in Money in a much greater Degree, with other Qualities that Silver has not, and is more capable of being made Money than any thing yet known. Land is what is most valuable, and what encreases [*sic*] in Value more than other Goods; so the Paper Money issued from it, will in all appearance not only keep equal to other Goods, but rise above them.[34]

Like Feuillet's symbols that could be combined and recombined in innumerable ways, paper money generated whole new systems for creating wealth in the form of credit and debt. The principles of movement indicated in the symbols, like the land quickly transforming into property, secured the value of movement.

Like the implementation of paper money, the notating of dances could even assist in the colonial expansion from Europe and England into the rest of the world. The fact that dance's ephemerality had been conquered by notation intimated success in all kinds of colonizing projects, as this excerpt from Soame Jenyns's poem "The Art of Dancing" written in 1729 suggests:

> Long was the *Dancing Art* unfix'd and free;
> Hence lost in Error and Uncertainty:
> No Precepts did it mind, or Rules obey,
> But ev'ry Master taught a diff'rent Way:
> Hence, e're each new-born Dance was fully try'd,
> The lovely Product, ev'n in blooming, dy'd:
> Thro' various Hands in wild Confusion toss'd,
> Its Steps were alter'd, and its Beauties lost:
> Till *Fuillet* [*sic*] at length, Great Name! arose,
> And did the Dance in Characters compose:
> Each lovely Grace by certain Marks he taught,
> And ev'ry Step in lasting Volumes wrote.
> Hence o'er the World this pleasing Art shall spread,
> And ev'ry Dance in ev'ry Clime be read:
> By *distant Masters* shall each Step be seen,
> Tho' Mountains rise, and Oceans roar between.
> Hence with her Sister-Arts shall *Dancing* claim
> An equal Right to Universal Fame,
> And *Isaac's Rigadoon* shall last as long
> As *Raphael's Painting*, or as *Virgil's Song*.[35]

In Jenyns's estimation seventeenth century dance had been saturated with uncertainty and confusion because it lacked rules or precepts, and hence, each teacher could interpret it differently. The transformation in form resulting from the person-to-person transmission of dances compromised or even contaminated their original beauty. Only the invention of Feuillet notation at the beginning of the eighteenth century imbued dance with a composed permanence and newfound clarity, creating a parity with dance's sister-arts of painting and poetry, and also an opportunity for dances to travel around the world. Notation hardened dance, giving it a masculine status and securing its equal rank within the arts.

In Jenyns's ambitious vision, the fact that dances could now travel to every climate of the world confirmed the triumph of rules and order over undisciplined variation. Notation could likewise introduce the world's dancers to the finest accomplishments of a colonial power, or at least maintain a crucial aesthetic continuity between those living at home and those living in colonies. Perhaps this kind of transportability could also assuage anxiety over the profuse varieties of cultural difference that colonists encountered and the impact that such difference might have on British culture.

The earliest British colonists in the New World arrived on the East Coast of North America in the same decade that Arbeau was writing his treatise. In Jamestown and subsequently in Plymouth, the British observed native dances and also indigenous practices of documenting their history. Algonquians, for example, typically archived negotiations and treaties through the beading of wampum belts and the decorating of hides. Edward Winslow of Plymouth noted yet another practice among the Wampanoag for preserving a memory of events which he described in these terms:

> Instead of records and chronicles, they take this course. Where any remarkable act is done, in memory of it, either in the place, or by some pathway near adjoining, they make a round hole in the ground, about a foot deep, and as much over, which when others passing by behold, they inquire the cause and occasion of the same, which being once known, they are careful to acquaint all men, as occasion serveth, therewith; and lest such holes should be filled or grown up by any accident, as men pass by, they will oft renew the same, by which means many things of great antiquity are fresh in memory. So that as a man travelleth, if he can understand his guide, his journey will be the less tedious, by reasons of the many historical discourses will be related unto him.[36]

Winslow's account identified the process of documentation as one that involved distinguishing events that were "remarkable," commemorating these events by marking the site where they occurred, and transmitting a verbal account at that site to those who passed by so that the entire community became a repository and maintenance system for the knowledge.

Not unlike Arbeau's dialogue with his student, the Wampanoags that Winslow observed required the sustained presence of individuals to receive and pass on the information. Their archive was maintained through the physical labor of traveling to the place where history was made. Events deemed of historical worth could not be separated from the land on which they were enacted. Knowledge was passed along generationally through the labor of all the individuals who assisted in witnessing the telling of the past.

By the time Feuillet notation recorded dances on paper, native lands and practices of historical preservation had been disrupted or eradicated by colonial expansion. In the way that it was constructed, the notation made evident how this colonization could be so successful. By breaking steps down into component parts, and specifying how each of these parts should be performed, the notation stipulated foundational units out of which all movement was derived and clear guidelines regarding the execution of all steps. These kinds of guidelines assisted those who followed Winslow to the New World by confirming the existence of standards for comportment and exchange. Practicing a dance from the notation, the dancer enacted a connection between step and written symbols that objectified the movement so that even as one was performing the step one was aware of its proper features. The notation thereby took the dancing out of the body, and away from body-to-body contact, and placed it in circulation as a codified symbolic system.[37]

Although a satiric exaggeration of the practice of learning and teaching from notation, a letter in *The Tatler* from 1709 vividly conveyed this connection between symbol and step. In it the author claimed to have been suddenly startled awake by a convulsive sound, repeated several times. Conferring with the Landlady and then heading up the stairs, he peeked in the keyhole,

> and there I saw a well-made Man look with great Attention on a Book, and on a sudden jump into the Air so high, that his Head almost touch'd the Sieling. He came down safe on his Right Foot, and again flew up alighting on his Left; then look'd again at his Book, and holding out his Right Leg, put it into such a quivering Motion, that I thought he would have shak'd it off. He us'd the Left after the same Manner, when on a sudden, to my great Surprize, he stoop'd himself incredibly low, and turn'd gently on his Toes. After this circular Motion, he continu'd bent in that humble Posture for some Time, looking on his Book. After this, he recover'd himself with a sudden Spring, and flew round the Room in all the Violence and Disorder imaginable, till he made a full Pause for Want of Breath.[38]

Knocking on the door, he was greeted by the young man who obligingly responded to his request to see the book. However, when the author asked that it be explained to him, the dancer replied, "It was one he study'd with great Application; but it was his Profession to teach it, and could not communicate his Knowledge without a Consideration."[39] He went on to explain, "That now, articulate Motions, as well as Sounds, were express'd by proper Characters; and that there is nothing so common, as to communicate a Dance by a Letter."[40]

Although a very small number of individuals mastered the system, those who could read and write it probably achieved considerable facility at translating the dance from page to motion. Perhaps they even devised new dances through writing them down, able to rehearse the sequences in their imagination. As *The Tatler* story depicts the process, the choreographer studied the page briefly and then tore into violent and disordered motion, leaping around the room. The symbols, however, confirmed that there was a logic and order to his motions. What is more, they consolidated a livelihood in the form of a precious source of knowledge that could be shared only by agreement and for a price.

Like the new system of money, Feuillet's symbols constructed a sign that authenticated the existence of the step. In so doing, the symbols also produced the potential for an excess to be borrowed, and increased or lost. Both in dance and in the economy, the new system of symbols created the possibility for credit. In Arbeau's time worth was asserted through the mutually defining actions of the individuals who performed and watched one another. Now it was amassed through the existence of a sign that stood in for and certified that worth. Credit, the theoretical capacity to borrow and expand wealth, and the wild fluctuations in value and worth that it provoked, became a major preoccupation of the eighteenth-century English economy. Similarly, in dance, because the step itself now existed apart from any particular execution of it, new criteria for excellence were consolidated to evaluate various enactments of it, and along with these criteria, the very possibility of superseding them in the exceptional or virtuoso performance. Virtuosity in dance emerged as the equivalent of financial credit and with it, dance expanded to include the dazzling, astonishing, and unspeakably brilliant performance.

Both credit and virtuosity acquired reputations as fickle and unreliable.[41] Editor of *The Spectator* Joseph Addison even reported having a dream of a ballet in which Lady Credit, as the symbol of credit's nefarious changeability, played a central role. Surrounded by phantoms of tyranny, bigotry, atheism, and anarchy, dancing "together for no other end but to eclipse one another," Lady Credit faints, the sacks of money against which she is propped change into bags of air, and the piles of gold transform into bundles of paper.[42] Yet in the midst of this seeming crisis, amiable phantoms enter, performing measured duets that pair Liberty with Monarchy, and Moderation with Religion, prompting the bags to reswell with guineas. The spectacular performances of the phantoms, working only to "eclipse one another," highlighted dance's newfound capacity to acquire wealth, not through the system of mutual indebtedness but through its ability to project a value beyond that of the step itself. Although the measured duets of Liberty and Monarchy might momentarily restore order, the appeal of the virtuoso performance, like the lure of credit, would eventually prevail.

Authorship, narrative, and technique

By the 1740s and 50s, the limits of choreography as a system for documenting dancing were clearly recognized. Although it assisted in consolidating a repertoire of English social dances early in the century, it fell short in preserving the actions of the face and arms, the positioning of dancers in relation to one another, and their interactions. These elements of dance, increasingly evident on the concert stage, began to carry more of the dance's significance than the footwork and pathways stipulated in the notation. Collections of notated dances stopped appearing in the 1730s, with Tomlinson's publication, originally organized in 1724, issuing in 1735 as one of the last. Even though Louis de Cahusac featured the system in his essay for the *Encyclopedie* in 1755, it had long fallen out of use. In 1760 Jean Georges Noverre, composer of a large number of full-length story ballets, railed against Feuillet notation as obsolete and incapable of capturing stage action, particularly facial expressions and groupings of bodies.[43]

Weaver, shortly after translating Feuillet into English, contributed substantially to the obsolescence of choreography by embarking on a series of experiments with pantomime that helped to launch the new genre of the story ballet.[44] His pantomime ballets also inaugurated a new approach to documenting dance – the narrative account of the story and action. Responding to continental *comedia del arte* productions, seen in London since the 1670s and working alongside a growing number of English artists experimenting with pantomime, Weaver investigated the use of rhetorical gesture in creating danced dialogues that could convey a plot without the aid of spoken or sung text. The fact that these dances were relatively short, appearing as *entre actes* between acts of a play or between different genres of entertainment, allowed for flexibility in developing the new form, and these danced vignettes began to be mined intensively for the innovations they could produce.

Weaver's scenario for *The Loves of Mars and Venus* (1717) made evident the discrepancies between Feuillet's capacity to document dance and the kind of action increasingly seen on the stage. It also demonstrated the relative lack of familiarity at reading this new action that Weaver assumed on the part of his viewers. Following its production at Drury Lane, Weaver published a thorough description of the plot and action. Scene Two began as follows:

> After a symphony of Flutes, etc. the Scene opens and discovers Venus in her Dressing-Room at her Toilet, attended by the Graces, who are employ'd in dressing her. Cupid lies at her Feet, and one of the Hours waits by. Venus rises, and dances a Passacaile: The Graces joyn her in the same movement as does also the hour. The Dance being ended the Tune changes to a wild rough Air. Venus, Graces, etc. seem in Surprize; and at the Approach of Vulcan, the Graces, and Cupid run off.
>
> Enter to Venus, Vulcan: They perform a Dance together; in which Vulcan expresses his Admiration; Jealousie; Anger; and Despite: And Venus shews neglect; Coquetry; Contempt; and Disdain.[45]

Weaver then continued by recounting in detail the physical appearance of each of these feelings:

> This last Dance being altogether of the Pantomimic kind; it is necessary that the Spectator should know some of the most particular gestures made use of therein; and what Passions, or Affections, they discover; represent' or express.
>
> Admiration is discover'd by the raising up of the right Hand, the Palm turn'd upwards, the Fingers clos'd; and in one Motion the Wrist turn'd round and Fingers spread; the Body reclining, and Eyes fix'd on the Object; but when it rises to
>
> Astonishment, both Hands are thrown up towards the Skies; the Eyes also lifted up, and the Body cast backwards.[46]

Weaver carefully described the gestures, facial expression, gaze, and bodily positioning for each of the fourteen passions from which the danced dialogue was composed.

Weaver pioneered in crafting such gestures into danced action, and he also helped to promote interest in how emotions should be represented by physical action. John Bulwer had published a comprehensive study of rhetorical gesture, *Chirologia: or the Natural Language of the Hand, and Chironomia: or the Art of Manual Rhetoric*, in 1644. Drawing on classical writings, Bulwer argued vigorously for greater attention to the physical presentation of an argument, detailing hundreds of actions for hands and fingers that would express a speaker's ideas. His description of admiration was remarkably similar to Weaver's: "The palm (the fingers all joined together) turned up, and by the return of the wrist, in one motion, spread and turned about the hand, is an action convenient for *admiration*."[47] By the time Weaver began to investigate pantomime, Bulwer's study and others such as Charles LeBrun's *Méthode pour apprendre dessiner les passions* were being consulted by actors and visual artists in their efforts to expand the range and specificity of their portrayals of feeling. Acting theory, as Joseph Roach explains, outlined the actor's craft as one of assuming the poses in a sequence of passions, rhythmically structured with pauses for particularly climactic tableaus.[48] This general burgeoning of interest in the representation of the passion affected many aspects of public culture.

As representation of the passions increasingly dominated the action in theatrical performances of dance, audiences lost interest in the body's perambulations along a path through space, and instead, became absorbed with the body's ability to paint a picture as it moved from one gesture and position to the next. Most often adapting well-known myths and familiar classical stories, the Dancing Master, as he was called, now translated these narratives into danced pictures. The brief vogue in committing dance to symbols and the livelihood that it promised was replaced by a new enthusiasm for sequencing feelings and arranging the responses of others to those feelings. Likewise, the potential that notation had offered to serve as a kind of copyright of one's own inventions was eclipsed by the new interest in which stories might be best adapted to stage and how to accomplish their translation into dancing. The capacities for classification and exchange that notation had promised were eclipsed by the possibility to tell a story and represent feelings through movement alone.

Despite its failure to deliver as pedagogical tool, fashion template, or portable collection of dances, Feuillet notation nonetheless helped lay the groundwork for the subsequent development of dance technique, and it asserted the criteria upon which virtuosity in dancing could be evaluated. In her comparison of mid and late eighteenth century dance manuals, Sandra Noll Hammond shows the consistencies in their cultivation of the basic principles of movement that Feuillet had identified.[49] Students practiced each position and the accompanying posture necessary to perfect its presentation, and then they practiced the *pliés* and *relevés*, formerly sinkings and risings, that prepared the body to execute more complex steps and sequences. These positions and basic steps entered both concert and social dance repertories, offering a skeletal pedagogy upon which to build instruction in dancing.

Analogous in many respects to the musical exercises practiced by students acquiring expertise at instrument playing, these sequences confirmed the suggestion, implicit in the notation itself, that music and dance were separate yet related arts forms. In Arbeau's analysis of dancing, the musical meters and rhythms were discussed first, and the movements were presented as a translation or emanation of musical structure in steps. Feuillet notation, in contrast, presented a catalogue of possible types of steps, without making any mention of musical types or rhythmic structures that would necessarily correspond to these steps. The several collections of dances that used Feuillet notation likewise detached dance from music, placing the musical notation at the top of the page and the notated dance below. Dance movement thus began to acquire a materiality, one that suggested an egalitarian relationship, rather than a fusion, with music.

When Feuillet notation was devised, the acts of composing a dance, learning a dance, and learning to dance were conceptualized as overlapping, if not identical projects. The Dancing Master performed professionally, and also taught students to dance, not so much by training them in a profession of exercises, but by teaching them progressively more complex dances. The analysis of dance movement that the notation offered implied a new status for dance in which these three functions, composing, performing, and practicing would, over time, become distinct practices. It laid the groundwork for the acquisition of skills based on a progressively more difficult set of exercises. And it imparted an objecthood for dancing as a pursuit separate from music or theater. Not only were movements broken down into their most basic units, but each movement was located within a specified sequence, one that could be altered in the same way that the individual moves could be varied and embellished. The arrangement and rearrangement of movement thus emerged as a practice through which an individual achieved recognition as the author of those arrangements.

The term "Dancing Master" or "Ballet Master" continued to refer to the creator, arranger, and teacher of dances, yet the role and responsibilities of this person began to change. Required to create a variety of dance presentations – divertissments, entre-actes, dances within operas, and short and full-length story ballets, Dancing Masters were credited by name in programs, and their work evaluated in the press, but the specific selection and sequencing of movement was never documented. Only when they devised scenarios for story-ballets was their work given fuller description. Printed as part of the program, the scenario, rather than any form of notation, began to serve as the document of the danced action.

Addressing the new responsibilities of the Dancing Master, Noverre identified an impressive number of skills which they needed to acquire: painting (for its depiction of groups); poetry (for renditions of emotions); anatomy (for how to train the dancer); history (for subjects suitable for ballets); music (for combining movements in the dance); and daily life (for the variety and liveliness of its characters).[50] The Dancing Master needed to become a discerning imitator of Nature by finding a persuasive and visually acute story to tell, and rendering the narrative with innovative and appropriate movement carefully matched to the music. Like Weaver who wrote on dance history and anatomy while also working as a Dancing Master in devising pantomime ballets, Noverre divided his attention between the knowledge necessary to create a story ballet and the insights emerging from the new discipline of anatomy that pertained to a dancer's training. These constituted distinctive arenas of study, all under the command of the Dancing Master.

In the early nineteenth century, Carlo Blasis, an Italian Dancing Master who worked in London from 1826 to 1830, identified a similar set of skills that reflected this dual importance of teaching dance and creating dances. Blasis produced two lengthy studies of dance; the first, *Traité Elémentaire Théorique et Pratique* (1820) set forth a training program for the dancer that included a remarkable set of drawings indicating correct placement of the limbs while performing various steps. The second, *The Code of Terpsichore*, translated into English and published in London in 1828, incorporated and expanded upon the first book while also adding major sections on the history of dance, pantomime, and most noticeably, an extensive consideration of "The Composition of Ballets." Although Noverre covered many of the same issues, his organization seems haphazard in comparison with Blasis's systematic breakdown. Blasis discussed in detail the crafting of the plot, its beginning, middle, and denouement; the evaluation of potential stories for use as ballets; the implementation of dramatic gesture; the need for spatial organization onstage and also variety and contrast between scenes; and the relations between dance and the arts of music, costuming, and scenography.

Blasis's extensive coverage of composition reflected the new status of the story ballet as a distinctive and popular genre, and he was among the first to identify the distinctive labor entailed in creating a new dance, as suggested in this passage addressing the Dancing Master's pedagogical duties:

> Finally, to create the accomplished artist, the master must infuse his pupil with the spirit, sensibility and enchantment of his art. Should the student have a flair for composition and show imagination the wise master will encourage it by letting him arrange dances and instructing him in design and the beauties of choreography.[51]

Here choreography refers to the art of making dances, one of its first and very rare appearances with that meaning throughout the nineteenth century. As described by Blasis, this process of composition consisted largely in selecting and arranging steps congenial to one's physical appearance, aptitude, and temperament, but it did not include the invention of new steps. Blasis advised dancers who showed talent to pursue the art of arranging dances, and he also noted that many soloists arranged their own solos to feature their specific proclivities and accomplishments.[52]

Blasis's theories of composition retained much of Noverre's aesthetics, however his drawings of proper positions and steps showed the dancer in an entirely new relationship to geography and geometry. Instead of the "wavings of the feet" (Feuillet's term) and the markings along the horizontal plane that documented the dancer's progress, Blasis's dancers posed on a tiny line that represented the floor with no particular location or perspectival relationship to a landscape. Shown in a variety of positions that inventoried different relationships among arms and legs, the dancers' placement in each position was highlighted by a dotted line running along each limb. These lines emphasized the geometric designs the limbs should make – right angles as the leg was lifted, perfect ovals as the arms were raised overhead. They also illustrated the vertical orientation of the body with respect to the floor. Rather than follow a line along the floor as Feuillet's dancers did, here, the line was internalized, embedded within the flesh, with the musculature wrapping around it.[53] It was as if the geometry in which the dancer had been located by the notation was now absorbed into the body and capable of being reproduced through the correct movement of the limbs. Not only had the sinkings and risings evolved into *pliés* and *relevés*, but the geometric designs of the floor-patterns were transformed into geometric patternings within the body.

The Code of Terpsichore also included a markedly new history of dance, one that focused obsessively on the influence of an African dance known as the *chica*. Unlike Weaver, who located the antecedents of

FIG. 10   FIG. 11

Figure 1.5 In these drawings from Carlo Blasis's *An elementary treatise upon the theory and practice of the art of dancing,* the dotted lines running through the limbs seem to indicate the proper geometric relations and proportions among parts of the body.
Carlo Blasis. *An elementary treatise upon the theory and practice of the art of dancing.* Translated by Mary Stewart Evans. NY: Dover Publications, Inc. 1968.
Fig. 10 & 11: grands battements

contemporary dance in the Greek and Roman theaters, Blasis organized his remarks according to nation state, reviewing Greek, Roman, and then Italian accomplishments before taking up the problems with Spanish dancing. The first historian of dance to elaborate a theory of climate's influence on temperament, Blasis argued that tropical heat induced excessive wiggling of the hips and an unrestrained enthusiasm for performing movement that produced a dance known as the *chica*. Migrating from central Africa via the Moors into Spain, the *chica* transformed into the Fandango and other related dances, ennobled in some cases by the "pride" that the Spanish took in their dancing. Both women and the "lower orders," Blasis cautioned, were susceptible to lasciviousness and vice following their exposure to the *chica*.[54]

Unlike the lively dances of Gypsies, Scots, or Hungarians, the unruly wiggling of the *chica* threatened to compromise the artistic standards of ballet. Still, if properly restrained, it, like the other national dances, promised to enrich the story ballet with exotic differences. The very lines that composed proper positioning of the dancer for Blasis could be utilized to docilize the foreign forms, giving them intrigue and novelty while assimilating them into a standardized style of execution. Thus a large number of ballets set in various locations around the world began to appear on the early nineteenth century stage. Rather than a parade of different types, held together by a single narrative proposition as in early eighteenth century ballets, these productions began to be staged with various exotic populations and their customs. Gypsy, Native American, Caribbean as well as Scottish, Hungarian, Italian and Russian dances, all assimilated into the vocabulary and style of classical ballet, imbued each ballet with local color while simultaneously displaying the ballet's mastery over all forms. Where the eighteenth century representations of foreigners typically borrowed a stereotypic gesture or piece of attire to signal the culture, nineteenth century productions balleticized actual phrases of movement. What had begun in notation as a rubric for collecting dances had now evolved into a system for assimilating them into the dancing body. Whether a Scottish Hornpipe or a Spanish Cachucha, all foreign dances were infused with an emphasis on the geometric shaping of the body and the metered timing of the steps. (See figure 3.5 from Chapter 3.)

Blasis argued that the Ballet Master who knew about these different dances could use them to infuse the ballet with diverting innovations. When combined with the ability to translate a gripping narrative to danced action, the incorporation of exotic movements would produce a successful ballet. Even individual dancers responsible for arranging their own solo variations, or *pas*, could surge to prominence through the judicious arrangement of foreign material. When such innovation was executed with technical brilliance, also defined by ballet's criteria for virtuosity, the result would ensure a marketable product and a successful career. Instead of dance supporting an economy of mutual indebtedness, as in Arbeau's time, dance now offered an opportunity to fashion individualized commodities for public consumption.

The gendered division of labor in accomplishing this marketability relied upon the female dancers to excel at the display of dancing while male dancers, although playing a supporting role onstage, typically crafted the narratives and arranged the steps. Men were thus empowered as creators and producers of ballets, and women functioned as performers. Whereas choreography as notation had secured a masculine permanence for dance by fixing the steps and documenting specific dances, as Jenyns proclaimed in his poem, once narrative took over as the principal form of its organization and documentation, and the largely female cast literally fleshed out its story, dance moved to the margins of the arts. Dance was severed from the symbolic system that had given it materiality and parity with the other arts. Without that system, the guarantor of movement, equivalent to the land or government that secured paper money, dance was reframed as the most feminized and trivial of accomplishments. As Hegel observed, dance was not a "real" art, since it did not evolve from a fundamental medium of expression.[55] Instead, it merely ornamented story with movement.

Along with the collections of notated dances, the term "choreography" generally fell out of use during the late eighteenth and nineteenth centuries in both French and English languages. When it was utilized in newspaper reviews or journals, it named indiscriminately the acts of dancing, learning to dance, or making a dance.[56] Choreography's legacy as a system of symbols that defined the steps was to determine the repertoire of exercises through which the body was trained for dancing. Clearly specified in that repertoire were the limitations on what could constitute dance movement as well as what superior execution warranted the status of virtuosity. Instead of supporting variation through the infinite variation and combination of specific positions and steps, the system now enforced its own borders, allowing in fragments of the foreign to rejuvenate its appearance. Leaving to narrative the task of documenting the dance, choreography as notation disappeared into the *pliés* and *tendus* of the dancer's daily regimen.

Revealing and testifying

At the beginning of the twentieth century, the term "choreography" came into widespread and new usage, both in Britain and the US. No longer a vague and infrequently used appellation for dancing, it now named specifically the act of creating a dance. Although its use coincided with the emergence of the new genre known as modern dance, the term "choreography" was not initially applied to that work. As Martha Graham reminisced about her earliest training, from 1914 to 1923 with Ruth St. Denis and Ted Shawn: "I had never heard the word choreographer used to describe a maker of dances until I left Denishawn. There you didn't choreograph, you made up dances"[57] Although Graham clearly specified the act of making a dance, there was no special name given to it.

Instead, the term was first used in response to the innovations in ballet introduced by Nijinsky and Fokine when their works toured to Britain and the US.[58] *Le Sacre du Printemps* prompted a large number of reviews when it premiered in 1913 that invoked choreography to identify Nijinsky's radical innovations in vocabulary and sequencing of movement. Many of the other Ballets Russes productions likewise inspired the use of choreography to name the new blendings of classical steps with other sources of movement. As one anonymous source explained, the

> sources of choreography are three. The interpreters use the ballet steps and movements that have been universally known and practiced for generations, as in *Papillons* and *Les Sylphides*; they introduce the barbaric, startling native dances of their steppes as in *Prince Igor*, and they freely empoly [*sic*] the oriental and classical, as in *Scheherazade, Cleopatre* and *L'Après-midi d'un Faune*.[59]

Uses of the foreign, implicit in Blasis's analysis of dance-making were evidently explicit in the general reception of the Russians' works, and their use of "barbaric" and "oriental" materials foregrounded the creative labor of constructing new movement as well as arranging well-known steps. St. Denis likewise integrated foreign movement vocabularies into her dances, yet perhaps because she did not weave together classical and unfamiliar steps so much as she assimilated foreign poses and motions into a new matrix of movement, her dances were not credited as a specific kind of innovation. Or perhaps the eighteenth century term "choreography," originally allied with the Dancing Master and subsequently translated into ballet, resurfaced, renewing its attachment to ballet by specifying a new function.

Whatever the causes of the transformation, the terms "choreography" and "choreographer" quickly gained momentum and, by the mid 1920s, specified the contributions of an arranger of movement in a variety of genres including Broadway musicals and reviews.[60] The terms were used regularly in concert programs and newspaper reviews where they specified the author of an original work and highlighted the inventive engagement of the artist in crafting movement.[61] Taken up enthusiastically by those involved in the new modern dance, choreography began to specify the unique process through which an artist not only arranged and invented movement, but also melded motion and emotion to produce a danced statement of universal significance. In 1933, dance critic and apologist for the new modern dance John Martin asserted this apocalyptic vision of the role of the artist:

> The major purpose of the artist is to make known to you something that is not already known to you, to make you share his revelation of something higher and nearer the truth, to rob the material symbol of some of its appearance of substance and disclose the essence, the reality, of which it is a transient representation.[62]

Unlike entertainment, which offered only a momentary escape, genuine art should lift viewers up, giving them a permanent new vantage point from which to glimpse either the ultimate or the infinite.[63] Dance as an art form used bodily movement, arranged in such a way as to transcend any individual's power to express by rational or intellectual means. Even though people did not speak a common language, Martin explained, they moved "in generally the same way and for the same reasons," and as a result dance had the capacity to communicate across all cultures, classes, and ages.[64]

The use of choreography to name the creative act of formulating new movement to express a personal and universal concern was supported by the new pedagogy in dance education entering universities across the US. One of the first dance educators, Margaret H'Doubler, who was hired in the Women's Physical Education Department at the University of Wisconsin to develop a course of study in Dance in 1917, argued that dance is the translation of emotional experience into external form.[65] In order to accomplish the development of feeling into movement, H'Doubler set forth a curriculum in which the body's responsiveness as a physical mechanism could be mastered. Advocating a kinesiological understanding of the body's movement capabilities as a way to understand its propensity to move, H'Doubler often worked with her students blindfolded, asking them to explore the range of motion at each joint, based on their study of the human skeleton. Abhorring any pedagogical approach based on imitation of movement routines, H'Doubler arranged classes so that students improvised most of the movement rather than copying combinations performed by the teacher. Eventually, this training would enable students to produce "Art," defined by H'Doubler as the free translation of internal emotional experience into external bodily form.[66] Thus each student investigated her own impulses to move, and her own anatomical proclivities to realize such impulses.

Where Feuillet's legacy inculcated an awareness of the relationship between bodily structure and horizontal and vertical grids, H'Doubler's approach traced the connection between impulse and its kinesiological realization. For H'Doubler, mastery over the body entailed an understanding of the "intelligent appreciation for, and application of, force and effort."[67] This awareness would empower students to overcome inhibitions and obstacles to their freedom of control. Unlike Feuillet notation, which implied standards of execution to which the body could be trained to adhere, H'Doubler envisioned her pedagogy as undoing obstacles to a natural and hence desired performance. This approach to training would construct the foundation upon which students could produce new dances.

Figure 1.6 Here, in a master class at Mills College in the 1970s, Margaret H'Doubler asks students to locate and feel the actions of the shoulder girdle in relation to a skeleton.
Courtesy University of Wisconsin Archives
Photo by James E. Graham

To her scientific exploration of bodily capacity, H'Doubler added sessions in which students collaborated, under the teacher's guidance, on the making of a dance. For their first experiments in learning composition, she argued, students could work on devising movement sequences for a select piece of music. She explained:

When the phrasing is understood, have the class skip to the right for one phrase . . . Then ask the class what to do next. Some will suggest going on in the same direction for another phrase; others will recommend going back to the left. Try both. The class will discover that skipping back for a phrase gives balance. Now ask the class if they have a satisfying sense of completion, or if they feel the need of repeating what has been done. Of course, some will want to repeat. So this should be done. They will soon realize that in this case repetition makes for monotony.[68]

H'Doubler guided her students through the process of exploring different effects that resulted from the addition of different materials. Her own aesthetic preferences, masked beneath the investigatory rubric of trying different options, clearly led students in a certain aesthetic direction, cultivating their ability to craft phrasing, floor path, and ensemble shapes, and to detect the interesting from the monotonous. From these discoveries, students could extend themselves further into composition. However, the underlying intimacy established between idea and action continued to inform their explorations, and the potential for this inquiry to yield new insights would undergird dance pedagogy for decades.

In response to the growing popularity of modern dance on the concert stage, as well as the pedagogical efforts of educators such as H'Doubler, Bennington College launched a summer program of study in 1934, one which attracted an impressive number of students who went on to become university educators of dance. Beginning in 1935, the curriculum distinguished among technique, composition, and choreography courses.[69] Where H'Doubler asked students to improvise much of the movement generated in class, by the 1930s, one trained to become a modern dancer using a more prescribed regimen of exercises, often devised by the choreographer, that, on one hand, exemplified the choreographer's aesthetic vision, and on the other, embodied "universal" principles of motion. Where H'Doubler based her course plans on the body's kinesiological capacity to move in any and all ways afforded by its structural organization, Bennington technique classes, taught for example by Martha Graham, Doris Humphrey, and Hanya Holm, proposed distinctive sets of principles as the underlying foundation for dance movement.[70] Students enrolled in two-week courses with two of these four choreographers, and they also studied continuously with Martha Hill in a course entitled "Principles of Movements."

Hill's Principles of Movement, like her approach to composition, implemented universal conceptions of space, time, and weight. Whereas

Figure 1.7 Martha Hill dancing the power and momentum of the volumetric body at Bennington College c. 1935
Courtesy of Janet Mansfield Soares & the Martha Hill Archives.

Feuillet notation located the body spatially in relation to horizontal and vertical axes, and temporally in relation to a metricized progression across space, Hill envisioned space as a void into which the body projected various shapes and energies, and time as a measure of the quickness or slowness of motion. Rather than positioning the body at the calm center of an embroidering periphery, as Feuillet indicated, Hill activated a momentum-filled relationship between central and peripheral body. Both Feuillet's and Hill's systems imagined that they could accomplish an analysis of all dance movement, but Feuillet notation assumed that this was possible because all bodies share the same mechanics – the ability to rise, sink, turn, and so on – whereas Hill, borrowing from Rudolph Laban and Emile Jacques-Dalcroze, assumed that all movement shares the same fundamental properties of shape, rhythm, and force. Where Feuillet notation located all movement along a universal horizontal plane, the new modern techniques foregrounded gravity as a universal within and against which the body articulated its dynamism.[71] In the same way that Feuillet notation occluded the labor of moving from one place to the next, so this conception of gravity rendered equivalent the efforts of all bodies in all places.

In Composition courses students learned structuring principles that imparted an ability to analyze movement in terms of space, time, and weight, creating short studies that demonstrated their understanding of the possibilities for shaping the body as a three-dimensional object in space, and for sequencing those shapes according to various musical structures.[72] Drawing on musical structures such as theme, contrasting theme, return to theme, ABA, or the rondo form ABACADA, students explored how movement could be developed from an original phrase into its repetition, inversion, amplification, or contraction. They also explored strange, asymmetrical positionings of the body and dissonant and contrasting textures.

Familiarizing themselves with movement as a malleable material that could be shaped and re-formed in diverse ways, students could then investigate potential connections between movement's attributes and various psychological states. Influential teacher of composition, Louis Horst, who was also composer, accompanist, and adviser to Graham, introduced his Pre-Classic Forms and Modern Forms courses at Bennington in which he proposed style as a feature of movement that tied individuals to a social temperament. For each style, Horst delivered a succinct summary of movement qualities and characteristics.[73] In "earth primitive," for example:

> The dancer is alertly sensitive to the feel of the earth under his feet. It is the genesis and grave of all living things – the source and the finale. The movements are in the lower areas and oriented to the floor. They can be clumsy and animalistic. They can be brutal and threatening. They can project the lyricism of wonder, or the

tenderness of the giver of life. They may have a drum-like percussiveness. But always they are simple and meagerly articulated; lean and taut.[74]

Here the notion of the primitive as both a psychological and social attribute was mined for the spatial and temporal characteristics associated with stereotypic images of it. Horst drew from these characteristics feelings states such as brutality or tenderness, and he intimated connections between movement and psyche in word choices such as "lean" and "taut."

In addition to the more historical and psychological forms, Horst associated styles with particular peoples and regions:

> The Air Primitive has to do with uncanny airy things; with birds, feathers, witches, fire and fire magic, with omens, apparitions, and enchantments, and with the sun and the wind. The Southwest

Bird Spell — Iris Mabry   Photograph by Louise Dahl-Wolfe

Figure 1.8 Iris Mabry performing an example of Horst's "Air Primitive"
Photo by Louise Dahl-Wolfe
Courtesy of Louise Dahl-Wolfe Archives: Center for Creative Photography, University of Arizona, Arizona board of regents

Indians begin their dance prayers with aspirants such as "hey-ah." Their gods are the Great Spirit (Great Breath) and air-borne divinities such as fire gods, the Thunderbird, the Plumed Serpent [. . .] all of Europe, except Spain, is earth-minded, while the aboriginal cultures of the Americas (Spanish and Indian) are air-minded.[75]

In contrast, Jazz style "retains attributes brought from Africa: jerky, percussive movements and accents. It displays qualities of syncopation which grew out of a disintegrated people: a melancholy and lassitude, resultant of slavery."[76] "Americana" consists of "big, free and extended movement . . . It is swinging and out-going – a wide stance in the legs . . ."[77] As these latter examples make especially clear, Horst conflated individual and cultural stereotypes, assuming that personality or temperament could stand in for or symbolize key cultural values and ways of being. The well-made study would transcend the stereotypes through its innovative interpretation of both the individual and the cultural and also through its mastery of movement's thematic development.

Unlike Blasis and other nineteenth century Ballet Masters who borrowed actual sequences of steps from various regional dance forms, but then imbued them with the essential characteristics of ballet's aesthetics, Horst assumed that each style of moving could be assessed in terms of spatial, temporal and qualitative attributes that could then be absorbed into one's own original study. Nineteenth century ballets transformed regional dances by making the bodily shapings more geometric, the timings of steps more precise, and the spatial orientations of dancers clearly presentational towards the viewer observing the contents of the proscenium. The zest, ferocity, or charm in the dances that remained, a product of the unique rhythms of steps or carriage of the body, referred back to the "spirit" of the people that originated them. For Horst, in contrast, dance movement consisted not of steps and positions but instead of patterns within motion. Aspiring choreographers who could observe, analyze, and reproduce the "swinging, outgoing" quality of Americana or the "syncopated lassitude" of post-slavery African-Americans could incorporate the specificities of a time or culture into their larger statement about the human predicament.

In Composition classes, students probed the complexities of motion's patterns, but they did not create "dances," conceptualized as the development of a vision or argument in movement. Only in the Choreography Workshop, where an already recognized artist created a new work for students in the course, could dancers witness and assist in the birth of a dance. When in 1936 Bennington added a new Program in Choreography, a course in "independent composition for advanced students," who each "completed and presented two full-length compositions," it reaffirmed this elite conception of choreography by identifying an exceptional few students as eligible for its study.[78] Both studies and dances, however, were envisioned as outcomes of a hyper-personalized process wherein the individual became origin of the movement, host to the creative process, and craftsperson of the dance's development. The choreography, as the outcome of the creative process, was seen as the property of an individual artist, not as an arrangement of steps that were shared amongst a community of practitioners, as in Feuillet's time, but rather, as a creation of both the movement and its development through time. The choreographer was one who could synthesize the knowledge gained through the study of compositional craft with a unique, inspired vision, a process that replicated and reinforced the mandate for a dance to fuse personal and universal concerns.[79]

Reflecting back on the burgeoning of what she called "choreographic theory" in the 1930s, Doris Humphrey speculated that the social upheaval provoked by World War I prompted dancers to reevaluate their mission as artists:

> In the United States and in Germany, dancers asked themselves some serious questions. "What am I dancing about?" "Is it worthy in the light of the kind of person I am and the kind of world I live in?" "But if not, what other kind of dance shall there be, and how should it be organized?"[80]

For Humphrey, the new modern choreographers were galvanized by a social conscience that aspired to redress injustices and create new visions of the potential for human society. Yet, as Susan Manning has demonstrated, the new conceptualization of choreography functioned in an exclusionary capacity because of the prejudicial aesthetic criteria applied to artists of color. The universal subject posited by choreography was, in fact, an elite white subject. Thus, black artists, in particular, were expected to produce "natural" and "spontaneous" movement, and this assumption either barred them from dance-making or else discredited their compositional labor. A number of critics, including John Martin, who taught criticism at Bennington, frequently rated African-American choreographers who followed the modern dance approach to choreography as "derivative" rather than "original" artists; whereas when they foregrounded Africanist elements, he, along

Figure 1.9 Ted Shawn in *Invocation to the Thunderbird* (1931), one of his
many works utilizing imagery from Native American dances
Courtesy of Jacob's Pillow Festival, Inc. Photo by Robertson.

with other critics, considered them "natural performers" rather than "creative artists."[81]

At the same time, white artists such as Graham, Ted Shawn, and Helen Tamiris felt empowered to represent all the world's peoples in their dances, casting their own white bodies in the performance of Negro Spirituals, Native American dances, and Cakewalks. Because the choreographer was an artist who could tap the universal fundaments that all movement shared, they could dance out the concerns and values of all peoples of the world. However, when Katherine Dunham used "primitive" forms from the Caribbean as the raw material for her modernist dances, she was criticized for being too sexual and therefore too commercial. As Gay Morris has documented, the white choreographic practice of modern dance ensured its elite status by working to exclude both social dance and forms of dance that purveyed entertainment.[82] Increasingly, the choreographer, an inspired individual artist, took on a new luster in comparison with the roles of social dance teachers and arrangers of dances, such as those who were setting pieces for revues, night club entertainments, or other Broadway attractions. Even after World War II, when a larger number of African-American artists appeared on concert stages, their works were required to display the values and issues associated with their specific racial communities, while white artists could continue to "experiment" with an unmarked radical newness in form and meaning.

Still, African-American choreographers such as Dunham, Pearl Primus, and Talley Beatty among others persevered in exploring the parameters set forth by modern dance, while at the same time challenging its epistemology. Their works subtly undermined the claimed separations between elite art and entertainment, between dance as the product of an extra-sensitive individual and the community that surrounded and supported that artist, and between the innovative and the traditional. Dunham, for example, contested the image of the choreographer by earning advanced degrees in anthropology and conducting extensive fieldwork on African diasporic dance forms. She produced work in highly commercial as well as elite venues, and she often integrated folk and social vocabularies into her dances in such a way as to preserve their identity while also refashioning them for the proscenium and blending them with balletic technique and modern dance syntaxes.

Although African-American choreographers began to carve out a space on the modern dance stage, the new conception of choreography continued to function as exclusionary by securing a special place for dances authored by a single artist as distinct from forms of dance

Figure 1.10 Lucille Ellis and James Alexander in the 'Fertility Section' of Katherine Dunham's *Rites de Passage* (1943)
Photo by Roger Wood
Copyright Roger Wood Photographic Collection, Royal Opera House Collections
Courtesy of Jerome Robbins Dance Collection, New York Public Library

practiced worldwide that could not be traced to a single creator. Implementing the opposition then asserted in anthropology between tradition and innovation, many white modern choreographers claimed that the movement vocabularies they devised were entirely new. Although they borrowed extensively from Native American, Asian, and various folk forms, along the lines suggested by Horst, they distanced themselves from these "unchanging" and "deeply embedded" practices even as these dances were becoming more familiar to audiences through photographic, cinematic, and sometimes live presentations of them.[83] Thus alongside the modern dance artists who experimented with "new" forms of movement, the "ethnological dancer" emerged as one who studied and mastered various enduring world forms.

Russell Meriwether Hughes, known as La Meri, claims to have invented the terms "ethnic dance" and "ethnological dancer" as ways to distinguish dances that "reflect the unchanging mores of the people of all classes . . . of a particular land or race" from ballet, the product

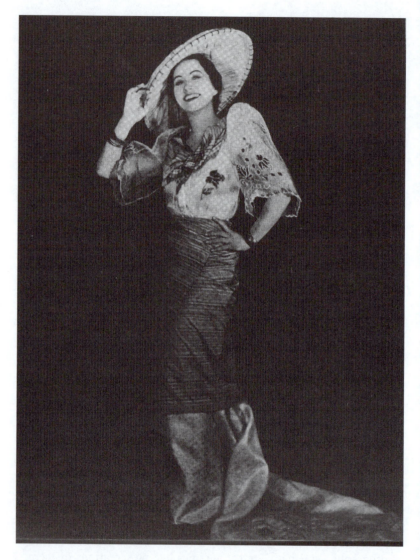

Fig 1.11 La Meri Dancing an Arabian café dance, Chethat-al-Maharma.
John Martin. *The Dance: the story of the dance told in pictures and text.* Tudor
Publishing Company: NY. 1946

Figure 1.12 La Meri dancing the Philippine dance-game Tinikling. Although the costume and arm positions differ from her version of the Chethat-al-Maharma, the smiling face and welcoming stance are remarkably similar. By performing various dances one after another and implementing similar production values for each, La Meri suggested an equivalent status for all the world's dances.

Martin, John. The Dance: the story of the dance told in pictures and text. Tudor Publishing Company: NY. 1946 of an international elite, and modern dance, the reflections of a genial individual.[84] La Meri studied Flamenco, Bharata Natyam, Javanese dances, and several European folk forms, and then arranged her own versions of the dances which she performed one after another on a single concert. Acclaimed by audiences around the world throughout the 1930s and 40s, the concerts seemed to offer a window onto diverse societies, signaling the desire to know and communicate with foreign cultures, but also displaying those cultures as small, collectible, and lacking in complexity. Not unlike Feuillet's notation of various regional dances, her concerts removed the dances from their original locations, reframing them within the space of the proscenium and suggesting that they had not and would not change over time.[85]

According to La Meri, these dances had been spawned by a universal dance of life, a more fundamental and generative energy than that evinced in either ballet or modern dance forms. In this assertion La Meri reiterated the views of Curt Sachs, whose *World History of the Dance* (1937) presented the first attempt to collate and compare dances from around the world, and who argued that all dance originated in an "effervescent zest for life."[86] Both agreed that cultures look different on the surface, but their underlying structures reflect the contours of the human predicament. Thus, dances may manifest in a vast diversity of forms, yet they are unified by their common function of providing an ecstatic alternative to quotidian life. Also like Sachs, La Meri found in all dances formal elements which she identified as aspects of their choreography. Sachs, however, focused his discussion of choreography on the range and variety of floorpaths or patterns of locomotion through which dances were organized. La Meri, in contrast, looked at the development of movement motifs, their dynamics, design, and rhythms, as signifying eternal elements of the human condition.[87]

Even as she endeavored to embrace the world's dances within a single conception of choreography, La Meri upheld fundamental differences between Western and Eastern forms. Offering her readers a list of some of the most essential contrasts, La Meri observed that occidental dances were built on broad lines that harmonized the entire body, whereas oriental dances manifested infinite shadings wherein each part of the body had a life, a line, and a rhythm of its own.[88] Occidental dances were eccentric and emotionally expressive whereas oriental dances were concentric and compressive.[89] The two traditions also differed in their overall dramatic shape, with occidental dances striving to excite by building to a brilliant and exciting climax, and oriental dances working to sooth by maintaining an emotional level that increased only in intensity.[90] La Meri's comparison extended

BALANCED CHOREOGRAPHY

Figure 1.13 This drawing exemplifying La Meri's conception of "balanced choreography" presents the dancers in an unidentifiable blend of costumes that nonetheless appears authentic because of the simplicity of the dancers' stance and spatial configuration.

La Meri. *Dance Composition: The Basic Elements.* MA: Jacob's Pillow Dance Festival, Inc. 1965.

Drawings by Cary

Courtesy of Jacob's Pillow Dance Festival, Inc.

BROKEN CHOREOGRAPHY

Figure 1.14 This drawing exemplifying La Meri's conception of "broken choreography," like her "balanced choreography," blends costuming details and also arm and hand positions from various dance forms into a single ambiguous evocation of the exotic.

La Meri. *Dance Composition*: The Basic Elements. MA: Jacob's Pillow Dance Festival, Inc. 1965.

Drawings by Cary

Courtesy of Jacob's Pillow Dance Festival, Inc.

to include contrasts in conceptions of art itself – occidental dances were motivated by courtship whereas oriental dances were born in the temple; occidental dances prized novelty and originality whereas oriental dances adhered to ancient rules; and occidental dances pointed to their own accomplishments so that their physical difficulty was appreciated whereas oriental dances masked their mastery of the form.[91]

Although La Meri's comparison claimed essential differences between East and West, it utilized the tenants of modernist aesthetics to make its argument. Space, conceptualized as a universal medium, and movement worked together to signify the journey of the psyche as the dancer's motion either expanded, radiating away from the body, or contracted, compressing in towards its center. Movement itself was a tangible and observable substance through which the dance presented a representation of self and world. Costuming, props, and lighting, although they made a critical contribution to the impact of the dance, were all treated as effects that were added after the fact to the basic substance of the dance – its movement. La Meri's approach to dance composition thus installed modernist assumptions at the core of the creative process, embracing all forms of dance while at the same time establishing itself as the meta-practice through which all forms could be evaluated. Feuillet's notation had similarly offered a set of principles through which all movement could be assessed and compared, but its principles remained separate from any emotional or interpersonal significance. Modernist principles, such as Horst's or La Meri's permitted a psychologization of culture and an appraisal of cultural difference in terms of personal as well as social attributes.

Making and collaborating

Beginning in the 1960s, the terms "choreography" and "choreographer" began to undergo yet another set of modifications due to the changing nature of dance composition and performance in the U.S. and Britain. The 1960s and 1970s also witnessed the burgeoning of performances by newly formed companies touring from around the world. In addition to numerous ballet companies, a large number of folk dance ensembles, including companies from Hungary, Poland, Mexico were presented on an international circuit along with national ballets from Cambodia, Morocco, Senegal, and Guinea, among others. Participating in the project of cultural diplomacy, these performances promised via dance to provide a vital and immediate window onto the character of a people and their way of life. They also tacitly challenged the concept of choreography by exemplifying collective forms of dance-making and by embodying the connectivity between dancing, music, and costume such that dancing as a discrete pursuit could not be separated from them.

At the same time, the collaborations between Merce Cunningham and John Cage provoked an altogether different sense of dance composition and the relation of dance to music. Both in the US and on tour, their use of chance procedures for sequencing events and the seeming disjunction between dance and music challenged the prevailing conception of the artist as expressing an inner subjectivity. In addition, many artists such as Daniel Nagrin and Anna Halprin began working with improvisation and alluded to the changing outcome of each performance by referring to themselves as the director, rather than the choreographer.[92] The new interest in utilizing "found" movement, such as the pedestrian tasks and activities deployed by Judson choreographers, also provoked a decentering of the artist-as-genius model of authorship. Artists studying at the newly founded London School of Contemporary Dance likewise explored a variety of new sources for movement vocabulary, expanding out from the Horst-based curriculum in composition to explore new methods of arranging movement through work with sculpture, film and slides, and spoken and recorded text.[93] As a result, many artists simply titled the work and then used the phrase "by," rather than "choreographed by."[94] The subsequent emphasis on borrowing movement from multiple sources and also on integrating dancers' choreography into the piece resulted in yet other nomenclatures, such as "conceived by," "directed by," or "arranged by."

These various artistic initiatives reflected a new status for the artist as more craftsperson than inspired luminary. The terms "making dances" and "making new work" came to signify a daily decision to enter the studio and construct movement or to sequence phrases of existing movement, thus signaling a redefinition of the artist as laborer and collaborator who worked with the materiality of movement. Feuillet notation had secured a substantiality for movement, but as a lexicon of established principles that could be combined in different ways to create new vocabulary. Horst had imparted a sense of its materiality by showing its possibilities for repetition, variation, and reiteration. For Horst, however, movement was always placed in the service of the choreographer who transformed it into psychological and universal expression. In contrast, the artist as maker of dances assembled movement from diverse sources and arranged it, not as personal expression, but as a statement about movement itself. This imbued the dance with a significance separate from that of its maker's intent, and at the same time, it reinforced the dance as a made event distinct from its execution. The choreography, now allied with the process through which it was made rather than the feelings or desires of its maker, became increasingly separated from both the choreographer and the dancer, even as dance companies from around the world demonstrated the interrelationship of movement, feeling, and worldview.

One of the influential exponents of the Cage/Cunningham conception of choreography was Robert Ellis Dunn who taught workshops that resulted in the renowned experimental concerts performed at the Judson Church. Dunn had been a student of John Cage where conversation focused on problem-solving and the philosophy of each student's pieces. Dunn's orientation for the course followed Cage's experimentation with chance procedures for composition and translated his precept that any sound is valid to the realm of movement where any kind of motion could be a valid part of a dance "whether it's a cough, a sniffle, or natural movement."[95] One of his first assignments "was to make a dance by combining sets of choices for body parts, durations, parts of the room, and left or right directions in space."[96] In responding to work that was presented in the class, Dunn asked students to distinguish between evaluation and perception. He worked to eliminate value judgments from the conversation, and instead asked students to contemplate the relation between the compositional process and its results: "What did you see, what did you do, what took place, how did you go about constructing and ordering. What are the materials, where did you find or how did you form them, etc."[97]

These workshops differed radically from the Bennington model in several respects: Not only did they not offer dance technique, but they even seemed to disregard technique in favor of fresh approaches to composition. Students took different technique classes on the side, but these were seen as peripheral and even incidental to the central mission of dance-making. Also unlike Bennington, the choreographic studies themselves, as a product of periods of investigation in the studio, were not so much the objects of scrutiny as the processes through which the choreography was realized allowing students to contemplate the array of procedures that existed for inventing and arranging movement.

Rather than an integral part of learning to dance, as it had been in the eighteenth century, technique, as developed by artists as diverse as Cunningham and Halprin, became a process of breaking down the body into constituent parts so that one could investigate all the combinatory possibilities for movement. Rather than a preparation of the body as vehicle of the choreographer's message as in the early modern dance, technique now cultivated the body's potential for articulation, for displaying a variety of combinatory possibilities for

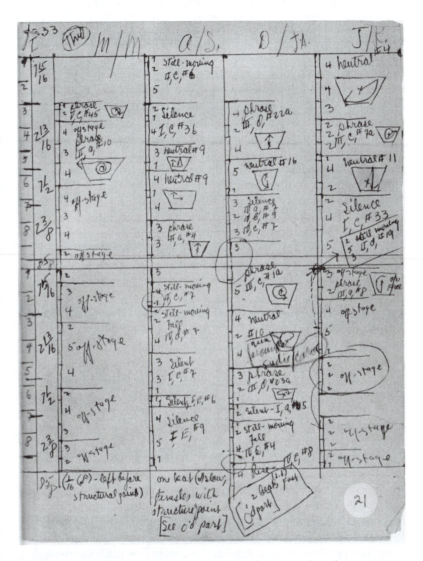

Figure 1.15 In this excerpt from the score for *Suite by Chance* (1953), Cunningham identifies locations and actions for each of the dancers. Other sections of the score indicate how to use chance procedures to determine parts of the body, motions, and durations.

Merce Cunningham, *Changes: Notes on Choreography*. New York: Something Else Press, 1968.

Permission granted Courtesy of Merce Cunningham Estate

moving. The body was disciplined, not so as to be able to fuse with the self in order to enwrap a given message, but to be able to articulate its various parts so that these could be combined or sequenced differently to produce distinctive physical effects. Dance movement, now seen as entirely separate from music, presented physical effects that were determinedly separated from any connotations of the spiritual or the emotional. Dance makers saw the body itself as meaning-filled, and they believed that the pragmatic execution of movement offered a glimpse into the self of the performer that felt more real and revealing than any performances in which the dancer enacted a character.

The avant-garde initiatives set in motion by Cage's theories of composition not only redefined technique but also the concept of virtuosity. For choreographers allied with the Judson tradition, virtuosity consisted not in distinguishing oneself by an exceptionally brilliant performance, but instead, in dissolving the self and its achievements into the movement so that the actions themselves were broadcast. Disdaining virtuosity as the act of surpassing what was stipulated in the choreography, they aspired to create a more modest and workmanly image for the dancer. At the same time, African-American choreographers such as Alvin Ailey and Donald McKayle, drawing on a heritage of virtuosity as an affirmation and celebration of communal values, pursued the exceptional execution of diverse vocabularies. Where white choreographers hoped to modify the artist-as-genius model with its claim to express universal issues within each body, African-American artists continued to synthesize the universal with the individual, not as a sign of individual entitlement, but as a contribution to community.

As in modern dance whose universal subject could express any human condition, so in the avant garde the alleged liberatory potential contained in the notion of choreography as a selection of processes and technique and virtuosity as the simple execution of those processes functioned as an unmarked and white set of claims. For example, Cage, Steve Paxton, and many others repeatedly acknowledged the influence from Asian philosophies of mind and art on their work, esteeming Zen and Taoist religious practices for helping them to break through habitualized boundaries and opening up new kinds of aesthetic possibilities. Paxton and those who developed the radical new practice of contact improvisation, borrowing many of its principles from Aikido, asserted the universality of its aesthetics of touch. At the same time, Asian artists were largely denied access to the experimental stage. Critics and many viewers continued to require Asian artists to represent classical artistic practices rather than new and experimental approaches.

Like the African-American artists of the 1940s, Asian artists of the 1960s and 70s were criticized as derivative if they produced experimental work and as natural when they showed more traditional works.[98] As Shobana Jeyasingh remarked in her interrogation of the politics of dance production, Asian-British artists, even as they endeavored to produce experimental and hybrid work, were housed in theaters reserved for "world" dance rather than for white British contemporary artists.[99]

The misunderstandings around these exclusionary operations of choreography and their attendant criteria of excellence predicted even larger epistemological faultlines that became increasingly evident as dance companies from around the world continued to tour to and from the US. Under the loose rubric of multiculturalism, "traditional" dance forms from many countries were being programmed and presented, maintaining the modernist distinction between single authored contemporary work and ambiguously authored ethnic or world dance. Where experimental choreography assumed the role of challenging viewers' expectations as to the nature of art and movement, these concerts were regarded as purveying joy, exotic excitement, and dazzling physical skills, while providing an "authentic" glimpse into another culture's values. At the same time, they raised serious questions about the separation of dance into sacred and secular, the assumed autonomy of dance movement from music, poetry, and costume, and the role of the dancer's performance in relation to the choreography. These issues, however, never received substantive attention, and only in 1997 did the Dance Critics Association pose the question of whether critics should be informed as to the history and aesthetics of foreign dance forms that they might review.[100]

Buttressing this reception of world dance, university curricula slowly added courses in West African dance, Javanese dance, or Bharata Natyam, beginning in the 1970s. These were not studied as proposing distinct theories of choreography, but rather, as techniques that could enrich the student's awareness of the body while also offering a distinctive "cultural" experience. Taught in the spare modern dance studio, often without costumes, sometimes without live music, students focused on learning the movement first, acquiring technical proficiency, and then dancing a dance. Yet curricular and financial constraints inhibited them from acquiring substantive proficiency. As a result, pedagogy reinforced the image of these dances as traditional and unchanging, since students never learned how to improvise within the forms, how to collaborate with musicians, or how to arrange and rearrange material to meet the specific demands of a given performance.

As compositional ideas for how to make dances and subject matters for dances proliferated, the meaning of choreography began to transform yet again. The choreographer, no longer the visionary originator of a dance, or even its maker or director, became a person who assembled and presided over a collaboration. Unlike the modern choreographers, dance artists no longer formed companies, but instead worked from project to project, picking up a company of dancers with whom to collaborate.[101] Rather than focus on elaborating the singular artistic vision of an individual, or on a rigorous methodology for inventing and sequencing movement, these artists embarked on collaborations that were project driven. Generally, each project required unique skills, and specific repertoires of movement. Presiding over these projects, the choreographer was identified as the facilitator of the work being made.

Choreographers as facilitators began to work with dancers in several new ways: they asked dancers to invent some or all of the movement, to propose its staging and development over time, to suggest costuming, and so forth. Additionally, choreographers began working with dancers who brought distinctive sets of skills to the project, such as juggling, gymnastics, skate boarding, and various forms of popular dance including break-dancing, salsa, square dancing, etc. They investigated the movement of animals in relation to human movement. They worked with untrained dancers and with dancers of vastly different ages and training experiences. Inspired in part by a growing awareness of how disabled bodies had been stigmatized and desiring to promote a non-hierarchical affirmation of physical difference, they also worked with dancers of different abilities. Less interested in the physical articulation necessary to execute these actions than with the cultural resonances that these actions evoked, choreographers began to ask: How do these actions signify identity? What kinds of cultural milieus do they represent? What had begun with Cunningham as an embrace of all movement as articulation soon transformed into an interest in all movement as varieties of signifying cultural and individual identity.

Choreographers not only collaborated with dancers but also began working more intensively with artists from other mediums, exploring interdisciplinary modes of performance between dance and theater, film and video, lighting design, new digital media, and also working with set designers and sculptors. These collaborations took a variety of forms, sometimes juxtaposing performances in the different media, and sometimes constructing new intermedia genres in which neither form would exist without the other. Modern choreographers had integrated different media, based on the premise of an organic

Figure 1.16 AXIS Dance company members Judy Smith and Jacques Poulin-Denis.
Photographer Margot Hartford

functionalism in which each art made a distinctive contribution to the whole. As Doris Humphrey observed, music, by contributing a syntax, should serve as the perfect mate, but not master, for dance.[102] The new collaborations, whether as juxtaposed collages of diverse media or as intermedia integrations of aspects from each art, dismantled and contested any organic differentiation among the arts. Each medium worked with different materials, but did not, as a result, create unique forms of address. Instead, any and all the arts boasted the capacity to expand perception and illuminate one's apprehension of the world.

The emphasis on borrowing movement from multiple sources and on integrating dancers' contributions into the piece meant that the dance to be created had no integral relationship with a specific technique or training regimen. Instead, each dance utilized a pastiche or amalgam of movement skills. Dancers began to train in multiple forms and genres, including ballet, contact improvisation, and jazz, as well as various modern forms, hoping to piece together the necessary all-purpose physicality to accomplish an array of movement tasks. This approach to acquiring technical competence, celebrated in *So You Think You Can Dance*, severed the connection between training and dancing. At the same time, new adaptations of traditional techniques such as ballet, and new exercise systems informed by anatomical organization proposed to train a universal dancing body. These regimens, including body–mind centering, release technique, Pilates, and varieties of yoga, all claimed to produce an efficient and balanced musculature based on their understanding of the body's true design. Like H'Doubler they championed a kinesiological analysis of movement, one that would disencumber the body from the distortions produced by psyche and society and reassert its natural grace and integrity.

The new model of collaboration in choreography mirrored new structures of patronage and support for artists. Both public and private funding sources increasingly invited applications for specific projects. Artists applied to these institutions, not for support for the ongoing maintenance of their companies, but for funds for a specific event. Granting agencies also encouraged the leveraging of grants by matching money from various organizations. This resulted in a need for "buy-in" from many different funding agencies, which in turn placed increased pressure on the artist as promoter of one's own career and as someone who was an effective entrepreneur. The artists did not seek patrons as the early modern choreographers did, but instead, tried to identify new kinds of opportunities for funding and advertisement. The choreographer thus became a manager of a career and of projects. Not a genius, not a craftsperson, and lacking in the expertise to decode the specialized knowledge inscribed in notation, the choreographer now leveraged different funding opportunities in the same way that she or he facilitated the collaborative interaction among all participants. Where Arbeau's dancers had employed dancing to participate in the accrual of mutual indebtedness shared by all members of the aristocracy, choreographers now contrived to pitch projects that could secure a similar kind of mutual buy-in from all funding agencies.

The new awareness of funding structures and practices was well documented in the *Poor Dancers Almanac: A Survival Manual for Choreographers, Managers and Dancers* (1983) published by the staff at Dance Theatre Workshop, one of the primary theaters presenting fringe work in New York City. Never intended to give aesthetic advice to young artists or to teach them about how to make dances, the manual instead enumerated the various financial skills necessary to becoming a successful choreographer. Organized to address the needs of a young artist arriving in New York City to build a career, the manual began with instructions on how to use phone services, libraries, health and medical facilities. It explained how to get discounted tickets to performances, how to find living and working spaces and part-time employment, and how to benefit from government financial services such as food stamps and unemployment insurance. It then embarked on a detailed analysis of how to set up the management for one's career: whether or not to incorporate as a non-profit business, how to employ dancers and other artists, how to construct budgets, pay taxes, and copyright one's work. Having guided the choreographer through the process of setting up a management infrastructure, it then offered extensive advice on how to produce one's work: how to write a press release, obtain photographs, invite critics, produce mailings, posters, and all forms of advertisement; how to find a performing space, negotiate a contract, organize box office and front of house, utilize the stage space, and document the work. The almanac then concluded with chapters on funding and the marketplace for dance. It listed various agencies, federal, state, city, private foundations, and corporations that supported dance, and advised on how to write grants, employ booking agents, establish fees, construct a tour, and even arrange to have one's work shown on television. The choreographer had become a manager of a career and of projects, a person engaged in artistic and wealth management.

The proliferation of approaches to choreography generated by so many independent choreographers in the 1970s and 80s prompted a break down in any consolidated or systematic approach to the teaching of composition. The American Dance Festival (ADF), tracing its roots back to the Bennington College summer school, offered composition courses based in the model of those taught in 1930s up through the 1970s. These courses generally devised assignments for expanding students' awareness and mastery of movement's spatial, temporal, and dynamic aspects. Then in the 1980s, and with greater and greater frequency, composition appeared in one of two new hybrid forms: as a course entitled improvisation/composition or as one called composition/repertory. Improvisation/composition largely addressed the use of improvisation as a way to generate new movement possibilities for oneself or for a group of dancers with whom one might be collaborating. Composition/repertory was taught by some instructors as a traditional repertory course where a new work was set on the students, or as a blending of the instructor's and students' composition studies; or, as in this course description by Liz Lerman, as a collaborative process:

> We will make a dance/text piece about how each of us looks to the future. Using personal stories, historical and contemporary events and family recollections we will explore and share the unique visions each generation holds as they imagine what lies ahead. Students will develop unique movement to accompany these stories.[103]

The fact that composition began to be parsed into these two separate courses – improvisation and repertory – seemed to indicate that two kinds of skills were needed in order to create new work: ways to generate movement and to work with people, and ways to generate a vision or thematics for a specific piece. This second skill was honed as it had been in the 1930s by witnessing and participating in several different artists' approaches to the making of work.

Promoting the modernist notion of the choreographer as the creative source of the dance, but allowing for that process to be collaborative, the American Dance Festival instigated a major new initiative on teaching technique and dance-making worldwide, extending the framework of collaboration to facilitate international projects. In 1987 ADF was invited to send teachers to Guang Dong, China to establish a modern dance curriculum there, consisting of technique and repertory courses. Performing in the ambassadorial role of tacitly promoting democratic values, the curriculum emphasized the individual creative process and the necessity of artistic freedom in pursuing new visions of dance. This program was the first of many "linkages" developed by ADF worldwide supporting the exchange of teachers and artists.[104] These schools had, in turn, sent students and artists to ADF where they studied and shared work with US students and artists. The fact that so many choreographers from different countries took classes and taught repertory at ADF stimulated a new intensity of collaborative projects combining, juxtaposing, or otherwise fusing distinctive cultural dance traditions. Support for these projects was extensive, with the USIA (United States Information Agency), the Ford Foundation, and the Rockefeller Foundation all awarding major grants for cultural exchange in the 1990s.

These pedagogical exchanges helped to construct a new global stage where contemporary, rather than traditional dance companies from around the world offered up diverse aesthetics wrapped in the conventional appearance of the two-hour proscenium-framed spectacle. They also helped to inaugurate new intercultural exchanges wherein dancers trained in diverse traditions might share, juxtapose, or fuse styles and vocabularies. Choreography, in these exchanges, has taken on multiple meanings and valences. In some cases choreography is interpreted as having depleted the diversity and precision of dance forms, compromising, by interrupting their historical legacies, and erasing the nuance, value and meaning of specific practices in favor of standardized and commoditized movement displays. Here choreography functions much like eighteenth century notation as a process of uprooting, accomplished not by the symbolic encoding of movements principles, but instead, by the application of criteria of marketability, such as glamour, authenticity, and professional quality, that work to homogenize dancing for acceptable global circulation. In other cases, choreography is envisioned as providing an arena in which to encounter and potentially transcend the histories of oppression, colonization, or enslavement that form part of the corporeal legacies of potential collaborators so as to celebrate a common humanity. In both cases, the drive to deliver "product" for multiple funding agencies often means that there is insufficient time to sort through these kinds of differences.

Responding to the various mandates to place dance in global circulation, professional schools for dance training worldwide have embraced diverse traditions of dancing and offer advanced levels of study in forms ranging from ballet to Barata Natyam, Chinese Opera, classical Indonesian, Malaysian, Thai, Flamenco, various West African forms, and so forth. These technique classes are complemented by other courses, in release technique, Feldenkrais, Pilates, yoga or Tai-Chi, envisioned as enhancing the student's kinesthetic awareness of the body. Whereas classical or other forms of dance technique are conceptualized as culturally specific, these provide a "universal" training that is efficient, anatomically informed, and capable of cultivating the greatest versatility for the dancing body. Whereas dance techniques give entry into culturally specific values and aesthetics, these forms exist uncontaminated by culture, or as beyond culture. They help to groom the body for global presentation. Thus, what began with H'Doubler as a kinesiological investigation of the mysteries of the body, and continued with mid-century dance-makers as a charting or inventory of physical possibilities, has become a universal base that authorizes collaboration across any and all registers of difference.

The opening up of choreography to encompass investigations across ages, physical abilities, and cultures has yielded diverse hybrid bodies and movement forms that can impact the viewer in multiple ways. The universal message that Martin presumed dance could deliver has been replaced, not by a new singular experience of dancing, but by a vast range of engagements with dance producing distinctive visions of and knowledges about the body. When choreography occurs in such a way as to allow the time and resources to negotiate these differences, viewers may be edified by the results of the artistic labor to exchange points of view and types of skills. Where these differences are submerged or glossed over in the rush to present newness, choreography functions much like the traffic lights system in Los Angeles as a form of collision control.

Choreography first uprooted dances by relocating them onto a horizontal geometric plane and, subsequently, by applying to them a universal principle of gravity, both psychic and physical. In each case, choreography gestured towards the world's dances only by assimilating their differences into its economy of meaning. Now choreography is convening the world's dances in order to substitute for each dance's locale commoditized markers of alterity. In these projects it mobilizes a universally versatile body capable of mastering any and all traditions of dancing. Alternatively, choreography holds out the promise to affirm the local's connection to the global, recognizing the specific and intensive physical commitment that any body must invest in order to ground itself in the world.

2 Kinesthesia

Emerging from underground transportation systems in major metropolitan centers, one frequently encounters a map of the immediate environs. In Tokyo, Shanghai, and Taipei, these maps offer a depiction of the neighborhood directly behind the map as one stands looking at it. In New York, London, or Paris, the map details the area surrounding the subway station, as located with respect to the cardinal directions with North at the top of the map. In order to read the map, one must determine one's location in relation to North. This often entails walking away from the map to find an intersection that will help to identify North and consequently one's orientation with respect to the map. Tokyo, Shanghai, and Taipei maps, in contrast, do not require this reconciliation of one's position with respect to an absolute geometry. Instead, they simply present what is ahead. As a consequence, completely different maps can be found on opposite sides of the same placard. The cardinal directions are indicated on these maps, but North might appear in one corner or along any side of the map. Walking around the placard to view the map on the other side, North changes from the upper right corner, for example, to the lower left.

I describe these different experiences of encountering a map, not to gesture towards some essential difference between "East" and "West," but rather to emphasize the different kinds of kinesthetic awareness that maps can require. In order to know where you are with respect to your surroundings in New York, London, or Paris, it is necessary first to assimilate your visual perception. Only after determining your location within the grid is it possible to navigate using the map's information. And this procedure of self-location entails a recalibration of internal and external sensings of one's whereabouts. The body must perceive simultaneously its position, movement, momentum, and proximity to everything around it, and even its relationship to gravity.

How does one sense one's own movement and sense the orientation of that movement within the surrounding space? Over the course of the nineteenth century, the physiological mechanisms responsible for this ongoing process were identified as various neural sensors, located in the joints, the muscles, the skin, and the inner ear, that together provided information about each body part's position, motion, and relationship to gravity. In 1820, physiologist Thomas Brown observed that "our muscular frame was not merely a part of the living machinery of motion, but was also truly an organ of sense."[1] In the 1820s and 30s Sir Charles Bell identified "muscle sense" as responsible for three groups of sensations – pain and fatigue, weight and resistance, and movement and position – all of which resulted from sensations arising when a muscle contracts. The Pancinian corpuscles, muscle spindles, and Golgi tendon organs that all contributed to these sensations were identified in the 1840s, 60s, and 80s respectively.[2] And in 1880 neurophysiologist Henry Charlton Bastian was able to synthesize investigations of these specialized receptors with his own work on their connections to the cerebral cortex in order to assert definitively the sense of movement which he named kinesthesia.[3]

Deriving from the Greek *kine*, or movement, and *aesthesis*, or sensation, the term "kinesthesia" initially referred specifically to the muscular sense of the body's movement. Contemporaneous with investigations into joint and muscle receptors, but independent from them, physiologists also examined the function of the inner ear in sustaining balance and contributing to bodily equilibrium. These investigations culminated in the 1870s in the establishment of the vestibular system. Only with the work of perception theorist James J. Gibson in the 1950s and 60s, however, did Bastian's conception of the kinesthetic expand to include the synthesis of information provided by muscle and joint receptors along with information on orientation contributed by the inner ear.[4] Gibson, to whose work I will return, identified the kinesthetic system as one that integrated information about position, motion, and orientation with other visual, aural, and tactile information so as to construct a sense of one's location in the world. It is this synthesizing of information that navigation based on map-reading requires.

Much like map-reading, each of the implementations of the term "choreography" delineated in the previous chapter specify a distinctive organization of physicality, for both the practitioner and the viewer. In what follows, I will reexamine choreographies for the epistemological assumptions they contain regarding kinesthetic experience. What kinds of physical orienting do these notions of choreography imply? I will also look to a range of diverse practices including map-reading, programs in physical education and therapy, medical assumptions about posture and exercise, and to an even less likely source of information, the accounts of people experiencing an earthquake, in order to track how the sense of the body's motion has changed over time, even before the term "kinesthesia" was invented to name that experience.

Many of the discourses that contain information about one's experience of kinesthesia implicitly address specific types of bodies, although most do not acknowledge their substitution of a singular physicality for all human bodies. Sixteenth century exercise manuals, for example, took as their charge the cultivation of the aristocratic male body, so as to enhance his nobility and his skill in combat. Seventeenth and eighteenth century manuals as well as the burgeoning courtesy and therapy literatures likewise extrapolated from a male body, usually urban and from the middle or upper classes. The working poor and those living in the countryside were seen as receiving sufficient exercise or as healthier because they lived in more beneficial climates than city dwellers. Throughout this entire period, there is little attention to the female body and to programs of exercise or protocols that might enhance her awareness of the body. Such programs of exercise that did make mention of women generally offered advice based on male regimens reduced in amount and kind. At the beginning of the nineteenth century, however, a new recognition of fundamental differences between male and female anatomy prompted new sets of exercises and standards for female activity that differed markedly from male-oriented practices.[5]

In the twentieth century, various regimens of physical education have been devised to address the needs of diverse kinds of bodies as they have embarked on individualized pursuits in health, athletics, and recreation. Some of these have integrated the notion of kinesthetic awareness into their specific approach to bodily cultivation. At the same time, kinesthesia has been pursued largely as a scientific inquiry into nervous system and brain functioning. The focus of this chapter is not whether different physicalities and life experiences produce distinctive kinds of kinesthetic information. Rather, I look at how a range of practices in a given historical moment all shared certain assumptions about a standard physicality and actively promoted that standard as the universal body. By tracking these discourses over time, it is possible to see how physicality and with it a specific experience of the kinesthetic have changed radically.

Chorographies and anatomies

If John Essex did intend an analogy between the ways that chorographers studied the countryside and the ways that notation documented dance when he titled his application of Feuillet *A Treatise of Chorography*, what kinds of analytic frameworks did the two share? Chorography was identified by Ptolemy as the study of a specific region, in contrast to geography, the study of the earth as a whole. It emerged as a discipline in the sixteenth century as part of widespread inquiry into the art of well-ordered traveling (*ars* or *methodicus apodemica*) provoked by explorations of Africa, the mid-East and the Americas, and also by a new interest in regional specificity within parts of Europe itself. Where the geographer, according to Ptolemy, implemented mathematics, the chorographer needed to apply aesthetic sensibilities so as to register the specificity and individuality of a place.[6]

Essex remarked on the uniqueness of English Country Dancing, a mode of dancing practiced widely in the courts of Europe at the time of his publication. He conceived of his collection of these dances as a practice in cultural diplomacy, but also a form of nation-building. Feuillet, he observed, "has been so kind to his own Country, as to form it into a Character easie to be understood,"[7] and Mr. Isaac, sponsoring John Weaver, had reciprocated by translating the system into English. Essex then proposed to contribute to the exchange by notating dances in the English country mode both of his own composition and also of French invention. In so doing, he claimed for England a specific kind of originality, one that had exerted extensive influence abroad.

Chorography likewise contributed to consolidating and building the nation.[8] In his study of landscape and the body politic, Kenneth Olwig demonstrates the crucial role that chorography played in consolidating regions and proclaiming their sovereignty. Chorographic studies of Great Britain, for example, helped to forge a public sense of a united British Isles beginning in the early seventeenth century. Not only did they collect the regions into a single compendium, as Essex's treatise did, but they also established a way of looking that Feuillet and Essex shared. Constructing a commanding viewpoint from which to survey a designated territory, they also reinforced claims to ownership of a specific landmass. Commissioned first by monarchs, they were subsequently adopted by nobility and landed gentry, the group of capitalists who were providing the funds for colonial exploration and expansion, as evidence of the boundaries and extent of their estates.[9]

As outlined in the 1709 edition of *The Compleat Geographer*, a compendium of chorographies from around the world, the chorographer's study should include four distinct descriptions of a given region:

> geometrically, as it relates to the extent and boundaries of countries to which ought to be added the subdivisions into provinces or shires; . . . naturally, wherein the situation (with respect to the heavens) the climate, soil, and products, ought to be declared; . . . politically, wherein the government and history is to be considered; . . . and humanely, with relation to the inhabitants of them, their religion, manners, customs, etc.[10]

The delineation of this fourfold analysis presumed a separation of land from its inhabitants, first locating the region geometrically and identifying its physical resources before considering its political and social organization, and any customs worthy of note.

In describing the geographical features of a territory, chorographies typically began by identifying the various rivers or mountain ranges that defined the borders of the area under consideration. In order to convey a sense of these borders, they positioned themselves as facing north and established an ichnographic or bird's eye viewpoint, as if observing the land from high above.[11] From this vantage point, they depicted mountains as rising up from, and rivers as cutting through an otherwise blank horizontal plane.[12] This description of Virginia is typical:

> On the North is bounded by Patowmeck River, which parts it from Maryland; on the East by the Ocean, on the South by a ridge of hills dividing it from Carolina, and on the West the unconquer'd Country, which may be reckon'd a Part of New-France, or Hennipin's Louisiana, as being no great distance from the known Lake of Erie.[13]

Often, such descriptions included longitudinal coordinates that endowed the blank horizontal plane with geometric specificity.[14] Especially in colonies such as Virginia, the natural resources were then surveyed with emphasis on the potential for trade or cultivation. A cursory overview of inhabitants and their customs concluded the descriptions. The chorographies thus conveyed a process of sweeping away, eradicating even, all the features of a land and then reinstating them methodically in order of their importance.

Essex's application of Feuillet, like other English translations, implemented the blank horizontal plane onto which the paths of dancers

Figure 2.1 This chorographic type of map of the region known as Nova Virginiae was published in John Ogilby's *America: Being the latest and most accurate description of the New World*. London: Printed by the author, and are to be had at his house in White Fryers, 1671. Plate between pages 134-135 entitled "Nova Virginiae Tabula."
Courtesy of University of California, Los Angeles, Special Collections Library

were inscribed. Like Feuillet, Essex felt it necessary to remind the reader that in order to interpret the diagrams, the top of the page must remain aligned with the top of the room. Neither Feuillet nor Essex constructed an ichnographic representation of the dance, however, a slightly later adaptation of Feuillet notation, by Kellom Tomlinson, placed the dancers' pathways within just that perspective thereby creating the choreographic equivalent of a chorographic map. Tomlinson's dancers, whether side by side, or upstage from one another, were clearly positioned on a dancing floor, the traces of their previous and next movements graphed onto it. Located within a precisely measured plane, they were positioned so as to survey their own progress through the dance, looking out over the notation towards their partner or the vanishing horizon. Seeming to garner their substance and significance from the grid along

Figure 2.2 This image from Kellom Tomlinson's collection of dances suggests a lively duet for two men.
Kellom Tomlinson. *The art of dancing explained by reading and figures: whereby the manner of performing the steps is made easy by a new and familiar method: being the original work/first design'd in the year 1724, and now published by Kellom Tomlinson, dancing master.* London. The second edition. 1744. Book 1, plate XII
Courtesy of The William Andrews Clark Memorial Library, University of California, Los Angeles

which they traveled, they encouraged the reader to savor from an ichnographic point of view the specific moment in the dance that was depicted and also to imagine all other moments within the whole dance as it had been laid out on the floor. Authorized by founding principles, with access to an established vocabulary of movements, their dancing enabled them to extend into space, a pure space, unmarked and open, that existed prior to the entrance of the body into it.

Like Tomlinson's engravings, seventeenth and eighteenth century chorographies imparted a perspective intimate enough to give the reader a sense of walking down a particular road or past a landmark building, yet distant enough to convey a sense of the whole. Ptolemy had likened chorography to the study of a region of the body such as the face, and geography to the study of the whole body. Topography, a subset of chorography, investigated specific locations, analogous to the study of the eye or ear.[15] Thus chorography provided a sense of relations among specific features similar to the way that each of Tomlinson's dances was laid out, either on a single page or series of pages, in its entirety. Each dance suggested a different atmosphere and degree of intimacy and engagement on the part of the dancers, yet they all conformed to a standard way of presenting the dance.

Like Feuillet and Essex, Tomlinson went to great lengths to instruct the dancer in how to read the notation in relation to the room in which one was dancing. He warned the dancer to calculate differences in size and shape of rooms, some being square and others rectangular, and then to fit the floor path to that specific shape. Where Feuillet advised the dancer on how to hold the book while turning so as to maintain the correspondence between the top of the room and the top of the page, Tomlinson enterprisingly suggested that the dancer utilize two books, one placed flat and stationary on a table or the floor and the other to be carried as one marked out the steps. Alternatively, a second person, standing at the front of the room, could hold the book up for the dancer to consult.

Such detailed instructions regarding how to orient one's self in relation to room and notation suggest that an ichnographic way of looking was relatively novel. They underscore the ideological impact, as Olwig argues, that maps could exercise over those who viewed them. They also make evident the disciplinizing process through which any individual acquired the ability to navigate within a chorographically constructed world. To read a map and find one's location within it took practice at coordinating several kinds of kinesthetic information. Slowly over the course of the seventeenth and eighteenth centuries, this skill was, literally, incorporated into one's kinesthetic awareness.

Early chorographic studies established a strong connection between specific climates, landmasses, and human disposition. England, for example, was identified as unusually warm and mild in comparison with the rest of northern Europe and in contrast with the hotter and more arid regions of the Mediterranean. English chorographers argued that the climate was responsible, in part, for the unique political

Figure 2.3 Although the Canary performed by this dancer is a lively and fast-paced dance, a more modest atmosphere is suggested in this drawing of a single female dancer from Kellom Tomlinson's collection.

Kellom Tomlinson. *The art of dancing explained by reading and figures: whereby the manner of performing the steps is made easy by a new and familiar method: being the original work/first design'd in the year 1724, and now published by Kellom Tomlinson, dancing master.* London. The second edition. 1744. Book 1, plate XVI

Courtesy of The William Andrews Clark Memorial Library, University of California, Los Angeles temperament of English society, one that differed from the more aggressive tendencies of those from the north and the weaker proclivities of those from the south. Each region was seen as containing specific characteristics and qualities, based largely on the prevailing medical conceptions of the body's humours.

Following the influential Renaissance translations of Greek physician Galen, the body was seen as comprised of spongelike masses, soaked with mixtures of four kinds of fluids known as humours.[16] Forming a symmetrical grid of binary oppositions, the humours, blood, yellow bile, black bile, and phlegm, correlated with degrees of temperature and moisture as well as the four elements, the seasons, and the stages of life itself.[17] Motivating these fluids and interacting with them were three kinds of spirits, vegetable, animal, and intellectual. Specifically corporeal in nature, these spirits drew their sustenance from an aerial substance, the *pneuma*, as it was inhaled. The predominance of one humour or another, as energized by the fleshly spirits, accounted for the complexion, or external appearance, and the temperament of each individual, whether sanguine, bilious, melancholic, and phlegmatic.

Health resulted from an equilibrium among the humours, just as disease was a product of their imbalance. Since there was no conception of circulation, fluids mingled in the body by seepage, responding to physical exertion, diet, social interactions, or climate. Chemical properties inherent in foods or landscapes, or the product of conversations, or physical exertion acted upon the humours, fortifying or diminishing their potency. The resultant imbalances constantly needed to be addressed through application or elimination of substances that, again, shared the same elemental properties as the humours. Thus, apoplexy or stroke, the product of excessive blood, could be induced by drinking too much red wine, whereas frailty and timidity, the product of thin blood, could be cured by rich food and red meat. As in the court dances that Arbeau inventoried, where the proximities between dancers were continually adjusted so as to maintain social balance, so too the maintenance of health necessitated an ongoing effort to calibrate and maintain equilibrium. Travel, capable of restoring balance as one interacted with peoples and climates, was frequently undertaken in order to expose one's self to a full range of influences and thereby deepen that equilibrium.[18]

Within this paradigm of corporeality, the kinesthetic sense of one's orientation in space and movement through space was the product of the seeping and swaying gravitas of fluids saturating the body. Any exertion, such as the fast-paced swirling turns in the La Volta that Caroso warned his readers about, could result in the excessive excitation of one of the animal spirits, provoking disorientation. Described by doctors as the experience of seeing what was before one move in a circle, dizziness was diagnosed variously as the product of vapors in the brain catalyzing to form a whirlwind, or as phlegm or bile originating in the stomach or womb that could rise up and affect the animal spirits in the brain. Sometimes caused by over-exposing the head to the sun, in which case hemorrhoids in its veins would be inflated, dizziness could be treated by cupping or a small amount of bleeding, or through avoidance of all food, especially steamed, that produced "flatus."[19] Dizziness could also be provoked through the sympathetic witnessing of anything going round and round.[20] The trajectories and momentums of various fluids in the body were highly susceptible to disruption by forces located both within the body and in the environment. The La Volta was almost as dangerous to watch as to perform.

By the middle of the seventeenth century, however, Galenic versions of corporeality were increasingly contested, in part by the persuasiveness of Vesalius's interpretations of dissected corpses, and in part through the application of a new technology, the microscope, that enabled a far more detailed understanding of physical structure.[21] The explosion in new anatomical discoveries assisted by the microscope helped to revise the conception of physical systems and their functioning. Blood was now understood to circulate throughout the body, assisted by the actions of the heart.[22] Individual parts of the body, once exposed to microscopic analysis, shared a common structural composition; each was built from the smallest and most basic of entities called globules, or cells.

In utilizing the microscope, scientists implemented a geometrical framework not unlike that used in chorography. Robert Hooke, member of the Royal Society and author of the influential *Micrographia* (1665), explained that just as the mathematical point was the beginning for geometry, so too, in applying the microscope one should begin with an observation of a point, such as a needle, followed by a line, such as the edge of a razor, planes, such as woven material, and finally three dimensional objects.[23] Applying these principles of investigation, Hooke determined that most inanimate substances were formed from globules of different geometric shapes – triangles, squares, tetrahedrons, cubes, and so forth.[24] In the same way that chorography cleared the ground so that a precise survey could be made of its features, so too, microscopy required careful preparation of the specimen to be viewed. Just as chorography imbued each district with geographical coordinates, so too microscopy depended upon a careful calculation of the relative size of the specimen. Hooke, for example, placed a ruler next to his specimens and was able to look with one eye through the microscope and with the other at the ruler, so as to measure the exact degree of magnification.[25]

As a result of these inquiries, the human body began to transform from a sloshing container of fluids into an intricately composed machine. As Roy Porter explains:

> Investigators were spurred to view living creatures mechanistically, as ingenious contraptions made up of skillfully articulated components (bone's, joints, cartilage, muscles, vessels), functioning as levers, pulleys, cogs, pipes, and wheels, in line with the laws of mechanics, kinetics, hydrostatics, and so forth. The body became a *machina carnis*, a machine of the flesh.[26]

These mechanical parts, like the topographical features along the surveyor's route could be placed on a scale regulated by mathematical measurements.

Although microscopy's contribution to this new image of physicality began to decline by 1700, the burgeoning of discoveries about physical structure that it made possible culminated in a vision of flesh as composed of single units that expanded or contracted by a change in the amount of fluids that entered them. Contraction of the muscles, for example, whether they were seen as strings of small bladders (William Croone), or as rows of globules held together by a thin membrane (Van Leeuwenhoek), or as a weaving together of hollow fibers and small membranes (Grew), resulted from an augmentation in the amount of blood.[27] No neural or electrical involvement seemed essential. Thus, microscopy was seen as having laid the foundation for new scientific inquiry into the chemical and mechanical composition of the body. Like Feuillet's breakdown of dances into fundamental principles that permitted the cataloguing of steps, the discovery of cells established the fundamental building blocks out of which the bodies were composed.

The kinds of discoveries made possible by microscopic investigation along with sciences such as chorography continued to shape the epistemological underpinnings of knowledge production throughout the eighteenth century. Like the anatomy theater framing the cadaver, the microscope helped to construct for anatomists a static and stationary perspective from which to view any object under investigation.[28] Analogous to notation's analysis of movement, it reduced the body to its most basic properties and placed these within a comparative mathematical framework based on relative sizes and dimensions of related objects. Like chorography, its companion study of the land, anatomy stilled both the observer and the object of study and created an unmarked plane onto which the various features of the physical were located. Both sciences positioned the observer looking down upon the object of study. Choreography then taught that perspective to dancers as a sensibility to be maintained even while in motion.

With the bodies of the observer and the observed fixed in stillness, a new conception of kinesthesia began to emerge, eloquently detailed in Étienne Bonnot de Condillac's inquiry into the senses. In his *Treatise on the Sensations* (1754), Condillac posited the existence of a hypothetical statue, a motionless body frozen in marble, whose senses were enlivened one at a time:

> Our statue, deprived of smell, of hearing, of taste, of vision, and limited to the sense of touch, now exists through the feeling which she has of the parts of her body one upon the other – above all the movements of respiration: and this is the least degree of feeling to which one may reduce her. I call it fundamental feeling, because it is with this play of the machine that the life of the animal begins; she depends on it alone ... This feeling and her "I" are consequently the same thing in their origin.[29]

Utterly immobile, the statue nonetheless felt parts of her body touching other areas, and also the sensation of breathing. These sensations emanating from the viscera and muscles, especially during the act of breathing, formed a base-line state from which a sense of self emerged. However, insofar as the statue remained untouched and unmoving, "It cannot notice the different parts of its body. It cannot feel that one part is outside the other, or contiguous to it. It is as if it only existed in a point, and there is as yet no possibility of its discovering that it is extended."[30] Only through the action of touching itself did the statue gain a sense of the space it occupied. Unlike all the other senses, touch offered the possibility of a double sensation, that of touching and of being touched. Once the statue touched itself and compared that with the sensation of touching something else, it began to establish both self and otherness.

Movement was what extended the body outwards from a point, giving it an expanded sense of interior space, and touch gave the statue an awareness of itself as having a body that moved.[31] The statue thus learned that it did move, could move, and could will movement, which allowed for further discovery. Extension was the process through which the body came to exist in space and through which it took up space so that it became something that one "had."[32] As already designated in dance notation, space was a given within which the body and then a succession of objects or events were located. The body that existed in space and could be extended through space then assisted in the production of knowledge as a sequence of incremental, contiguous units, acquired through the action of moving and then registering the results.[33] Although it came to understand the world by moving in it, it nonetheless perceived the world through a binary process in which sensory information was encountered through movement, yet the receiving of that information was fundamentally passive, a process of imprinting sensation onto the sense organ capable of receiving it.

Although seemingly neutral, even clinical, in the conditions it set for investigating perception, Condillac's statue performed according to several tacit assumptions shared by chorographers, microscopists and choreographers. Observing the land, the specimen, or the physical body, the stilled viewer placed the object of analysis on a plane that existed prior to the entrance of the object onto it. Its parts were then located in relation to one another as they existed along that plane. The bird's eye view, so celebrated by chorographers and so emphasized by choreographers as an essential position from which to comprehend the dance, was projected inward, with the encouragement of microscopic study, to scrutinize the body's feeling of itself.

Trembling and orienting

In the very fact of stilling the body in order to fathom its sensations, Condillac refashioned physicality into distinct parts with exact coordinates. He also set up the conditions under which the self was separated from the sense of the body and actualized as a being that has a body. Not only did the subject have a body, but, as in the early choreographers' efforts to encourage dancers to maintain awareness of their progress through space, this subject could learn to observe its body from a distance and evaluate impassively its appearance and actions.

This new awareness of a self that had a body was vividly portrayed in an account of the Lisbon earthquake that occurred a year after Condillac's essay. Mr. Thomas Chase recounted his experience as follows:

> About three quarters after nine o'clock in the morning . . . I was alone in my bed chamber, opening a bureau; when a trembling of the ground, increasing to greater violence, alarmed me so much, that . . . I ran to a room at the top of the house, with windows all around . . . A prospect the most horrid that imagination can form, appeared before my eyes. The house began to heave to that degree,

that, to prevent being thrown down, I was obliged to put my arm out of the window, and support myself by the wall. Every stone in the walls, separating, and when I came to myself, supposed the earthquake to be over.[34]

Chase realized he had fallen into a high-walled space between two houses, and eventually crawled through an opening in the basement of one where he encountered

> a Portuquese [*sic*] man covered with dust, who, the moment he saw me coming that way, started back, and crossing himself all over, cried out, as the custom is when much surprised . . . This made me examine myself, which before I had not time to do. My right arm hung down before me motionless, like a great dead weight, the shoulder being out, and the bone broken; my stockings were out to pieces, and my legs covered with wounds, the right ancle [*sic*] swelled to a prodigious size, with a fountain of blood spouting upwards from it: the knee also was much bruised, . . . all the left side of my face swelled, the skin beaten off, the blood streaming from it, with a great wound above, and, a smaller one below the eye, and several bruises on my back and head.[35]

Running from the next shock, Chase found himself out on the street, where

> The people were all at prayers, covered over with dust . . . I turned, and saw the street below, filled with fallen houses. Then, in hopes of getting into the country, I advanced up the hill, till the same sad prospect presented itself above me . . . my strength failed me, and I fell prostrate in the middle, just where the three streets met.[36]

Like most other Lisbon accounts, Chase began by grounding the record of events in the facts of time and place, locating his physical presence within a scene and in the midst of an action. (Some accounts even specified barometric pressure, temperature, wind conditions, etc.)[37] Hoping to gain a perspective on the disaster, he ran up the stairs, only to have the vertical positioning, from which he viewed the world, alarmingly compromised. First, in the cupola; then in the chasm between houses, then crawling through an opening into the other house; and finally, outside, looking one direction and the other, Chase reasserted a static physicality as the source of all observations. Then, in a stunning reversal of that orientation, he regarded his body as if from outside, inventorying its wounds, even those he could not possibly see.

A contrasting account by an anonymous British merchant of the Port Royal quake from 1692 offered no such stable posture from which to view the surrounding events:

> Those houses which but just now appeared the fairest and loftiest in these parts were in a moment sunk down into the earth, and nothing to be seen of them; such crying, such shrieking and mourning I never heard, nor could anything in my opinion appear more terrible to the eye of man: Here a company of people swallowed up at once; there a whole street tumbling down; and in another place the trembling earth, opening her ravenous jaws, let in the merciless sea so that this town is becoming a heap of ruins . . . Several people were swallowed up of the earth, when the sea breaking in before the earth could close, were washed up again and miraculously saved from perishing; others the earth received up to their necks and then closed upon them and squeezed them to death with their heads above ground, many of which the dogs eat. Multitudes of people floating up and down, having no burial. The burying place at Palisadoes is quite destroyed, the dead bodies being washed out of their graves, their tombs beat to pieces.[38]

Appearing in the *London Gazette* shortly after the quake, this account depicted bodies tossed to and fro, witnessed by an observer whose own body was in motion. Rooms, houses, or streets did not compose a backdrop, even a changing one, within which action occurred. The earth itself took on the role of active agent. In the words of a fellow observer, "it threw down most of the Houses, Churches, Mills, and Bridges; it tore the Rocks and Mountains, and it destroyed Plantations and threw them into the sea."[39] Deploying images of intense vividness, such as the heads of victims sticking up out of the earth being eaten by dogs, the merchant catalogued the devastation while keeping bodies, buildings, earth, and sea in evolving relation to one another. Where Chase's account painted each successive scene, placing the author both in its center and as its principle beholder, the Port Royal merchant summarized the multiple kinetic reversals that had acted upon bodies so as to yield ruin. Like the Galenic body composed of humours and their various attractions, the parts of this quake, including the humans, swayed and sloshed as an ensemble.

Both narratives touched on the pathos of the situations – Port Royal's citizens cried, shrieked and mourned, and Lisbon's people prayed. The Port Royal account, however, incorporated these events alongside the actions of buildings and of the sea, whereas Chase's struggle – his terror and dismay in each successive situation – served as emblem of every citizen's plight. Constituting himself as the principal actor in each scene, the reader followed his character through adventures, keeping focus on his individual body as the entity that was acting and reacting. Thus his account registered his disorientation, first, as an inability to maintain a static, verticality, and subsequently as the inability to make sense of each scene in which he found himself. The Port Royal merchant, in contrast, was heaved up and swept away by forces greater than he, such that he could never maintain a stationary and static viewpoint. For him, disorientation resulted from a distortion of the normal motions of nature, objects and bodies. In response, he hurled events across the reader's path, whereas Chase painted a picture for them to behold.[40]

Inspired by the Port Royal quake, the anonymous author of the 1693 treatise *The Earth twice shaken wonderfully* reduced the large variety of previously categorized earthquakes – inclining, lifting, thrusting, and bellowing, among others[41] – to two sorts: Trembling and Pulsational.[42] Striving to regularize the quixotic tumult of vapors residing in the earth's core, the author seized upon longitude and latitude as the taxonomic rubric that accounts for the shaking of the earth along one axis or the other. Although Mercator had organized mapping into horizontal and vertical lines in 1569, the ability to orient one's self in terms of this geometry was not yet widespread.

In fact, three kinds of maps of Port Royal existed from the period of the quake: Portolan charts, depicting houses and mercantile establishments lining the coast, chorographic maps, picturing the entire port as if from above and off shore, and Mercator projection map, an enormous aid to all those who hoped to navigate the new world, projecting land masses onto a flat plane.[43] Where both Portolan chart and chorographic map specified precise viewing locations for the map-reader, the Mercator projection removed the viewer to an omniscient and all-encompassing vantage point.

Portolan charts, or portulanos, documented the early trade route maps of the Mediterranean from the fourteenth and fifteenth centuries, synthesizing visual information from the explorer en route with astronomical readings of stars. They were constructed from a network of intersecting lines, or rhumb lines, originating from sixteen equidistant points spread about the circumference of a hypothetical circle established by triangulation with specific celestial patterns. The Portolan charts enabled navigators to move along a coastline and then

Figure 2.4 A Portolan map of the Mediterranean with the rhumb lines and perpendicular labeling of geographical features clearly evident.
Prunes Chart of the Mediterranean and Western Europe, 1559.
Courtesy of the University of California, Los Angeles Young Research Library

aggregate each day's progress into a larger map. Spanish and Portuguese sailors conducted their early explorations of Africa and the Americas using these charts, making their way down the coasts or, occasionally circling out into open water before returning towards land, a navigational technique known as the "volta." Columbus executed a volta in traversing the north Atlantic in order to arrive in the New World.[44] It is possible that the dance known as La Volta, described in detail by Arbeau as producing dizziness in both dancers following the centripetal dynamism of the looping action, was so named for its similarity to this navigational maneuver.

The Portolan charts consistently placed the names of coastal towns and other large geographical features exactly perpendicular to the coastline regardless of its curve or direction. As a result, names often appeared at odd angles and even upside down when looking at the map. Yet they could easily be read if one was navigating along the water route at that place.[45] The chart thus registered the location of places in relation to a reader who was traveling. Similar to the changing

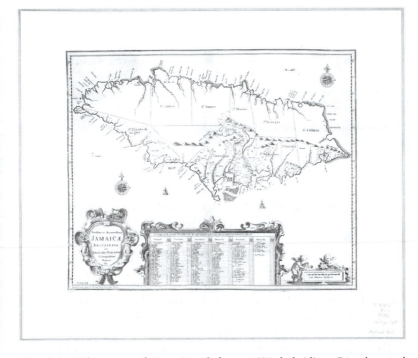

Figure 2.5 This map of Port Royal from 1681 hybridizes Portolan and chorographic map-making techniques. The city of Port Royal is shown from an ichnographic perspective with all the adjacent land carved into geometrically bounded shapes, while the coastline is represented in the manner of a Portolan map with all geographical features identified by names placed perpendicular to the coast.

Courtesy of the University of California, Los Angeles Young Research Library

socialscape in the Renaissance court dances that Arbeau documented, Portolan charts asked their readers constantly to reorient their placement in relation to all other bodies in motion.

Chorographic maps, in contrast, established the viewer/map reader in a static location, yet they also provided a kind of specificity that the Mercator maps abandoned. They registered each region as unique and emphasized its distinctive contours and features.[46] No longer in transit as the Portolan charts required, the chorographic viewpoint nonetheless specified locality. Mercator maps, based instead on the geometric rendition of the globe as sphere and then projecting the spherical placement of landmasses onto a two-dimensional plane, conveyed a more comprehensive and global sense of the world. Unlike the Portolan chart, whose only hint of an all-seeing viewer was that nestled within the rhumb lines connecting the arbitrarily but evenly spaced points, and the chorographic map that relocated and consolidated it in the eye of the reader, the Mercator map expanded the omniscience of the reader to encompass the entire surface of the earth.

Mercator representations of the world implemented the postulate, deriving from Ptolemy, of the globe as graticule, as a sphere composed of 360 lines of longitude converging at poles and 180 degrees of parallel latitudinal lines measured from the equator.[47] In contrast to both Portolan and chorographic maps, the graticule not only universalized the viewer's point of view, but it also, as Denis Cosgrove explains:

> flattens and equalizes as it universalizes space, privileging no specific point and allowing a frictionless extension of the spatial plot. At the same time it territorializes locations by fixing their relative positions across a uniformly scaled surface.[48]

Both Portolan and chorographic maps embedded within them the labor of the map-maker, as someone en route, or as someone perched high above the landscape. The graticule erased the representation of an embodied witnessing of the world.[49]

Tomlinson's drawings, resembling chorographic maps, conveyed a certain degree of specificity about the individuals who were dancing. However, Feuillet notation when printed as if from directly above the dancing, implied a theorization of movement that performed the same operations as the graticule. It positioned movement within horizontal and vertical planes. Regularizing each step, smoothing out all irregularities, it erased the labor of moving from one position or step to the next, and equally, the labor of anyone watching the dance. Collecting all dances into a single rubric, it territorialized them by charting their various components according to a universal set of principles.

In order to be useful, however, the reader of any notation needed to learn what Feuillet and his English translators were so deeply concerned to teach – an ichnographic perspective on their own actions. No longer a swaying sack of fluids, the body now consolidated as a hydraulics, governed by mechanical and chemical principles. Its anatomical structure and function, apprehended through scrutiny under the microscope, replicated the principles on which cartographic placement of land and waters was established. The body's movements could now be mapped, capable of being located precisely within a geometrized space. In order to read that map, the stilled body removed to its bird's eye perch then needed to learn to maintain that perspective while also reentering the space and moving across it. If Condillac's statue and Mr. Chase's account of his earthquake experience are any indication, the early choreographers were successful in helping to achieve that dual perspective. The body by mid-century came to be visualizable from outside itself. But what it saw from this exterior viewpoint was a picture or portrait of its own appearance.

From hardening to picturing

The very notions of having a physical appearance and presenting that appearance to others developed slowly over the sixteenth and seventeenth centuries, with exercise coming to play an increasingly important role in forming the body. Until the beginning of the sixteenth century, exercises were envisioned as activities to assist with the preparation of readiness for warfare. Upper class men exercised in fencing, horseback riding, and hunting as a way of acquiring skills necessary for going into battle. With the upsurge of interest in anatomy and the increasing awareness of the deleterious effects of urban living, educators and social critics began to promote the value of exercise for health.[50] Interpreted through Galenic models of the body, exercise began to function as an activity that promoted a balance of the humours, particularly effective in redressing problems that resulted from damp and cold physical conditions. Because exercise augmented the body's heat and increased circulation of all fluids, it dried and fortified the body. Thomas Elyot amplified on these general effects of exercise by explaining: "Moreover there be divers manners of exercises; whereof some only prepareth and helpeth digestion; some augmenteth also strength and hardness of body; other serveth for agility and nimbleness; some for celerity or speediness."[51] Although different kinds of exercise were acknowledged as contributing to specific improvements, exercise largely addressed the body as a whole.[52]

Exemplary of this holistic conception of exercise's effects on the body, Richard Mulcaster's 1581 publication *Positions Concerning the Training Up of Children* offered a comprehensive argument for exercise's role in childhood education. Equivalent in many ways to Arbeau's catalogue of dances and published earlier in the same decade, Mulcaster identified types of exercise and discussed the suitability of each form of exercise in addressing particular bodily dispositions. Exercises to be performed indoors included "lowd speaking, singing, lowd reading, talking, laughing, leaping, holding the breath, daunsing, wrestling, fensing [*sic*], and scourging the Top." Taking place outdoors were "walking, running, leaping, swimming, riding, hunting, shooting, and playing at the ball."[53] Each affected the body by invigorating and heating the flesh, yet each kind of exercise also exerted specific impact. Loud speaking, for example, "scoureth all the veines, stirreth the spirites through out all the entraulles, encreaseth heat, stutileth the blood, openeth the arteries, suffereth not superfluous humours to grow grosse and thick . . ." [54] In contrast, dancing "beside the warmth, driveth awaye numnesse, and certaine palsies, comforteth the stomacke, being cumbred with weaknes of digestion, and confluence of raw humours, strengtheneth weake hippes, faintin legges, freatishing feete."[55] By enhancing the circulation, conceived as a process of seepage from one interior location to another, exercise kept the humours from building up or from abandoning any given part of the body.[56] It also hardened the flesh, making it more capable of any kind of task.

Naming the tutor a "traynor," Mulcaster placed great emphasis on his ability to judge different body types and their various needs, in terms of disposition, habits such as how often they bathed, and inclination towards types of disease. (Those who bathed infrequently should avoid vigorous exercise.) He also advised the trainer on how to choose the appropriate place in which to exercise according to climate, the amount of time, and the quantity of exercise, and the manner, or vigor of the exercise.[57] Exercise rebalanced the body's interior, and it also attuned the body to its environment. Walking, for example, the single most effective form of exercise for man or woman, could vary in its effects according to the place of the walk, whether downhill, on sand, in a close room, in an open space, where birds abound, in shade or in sun, or in the morning or evening.[58] Each of these locales exerted specific influence on the body, with the healthiest settings being those that were dry, open, and elevated, and the least healthy being those that were low, near level with the sea or rivers, or where the air was moist or laden with putrid smells.[59]

Treatises such as Mulcaster's typically reviewed options for the male student, with occasional reference to exercises appropriate for young women. At the end of the seventeenth century, John Locke likewise addressed the education of the young man, noting that there would inevitably be differences between the rearing of sons and daughters, yet "where the difference of Sex requires different Treatment, 'twill be no hard Matter to distinguish."[60] Arguing that neither sex should be corseted, a practice that had gained momentum in the mid-seventeenth century, Locke encouraged loose clothing for open air play. Although he briefly mentioned swimming, fencing, riding, and wrestling, as pursuits that would improve health, Locke was most concerned that students acquire a civil and well-fashioned carriage. Not merely the physical appearance of the body, one's carriage included a "decency of gracefulness of Looks, Voice, Words, motions, Gestures, and of all the whole outward Demeanour, which takes in Company, and makes those with whom we may converse, easie and well pleased."[61]

Of all the exercises in which the Gentleman could engage, dancing was the most important, "being that which gives *graceful Motions* all the life, and above all things Manliness, and a becoming Confidence to young children."[62] If taught improperly, dancing could lead to affectations in the presentation of self. Careful instruction, however, cultivated an openness of countenance, a pleasant demeanor, and an ease in motion, all in the individual's carriage. Where Mulcaster envisioned each form of exercise as convening a relationship between action and place, Locke saw all pursuits as adding to the graceful and competent appearance of an individual. Like Elyot who conceptualized dancing as the enacting of various virtues, each corresponding to a specific pattern within the dance, Mulcaster defined exercise as an integrative process. Locke, in contrast, praised dancing for imparting graceful motion that would build up and enhance one's demeanor.[63] The body was slowly being drawn away from a communion with nature and society and towards a presentation of the self as a singular entity to be observed by others.

Although an increasing number of treatises were published over the eighteenth century that focused specifically on the education of young women, emphasizing the divergence in specifications for how women and men should cultivate physicality, the goal for both sexes was a specific image of how one should appear. This image, no longer the product of mutual engagement by all forces in the environment, whether social or geographical, now consolidated as an isolated entity presented to a hypothetical but singular viewer. In the seventeenth century, as Georges Vigarello has observed, all bodies were continually re-presenting themselves to one another as if "caught up in a web of intersecting glances."[64] In contrast, the spectatorial enthusiasm of the eighteenth century, as the popularity of the journal *The Spectator* suggests, was no longer produced through a dialogic encounter, but rather by one individuated body regarding another.[65] The mutual indebtedness that dancing built up through what Arbeau called "a mute form of rhetoric," was replaced by individuated figures displaying proper carriage performing for one another.

As the individuated body consolidated, posture assumed a more central role in evaluating one's appearance, and for the first time, it manifested, not as a set of external relations between body and surroundings, but as a set of internal relations evident in the outline of the body. Vigarello has shown how posture in the Renaissance, as in Leonardo Da Vinci's drawings, was figured through a calculation of surrounding points.[66] Similarly, the rider on the horse was advised to establish a posture determined in relation to the proportions and carriage of the animal. Early in the eighteenth century, posture began to be cultivated as an attribute of carriage in which spine, torso, pelvis, and legs all contributed to an aligned presentation of the person. It was the motions of this body that choreography as notation aspired to document in its careful analysis of options for where and how the upright dancer might progress through space. It was also this body, even in its sorry state, that Mr. Chase labored to present to the other stricken citizens of Lisbon and to his readers.

Nicolas Andry's *Orthopaedia: Or, the Art of Correcting and Preventing Deformities in Children* [1741] made clear the extent to which specific parts of the body each contributed vitally to an overall appearance.[67] One of the first kinesiology texts, explicating each part of the body's function in the positioning and movement of the body, *Orthopaedia* inventoried proper proportions amongst body parts as well as the deformities and conditions that resulted from their misalignment. Necks could be sunk, shoulders higher or thicker than one another, backs bunched, hollow, or crooked. Explaining that the chest was a box, upon which the neck, a pillar, supported the head, Andry provided detailed descriptions of the most pleasing proportions among all part of the body. Yet he also admitted that peoples of the world valued different proportions and distinctive attributes, all based on the relative size or shape of the body part. The Chinese, for example, were fonder of smaller feet and smaller eyes, especially in women.[68]

In order to display good posture, the two sides of the body should align symmetrically, and the front and back of the body be balanced so as to produce erectness. Since the bones of children were soft and malleable, they were prone to undesirable curvature, shortening, or shrinkage, often as a product of constricting dress, repetitious movement, or even improper furnishings. Pinched sleeves on gowns compressed the clavicles; soft beds or sinking chair seats produced crooked spines, just as work in a trade that demands constant repetition of specific motions yielded disproportionate strength or flexibility. Andry repeatedly emphasized the connection between daily habits and alignment, explicating in detail the influence that specific motions, such as carrying heavy objects, reading in slumped positions, or even straining to look out a window, could have on bodily shape.

Fortunately, since children's bodies were so pliable, a variety of remedies existed for correcting incipient deformities. All of these relied

Figure 2.6 A good posture and a bad posture from Nicolas Andry's *Orthopedia*.
Nicolas Andry. *Orthopedia*. Philadelphia, PA: J.B. Lippincott Company, Facsimilie Reproduction of the first Edition in English. London. [1743] 1961.
Engraving by Hulett Sculp

on the application of props or potions. Balancing an object on the head enhanced the straightness of the spine; different constructions of corsets ameliorated protruding bellies or backsides; canes could be used to encourage a leg to lengthen; even a convex chair seat could discourage slumping and improve erectness while seated.[69] Various oils and unguents softened tissue, and their effects were frequently enhanced by massage.[70] Andry likened the child's body to that of a young tree. In the same way that its trunk could be straightened by tying it to a rigid post, so a child's knock knees could be eliminated by wrapping an iron plate to the outside of the leg.[71] Thus, even as Andry emphasized how habitual motion produced deformity, the therapies for correcting physical problems relied on external aids that pushed and pulled at its silhouette.[72]

By the end of the eighteenth century, exercise, more than external aids, was seen as the effective means of achieving an elegant and sound physical appearance. Uprightness had replaced the gracefully curving contra posto aesthetic of the sixteenth and seventeenth centuries. In search of uprightness, specific kinds of exercises were invented that addressed problems concerning posture. Through the application of these exercises, the body itself, without the aid of external forces, such as the corset, slowly acquired the ability to erect itself and to maintain that erectness. In dance, the sinkings and risings that Feuillet had

Figure 2.7 In this illustration, Andry illustrates the similarity between the limbs of a child and the trunk of a young tree, whose curving tendencies can be straightened by being tied to a stake.
Nicolas Andry. *Orthopedia*. Philadelphia, PA: J.B. Lippincott Company, Facsimilie Reproduction of the first Edition in English. London. [1743] 1961.
Engraving by Hulett Sculp

identified as universal principles became embedded within specific steps that were practiced again and again in order to improve skill. Instead of learning to dance by learning simple dances, dancing now required the repetition of discreet movements that eventually built towards the steps in a dance. These movements parsed the body into discreet units that, when reassembled, constituted an erect posture. Each exercise contributed specific effects to the whole. Noverre, for example, railed against turnout machines, contraptions, like Andry's remedies, that secured the feet on movable platforms to be cranked apart in order to force the legs into a more turned-out position. He advocated instead for the *rond de jambe*, a circling of the foot from front, out to the side, and then to the back, arguing that it was far more effective.[73] Whatever specific assemblage of regimens was undertaken, however, the whole should present a pleasing picture of a graceful and upright bodily carriage.

Exercise and education treatises began to identify not only the relation of habits to specific postures, but also the role that exercise could play in producing certain physical attributes. Erasmus Darwin's plan for female education noted, like Andry, that writing, needlepoint, or drawing should not be undertaken for prolonged periods of time since they could fix the posture in a particular attitude. Unlike Andry, however, Darwin advocated for exercises that promoted a young woman's height and uprightness, and these included shuttlecock, swinging on a cord, and dancing. The ringing of a church bell or pulling of a weight over a pulley was productive since "it both extends the spine, and strengthens the muscles of the chest and arms."[74] Darwin also allowed for exercise of the arms by swinging leaden weights called dumb bells, but cautioned that these should be very light, "otherwise they load the spine of the back, and render the shoulders thick and muscular, and rather impede than forward the perpendicular growth of the person."[75] In his analysis Darwin connected the importance of uprightness with exercise, and he also noted the correlation between exercise and an increase in musculature. Muscles began to emerge as a category of the physical that could be altered and shaped.[76]

Like other manuals of the period, Darwin also discouraged the development of extensive musculature in a woman. Nancy Armstrong has noted how education and conduct manuals underwent a shift in subject over the eighteenth century from the aristocratic man to the domestic woman. Appealing to readerships of various levels and sources of income, the domestic woman appeared to resolve conflicts around human rights and equality that had emerged in Enlightenment thinking.[77] Formulated as a presence gracing and presiding over domestic space, this construction of the feminine was expected to conserve, to spend with discretion, and to regulate her own conduct and that of her children.[78] Participating in this overhaul of woman's role, the education manuals increasingly warned against vigorous exercise, public activities, and "frivolous" pastimes, and began to advocate for the sequestering of women within private spaces. Not unlike the corsets that increasingly limited women's ability to move, the social restrictions on women's activities and pastimes focused with greater intensity on what she should not do.

By the early nineteenth century, dancing, still seen as a viable pursuit because of the mildness of its actions, became an activity that many argued should be performed only in the confines of one's parlor. Where early in the eighteenth century, it could be improperly taught as excessive or ornamental elegance, associated with "bad" French dancing masters, dancing now assumed the power to over-excite, to lead astray, and to distract female subjects from frugality and piety.[79] Prompted by its exceptional popularity as a social pastime, especially among the working and middle classes, debates sprang up in medical and ethical domains addressing whether women's more frail systems would be overly taxed by vigorous exercise, especially the new forms such as the waltz, and also whether or not they would foment contagion by, for example, dancing while menstruating.[80] Similar to Carlo Blasis's criticism of the *chica* and its effects on Spanish dance, dancing itself now took on the capacity to unleash excess. Since the procreative responsibilities of the female body took the majority of her strength, it was essential to monitor all participation in exercise and even in public life.

Educator Donald Walker's separate and distinctive programs of exercises for men and women, published in the 1830s and 1840s, addressed these profound differences in male and female physicality.[81] Women, being fundamentally more feeble, needed to engage in only moderate exercise, primarily of the passive kind.[82] Swinging, see-sawing, and sailing, for example, improved the vigor of the organs, while at the same time avoiding the unsightly dilemma of perspiration. Men, in contrast, should advance into all forms of physical pursuit, including running, vaulting, swimming, riding, skating, and throwing the discus. Where women could avoid lassitude through mild activities, men would acquire strength and enhance the beauty of the physique, thereby conferring power and health on the muscles and organs.[83] Regardless of the differences between these programs, Walker's approach centered on exercise as an activity that in and of itself could improve alignment. Explicating physicality in terms similar to Blasis's geometric lines located inside the musculature, Walker explained that when the body was in repose, it was actually active because standing required an effort of the muscles: "The head, resting upon the first vertebra at a point of its base which is nearer its posterior than anterior part, cannot remain in an upright position, except by an effort of the muscles of the back of the neck."[84] Where Andry had noted the tendency of the musculature to become warped from different kinds of actions, such as reading in the wrong position, Walker discerned the contribution made by muscles to posture, whatever the action.[85] He also established a basic alignment from which the body was to proceed into any exercise, thereby securing symmetrical and equal development of all muscles.

Walker's treatises coincided with the introduction into Britain of Swedish gymnastics, developed by Per Henrik Ling. Like Blasis, Ling analyzed the body in terms of its internal geometry, showing the line through the arm and hand, for example, and sometimes using that line to indicate the motion of the exercise.[86] Not a program of prescriptions for the best way to run, vault, or swim, Ling proposed a systematic sequence of standing exercises that took the body or individual limbs from an upright standing position to off center poses and back again. Each set of joint articulations and weight shifts was repeated numerous times before moving on to the next exercise. Like Walker's basic

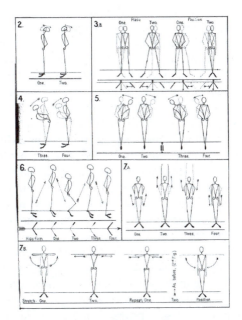

Figure 2.8 This illustration of some of Ling's exercises shows the interior sense of verticality to be maintained by the body as it progresses through a set of maneuvers that displace it from and return it to standing.
Ling's System. Swedish Gymnastics Part 1: A Manual of Freestanding Movements for the use of schools without apparatus. Compiled and arranged by J.D. Haasum, captain 2nd Swedish lifeguards. London: Librairie Hatchette & Cie. 1885. Plate 2.

positions from which exercises should proceed, Ling's system built up a strong sense of an erect alignment to which the body should always return. Because so many of the exercises did not rely on props or include actions proscribed for women, the system was adopted by women who had the leisure and privilege to cultivate the body as early as the 1830s, with private gymnasia that promoted its use springing up at mid-century.[87] At the same time, the goals promoted by the program focused around creating reliability of one's own actions, the ability to endure pain, and the ability to respond to any contingency with deliberation. Such attributes were considered to be the ideal standards for a man and a "true" warrior.[88]

Similarly focused on the acquisition of manly virtues, sports training in schools and clubs promoting activities for male students such as mountaineering, rugby, sailing, cycling, skating, boxing, hockey, lawn tennis, badminton, fencing, came into existence between 1850 and 1900.[89] Seen as an excellent venue in which to cultivate patriotism and moral virtues, enthusiasm for sports training accelerated rapidly, applying the kinds of insights tabulated in Walker's treatises. The emergence of "muscular Christianity" at mid-century, with its emphasis on manliness, virtue, mastery of rough sports such as rugby, and fist-fighting, reinforced the popularity of sports as a vehicle for building the physique.[90] Championed vigorously by working class men, muscular Christianity cultivated the connection between physical and spiritual purity, securing and fortifying a maleness that had been jeopardized by unemployment at home and failing colonial policies abroad. The spreading popularity of the Young Men's Christian Association in both Britain and the US likewise promoted sports as an ideal pursuit for the improvement of the self. Immediately voicing objections to men's exclusive access to sports clubs and training, early feminists protested the constricted conditions of women promoted by corsets deforming the body and by public policies and medical practice that denied women the opportunity to exercise more freely.

Despite the marked differences in training regimens for male and female bodies and for bodies of different classes, a new sense of the body began to emerge in the second half of the nineteenth century that suggested a more volumetric experience of physicality. No longer a pictorial presentation of self, propped and adjusted with the aid of externally applied prostheses, the body became an organism striving for erectness whose musculature contributed centrally to that effort. Whereas exercise as conceptualized in the Galenic model assisted the body in regulating itself through enhancement of internal circulations and exposure to beneficial external substances, all of which would improve balance, exercise now developed the physique as something separate from but necessary for social interaction and productivity. Erectness, redefined as an internally cultivated attribute, did not contribute to one's carriage and demeanor so much as it signified a morally upright character. Armstrong has noted how self-regulation was promoted for women within the domestic sphere as a desirable practice that augmented value for others.[91] Similarly, for men, self-regulation enabled the most effective participation in civic and patriotic duties. Assisting in this certification of citizenship was the body's ability to support and cultivate itself.

Encompassing and expressing

Just as this newly volumetric physicality began to consolidate, pressured by gender and class regulations regarding the training of bodies, but with an increasing focus on musculature as a defining constituent, kinesthesia was proposed as a naming of the sense that one has of the muscles' actions and our consequent sense of motion. The progressive identification of a variety of sense organs within the musculature – corpuscles, spindles, and tendon organs – coincided with the progressive focus on training the body's individual muscles. Even the terms "muscularity" and "musculature" were coined in the 1880s at precisely the same time that Bastian invented the term "kinesthesia." As an expanding labor force committed to routinized repetitions of specific actions in industrial production, and regimens for physical education began to develop each muscle separately, a newly volumetric apprehension of physicality began to emerge. Tensile and three-dimensional, any or all of one's muscles could be summoned into action, and by contrast, taught to relax.

In 1879, only a year before Bastian's publication naming kinesthesia, Dudley Allen Sargent was awarded a professorship at Harvard to establish the first program in physical education in the US.[92] There he devised an exercise regime that implemented pulley-weight machines that could be adjusted to the strength of the individual and focused around the cultivation of individual muscles groups. By 1912 Sargent boasted that 270 colleges offered programs in physical education; 300 city school systems around the US required it; and 500 YMCA (Young Men's Christian Association) gymnasiums with 80,000 members were utilizing versions of his machines.[93] Sargent's regimens, along with several other similar systems of exercise that worked with dumbbells, balls, and ropes, helped to forge an entirely new experience of the body as a musculature distinct from other physiological systems. Contributing

Fig. 19.

Exercise No. 10.

Weights. —

Times. —

Rate per minute. —

Position No. 10. — Stand with back to boxes, holding the hands extended behind the body, with body bending slightly forward. (See Fig. 19.)

Movement No. 10. — Bring the handles forward until they pass the body, the ropes moving under the arms, turning the palms inward, and straightening the body.

Principal Muscles brought into action.—P^4, D^1, T^{12}, A^{10}, E^4, E^3, E^{13}, E^7, E^6, E^{12}.

Simultaneously for both arms and sides.

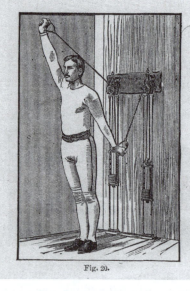

Fig. 20.

Exercises Nos. 11 and 12.

Weights. —

Times. —

Rate per minute. —

Position No. 11. — Stand with back to boxes; right arm bent sharply back over shoulder, with palm upward; left arm extended downward and backward, with palm forward, and handle level with the hip.

Movement No. 11. — Move both hands directly forward, at the same time straightening the elbows. (See Fig. 20.)

Position and movement in No. 12 the reverse of No. 11.

Principal Muscles brought into action. — No. 11: Part of P^4, L^1, B^1, C^3, B^4, P^{13}, F^7, F^9, F^8, S^{26}, P^2, F^{14}, F^{11} for right and left arms and sides.

No. 12: Same as in No. 11 changing arms and sides.

Figure 2.9 These excerpts from Dudley Allen Sargent's system of exercises show how the body must assert the interior fortitude to maintain an absolute rectitude while under the stress of pulling or lifting the weights. Sargent, Dudley Allen. *Handbook of Developing Exercises.* Cambridge: n.p., 1897. Exercises 10, 11 & 12

vitally to the health and well-being of the person, muscles now needed to be developed and maintained through regular exercise devoted specifically to them.

Sargent's regimen identified 156 individual muscles capable of development in diverse exercises that used pulleys and weights attached to the floor, wall, or overhead.[94] Planting the body firmly in front of the pulleys, the exerciser held firm while pulling the weights towards the body from a variety of locations. For each position and direction of action, Sergeant specified the muscle groups that would be developed, and a range of numbers of repetitions and speeds for the action. Although eighteenth century medical and exercise literature sometimes referred to the lever system of bones and muscles, it never specified the ways in which repetition of actions could alter muscle mass and strength. Sargent's innovations contributed to a vast new inquiry into the science of muscle development. His regimen also located the body comfortably in relation to a machine, thereby referencing favorably the new relations between bodies and machines that were transforming the workplace and all of daily life.

At the same time, a new fashion in physical culture was expanding primarily among women based on the work of French aesthetician François Delsarte. Taught widely in the US and Britain in schools of oratory and acting and in private salons, Delsarte's theories and exercises exerted massive influence on diverse presentations of the self in public from dance and acting to public speaking and recitation, including the delivery of sermons in church.[95] Promulgated in the US by dramatist and theatrical designer Steele Mackay and actress and rhetorician Genevieve Stebbins, classes in Delsarte's system of expression organized the body into zones identified with one of the three kinds of energy, spiritual, emotional, or vital. Large zones corresponding to these energy types were broken down into smaller and smaller areas, each maintaining a correspondence to an energy type. In addition to the zones, Stebbins classified positions of the body into three types – excentric, normal and concentric. Correlations between the kind of energy in each region and the position of that portion of the body yielded an array of character attributes, emotional states, and temperaments that would enhance the persuasiveness of public speaking. Alternatively, sequences of these positions could be arranged and then performed as mute testimonies to the power of physical expression and the beauty of the body.

In the seventeenth century, Bulwer and others had similarly argued for the concinnity of motion and feeling, yet their studies did not put forth the same kinds of underlying principles upon which Delsarte's

GRIEF.

Figure 2.10 A Stebbins-based pantomime depicting Grief enacted by five women, each of whom portrays a different aspect of grief.
Elsie M. Wilbor. *Delsarte Recitation Book*, 4th Edition, New York: Edgar S. Werner & Co. 1905.

system was founded. Bulwer, for example, inventoried variations on the stretching out, joining, or wringing of the hands, but he did not classify these as forms of excentric or concentric types of positions. Now, with Delsarte's theory of expression and Stebbins' application of his system, movement was seen as embodying types of energy and directions of energy flow that corresponded to types of feeling. Much like Feuillet's classification of types of movement, Delsarte's system also asserted universality of its principles. Yet where Feuillet located movement in relation to horizontal and vertical planes, Delsarte focused on central and peripheral directions and also on types of energy.

Stebbins devised numerous routines, called "pantomimes" or "artistic statue posing" that transited the body through various dramatic moments.[96] For example, greeting a dear friend who, in response, showed indifference, one might express surprise and affectionate protest by

Hand now expands into conditional attitude nor.-ex., animation; little finger pointing to normal zone of the torso. Forearm bends until little finger is brought to left side of normal zone. A moment's pause, then the shoulders lift; face expresses surprise; hand drops decomposed, position of arm retained. Now sink elbow, pressing upper arm against side, throwing decomposed hand into relative attitude con.-nor. Unbend elbow, which throws hand out and up into relative attitude ex.-ex.[97]

Stebbins tabulated shapings of eyes, fingers, etc. in terms of their normal (nor.), concentric (con.), or excentric (ex.) position and asserted their correspondence to various psychological states. For the hand, the combination of concentric and normal signified "indifference, prostration, imbecility, insensibility, or death," whereas eccentric with normal indicated "approbation and tenderness."[98]

In Delsarte's theory and Stebbins realization of it, mind, located in the brain, and body were intimately connected, especially via the emotions, also located in the mind. Emotion could activate the body's movements, or in the reverse process, the enactment of the actions associated with a given emotion could generate those feelings. Stebbins explained:

> Thus, when anger or love quickens the circulation and changes the breathing, we recognize the physiological correspondence to the psychic faculty which, if unobstructed, is further carried outward into pantomime. *Per contra,* the wilful [*sic*] expression of an emotion which we do not feel generates it by generating the sensations connected with it, which, in their turn, are associated with analogous emotions.[99]

Depending upon the intensity of the feeling, the body could be prompted into a full pantomime-like expression of feeling. Central to Stebbins's own approach, however, was the possibility that enacting specific shapings of the body would induce the feelings of "indifference" or "tenderness" as a product of that physical action. The pantomimes and poses, therefore, yielded healthful benefits, and they also enabled their practitioners to journey through numerous dramatic narratives.

Key to the successful realization of these bodily postures was the preparative training known as "decomposing," in which practitioners learned to relax and let fall towards gravity different parts of the body and even the body as a whole. Where Sargent's exercises cultivated awareness of muscular exertion, Stebbins's invited practitioners to sense the body's changing relationship to gravity, through relaxation or through the slow swaying of body parts.

Stebbins believed strongly in the power of relaxation to recuperate energy and thereby restore and equilibrate bodily functions. She encouraged her students to:

> Lie down on the floor, relax at once as completely as possible, so that the body shall be practically limp and lifeless, as though it was no part of you. The mental idea is a calm and perfect consciousness of your separate existence apart from and superior to any part of the body undergoing the exercise. This must be accompanied by rhythmic breathing, while in imagination the mind seeks unaided a pleasing but dreamy kind of rapport with the natural surroundings, if they are beautiful; if not, close the eyes and make a picture of sea and sky, rose garden or hill, lawn or bower.[100]

Similar to Condillac's statue in its assertion of the separation between consciousness and physical experience, Stebbins's supine figure was nonetheless a real person who, she argued, could learn to control all the voluntary musculature. Where Condillac posited a statue in order to reveal the existence of kinesthetic sensation, Stebbins, confident of its existence, could create statue-like relaxation as part of her cultivation of kinesthetic awareness.

In order to expand awareness of and control over the musculature, Stebbins developed energizing exercises, seen as complementary to the decomposing exercises, in which one muscle group would contract slowly while the rest of the body remained resolutely relaxed.[101] For example, standing with the right leg raised, "Inhale, and as you do so, gradually contract every muscle until the left leg is quite rigid at the fourth count. Hold the tension and the breath while counting four. Slowly relax while you count four."[102] Repeating this kind of exercise with different parts of the body, consistently monitoring increasing and decreasing tension through counting and the breath, one gained a satisfying sense of mastery over an entire interiority. Surveying from the distance intimated in Stebbins relaxation exercise, the body instantiated itself, not as an appearance, but as a volume.

From this enhanced awareness of specific muscle activation, Stebbins developed sequences of actions based on spiral and successional patterns. Delsarte had advocated for a law of opposition evident in the contraposto shapings of classical Greek sculptures which the poses sometimes imitated. Gradually transitioning from one pose to another, the body became integrated through the modulated flow of energy across and connecting the zones, displaying the much desired quality of sinuosity. Quoting Delsarte, Stebbins reminded her readers that,

"Dynamic wealth depends upon the number of articulations brought into play."[103] Repeatedly isolating each body part and then moving successively through them, the practitioner developed a strong connection to gravity and a sense of movement as tensile and three-dimensional. Within this volumetric and tensile physicality, wealth, according to Delsarte, depended upon the number of articulations within one's mastery. Unlike the Renaissance court dances where wealth accrued to those who demonstrated reciprocity, meeting each gesture from the other person with the appropriate response, in Delsarte's system wealth was internally produced and regulated. No longer dependent upon the naming of the steps that the eighteenth century choreographies had documented nor on the dancer's ability to execute perfectly a large number of these items, wealth now manifested in the sinuous integration of actions within diverse parts of the body.

In the US, Sargent's and Stebbins's work coincided with a period of mass migration into urban centers, where daily living offered far fewer opportunities for physical exercise. Exercise began to be seen as an effective way of building up nervous reserves. It both interrupted the depletion of those reserves brought on by laboring in the factory, with its highly repetitive phrases of motion that frequently interfaced with machinery, and at the same time it provided a respite from the nervous taxation of city life.[104] For many psychologists of the period, the whole body was seen as contributing to the energy needed to maintain mental and motor activity. They also saw the cultivation of the body as a manly pursuit, often with a religious dimension. Sustaining its popularity in both the US and Britain, "muscular Christianity" as the impetus to develop the physique, was rationalized by G. Stanley Hall in these terms: "We are soldiers of Christ, strengthening our muscles not against a foreign foe, but against sin within and without us."[105] Reversing the Puritan suspicion of bodily contamination of the soul, muscular Christianity advocated for men's regular involvement in exercise in order to combat sin and purify the person.

In contrast to muscular Christianity, Stebbins's advocacy of physical culture was taken up largely by middle-class white women who found in the regimen a new sense of freedom and control of the body divorced from the constraining limitations of the corset and the bulky limitations of fashionable dress. Although performed in parlors rather than in public spaces, their pantomimes displayed female physicality as graceful, dramatic, and vital. Serving a role akin to the relaxation that Stebbins so ardently promoted, they carved out a space for rejuvenation. Releasing the body from the habitual patterns associated with daily life, they enabled a recharging of the entire body.

As distinctive as Stebbins's and Sargent's regimens were, they partook in the common reorganization of kinesthetic experience that was occurring in relation to new technologies and new modes of work. Hillel Schwarz has argued that a range of new innovations, from the escalator to the zipper, privileged continuous motion, the kind that both Stebbins and Sargent were promoting in their various exercises.[106] Schwarz shows a preoccupation throughout childhood education with continuous and rhythmic motion, promoting it as a key factor in good penmanship, accurate drawing, and also reasoning. At the same time, new methods of organization within the factory stipulated repetition of discrete movement patterns, and scrutinized both the parsing of these patterns into actions assigned to individual workers and their performance of those actions in terms of efficiency. On the one hand, there was a celebration of the musculature and all that it could accomplish, and on the other, a strong mandate to economize on expenditure of effort, now seen as existing on a continuum between full exertion and relaxation.

Within this climate of growing interest in the musculature, neurological investigations of the perception of movement soon replaced the term "kinesthesia" with a new term, "proprioception," that focused specifically on how the sensors in muscles and joints were connected by nerves to the spine. In 1906 British neurologist C. S. Sherrington identified proprioceptors as those sense organs that deliver internal or afferent sensations about the status of the muscle or joint to the spinal cord and brain where they connect to motor, or efferent, responses.[107] Functioning at an unconscious level, proprioceptors were studied for their participation in spinal level reflexes that primarily assist in maintaining posture and balance, precisely the kind of effort that Walker had described for the person even while standing still. Proprioception was also seen as contributing to the learning and remembering of physical activities such as sports. Sherrington's pioneering studies of reflex actions and the role of proprioception in guiding and refining muscular action presumed a circuit that he called the afferent-efferent arc, a reflex pattern that transformed information reported about the status of a muscle into a necessary response. Sherrington's theory and research, based on the separation of incoming sensation and outgoing action, dominated the field for several decades.

Although kinesthesia fell out of medical and neurophysiological usage, replaced by the notion of proprioception, it continued to find relevance in psychology. Edward Titchener was among the first to aggregate as "kinaesthetic senses" the "muscular" sense, the "tendinous" sense, the "articular" or joint sense, and the capacity of these to convey a perception of movement, position, resistance, weight, and degree of activation. He also discussed the integral role played by the skin in contributing to continuous or interrupted movement and the amount of effort exerted, especially in relation to an object, calling this type of information "touch-blends." He included the vestibular system and its component parts, giving a lengthy explanation of its role in the experience of dizziness.[108] Instead of animal spirits rushing around in the head, the hairlike sensors and fluids of the semicircular canals, subjected to gravitational alterations, produced the sense of the world spinning around one.

Titchener argued that kinesthetic sensations, along with visual and auditory input, created images – traces in the mind of the body's actions. He conceived of kinesthesia as more ingrained and often unconscious in the organism, yet it nonetheless produced a kind of thinking. Rapid reading, the playing of a musical composition, or the changing into a different language as one greets a different person – all constituted meaning-making, even if they occurred without our conscious awareness.[109] A proponent of detailed self-observation of one's mental activity, Titchener explained that he had learned to become more keenly aware of his own kinesthetic sensations, noting that his entire physical attitude would change depending on whether he was sitting down at his desk to type professional correspondence, write to an intimate friend, or think out a lecture.[110] He argued that "originally, meaning is kinaesthesis," commencing in bodily attitude and the consequent sensations that it produces in response to any situation.[111]

Developing kinesthesia along similar lines, educators in dance and physical education explored it as the medium in which cultivation of physicality could be conducted. H'Doubler's courses, in which students studied the skeleton and then worked sometimes blindfolded to explore the range of motion at a given joint, were designed to enhance sensitivity to "kinesthetic" information. As H'Doubler explained:

> It has proved helpful to approach finished arm and hand work by considering the exercise as a test of the power of accurate discrimination of the student's kinesthetic sense, to see if he can tell by the report to his consciousness of the moving muscles and joints if all parts of the shoulder, arm, and hands have been included in the exercise.[112]

Kinesthetic sense was seen as essential to learning about one's own anatomical structure and proclivities. It also served to promote the students' abilities to overcome inhibitions and obstacles to their freedom of control.

As implemented by H'Doubler, Martha Hill, and other early pioneers of modern dance pedagogy, kinesthesia provided verification of the natural organization of physicality. It enabled students to delve beneath the habits acquired in socialization, many of which inhibited motion and produced deformities of posture and erratic or incomplete motion. Freed from the constraints of fashion and protocol, students would discover a whole new repertoire of motion by honing their sensitivity to kinesthetic information. Unlike eighteenth century conduct manuals that guided readers between the poles of uncouth disarray and pretentiously exaggerated politesse in order to achieve a naturalness of appearance and carriage, early twentieth century dance pedagogy presumed that a natural grace lay hidden beneath surface distortions. Where naturalness and grace of motion were cultivated in the eighteenth century, now they were discovered.

The identification of a specific sense system known as the kinesthetic and the robust awareness of muscularity that it entailed also provided the justification for the meaningfulness of the new modern dance. John Martin depended heavily on the notion of kinesthesis, giving it a central and vital role in establishing the importance of the new modern dance and its impact on viewers. In the second of his three major publications justifying the new genre, *America Dancing*, he explained:

> Nevertheless, a sixth sense, whether it exists officially or not among those who live by the book, functions most serviceably. It is primarily a muscle sense and is called kinesthesia – "movement-perception." Embedded in the tissue of the muscles and in the joints there are sense organs which respond to movement much as the organs of seeing respond to light; ... in conjunction with the semicircular canals in the ears, which tell us a good many useful things about balance, posture, and position, these humble organs, that have never been given anything but the generic name of proprioceptors, make it possible for us to know our own movement at first hand without seeing, hearing, touching, tasting, or smelling it. We can ascertain quite without effort whether we are upside down or rightside up, and be perfectly aware of the relation of one part of the body to another.[113]

Identifying kinesthesia as primarily deriving from muscle sensation but also involving vestibular information, Martin proposed that the kinesthetic sense was what enables familiarity with objects and actions, even when viewing them from afar. We know a ball is round and an eggshell fragile based on the history of our "neuromuscular coordinations" from previous contact with these objects.[114]

Like Stebbins, Martin believed in the close connection between movement and emotion. He extrapolated from the way that kinesthesia functions to our apprehension of a person's emotional state, arguing that another person's emotions would be evident to us based on the visible signs of those feelings which are already familiar to any observer. It was this reservoir of experience built up from all kinds of physical acts and interactions and stored in kinesthetic memory that informs how a viewer sees a dance.

> When we come into the presence of a man whose face and body are convulsed in rage, we do not have to stop to ask him what is the matter... If by some chance we had never experienced anger ourselves..., we would have no way of knowing it when we saw it. It is because our own body reacts in kinesthetic sympathy that we are enabled to recognize and escape the wrath upon which we have intruded.[115]

Because movement and emotion were so closely connected in life and in dance, the majority of "associational connotations" that the viewer experienced were states and developments of feeling.

Martin believed that as a product of Victorian educational values that promoted only intellectual and never physical education, kinesthesia had been undervalued and uncultivated for decades. Like Sherrington, he distinguished between one's "mental equipment" that determined when and where and how to move, and one's "motor equipment" that executed those commands.[116] More like Titchener than Sherrington, however, Martin believed that both mental and motor capacities could be brought into greater self-awareness. Dance in the US had suffered precisely because of the failure to acknowledge the importance of kinesthesia. Those with a meager or impaired kinesthetic sense, he argued, would have difficulty apprehending dance's power and message. The best way to awaken a deadened kinesthetic sense was to undertake the study of dance itself.

The technique classes that the new modern dance choreographers began to develop cultivated the musculature in distinctive ways, but each focused on the body as a volume subject to the laws of gravity and momentum, and each developed a relationship to the ground that contrasted radically with earlier forms of concert. Martha Graham's investment in the contraction and release and her exploration of the

Fig 2.11 In this photograph of *The Desperate Heart* (1943) choreographed and performed by Valerie Bettis, Barbara Morgan's double exposure suggests the volume and dynamism at the core of the choreography.
Photograph by Barbara Morgan.
Courtesy of The Barbara Morgan Estate

spiral suggested a body that no longer embodied a set of lines to be formed into geometric shapes, but instead, an amalgam of forces to be harnessed according to flow. Similarly, Doris Humphrey's investigation of fall and rebound foregrounded the body's weightiness and its ability to succumb to and then soar away from the force of gravity. Like the contraction and release, the fall and rebound fashioned the body as a vortex of endlessly repeating cycles. No longer dancing on top of an abstract geometric plane and tracking their progress across it, dancers now explored their dynamic relationship with earth, not as a specific piece of land, but rather as the abstract and universal but nonetheless palpable principle of gravity. The tensility of motion produced by the musculature as it enacted these cycles of engagement was the medium in which the drama of life was staged.

In the Galenic model, all bodies were governed by universal laws of attraction and repulsion that operated both inside and outside of the individual body. Now the inside of the body contained and replicated those universal laws. Much like Feuillet notation, that had presumed the universality of its basic motions, so, too, the musculature's responses to gravity explored by the new modern dance bespoke of a universal human condition. Yet whereas Feuillet notation had located the body with respect to an external geometry, this bodily responsiveness constituted an internal grammar and rhythm for both motion and emotion. In this way the conception of kinesthesia undercut all differences. Even if bodies of different cultures, classes, or genders, looked and moved differently, those differences were to be absorbed into a universal program of bodily cultivation based on the body's interior articulateness and integrity. Stebbins examined yogic breathing and Arab practices of relaxation. Ruth St. Denis taught yoga poses and sequences as part of the curriculum at her school Denishawn. The volumetric body, responding to the universal law of gravity, exuded and exerted a tensility to be regulated through exercise and relaxation so as to participate fully in the rhythm of life.

Synthesizing and simulating

The term "kinesthesia" came into new and more widespread use with the 1966 publication of James J. Gibson's influential study of perception *The Senses Considered as Perceptual Systems*.[117] Following Sherrington, scientists working in psychology and perception studies had upheld an absolute separation between perception and action. They agreed that afferent and efferent neural systems were distinct and incommensurate – the afferent processed incoming stimuli and the efferent conveyed the command for bodily movements. As it had been for Condillac's statue, perception was investigated as the passive experience of receiving input from distinctive kinds of receptors, individually responsible for sight, hearing, taste, touch, and smell. Gibson, in contrast, argued that perception was the active process of extracting information from the environment. A highly engaged project, perception required participation from both afferent and efferent systems. In fact, any given act of perceiving depended upon a complex sorting through of that which was invariant and that which was in flux within all sensory modalities. Gibson identified kinesthesia as central to that process.

Like Titchener, Gibson defined kinesthetic information as including sensory input from muscle and joint receptors but also from a wide variety of other sources: vestibular, cutaneous, and visual.[118] Unlike him, Gibson emphasized the integration of information that resulted from the combined contributions of these sense organs that provided a continuous sense of one's orientation with respect to gravity and one's motion through space as well as a generalized sense of bodily disposition – where one was tense or relaxed, expanded or compressed, even the precise angle of each joint. Gibson further proposed that any act of perception depended upon the detection of the just noticeable difference between sensory input and bodily disposition. The eyeball itself could tell us very little about the visual world around us, but the eyeball combined with the ocular musculature that surrounded it and the vestibular system that oriented it with respect to gravity could give very precise information about one's surroundings. Gibson identified this integrative processing of external and internal stimuli as the perceptual system. He further argued that kinesthesia played a central role in integrating all the senses.

Gibson's theory proposed an ongoing duet between perceiver and surroundings in which both were equally active. The environment did not impinge upon a passive observer. Nor did the perceiver survey the environment, as Condillac's statue had, from a static and omniscient position. Instead, the perceiver negotiated the perpetual flux of surroundings by determining that which was constant and that which was changing. Gibson argued that because vision was especially successful in determining these constancies, a sense of self was associated with the head. The "I" (head) and "my body" (the rest of my body) existed as identifiably separate, partially because of vision's extreme precision in coordinating with locomotion to navigate the world, and partially because of one's ability to see many other parts of one's own body. Because perception needed to be envisioned and investigated as something that occurs while the body is in motion, Gibson shunned experimentation using an immobilized subject in order to study an isolated reflex, and instead devised experiments that simulated the ways perception occurred as part of moving through one's surroundings.

Alongside Gibson's research a vast number of movement practices began to be pursued including numerous forms of meditation, martial arts practices, yoga, as well as new styles of social dancing. Dedicating themselves to experimentation with "altered" states of consciousness, some drug induced, practitioners of these forms endeavored to probe the boundaries of perception and its effects on subjectivity.[119] As Cynthia Novack has demonstrated, they conceptualized the body's movement as a potential conduit to new ways of perceiving and orienting oneself in the world. Movement held the promise of expanding consciousness. Like Gibson's understanding of the role that movement played in extracting information from the environment, movement could be tapped to give insight into new dimensions of reality.

Typical of these movements practices, the dance form known as contact improvisation asked participants to forge a moving point of contact between two bodies and to follow that contact wherever it led. The practice dramatized the ongoing duet between perceiver and world that Gibson proposed by encouraging dancers to develop lightning quick responses to one another's changing momentum as they rolled across the contours of body and floor. Rejecting the proscenium in favor of informal "jams" that took place in gymnasiums, art galleries, or dance studios, contact improvisation embraced the full sensorium in physicality, inviting viewers as well as participants to share in the topsy-turvy experience of moving in a new way. Recognizing the hierarchical arrangement of the senses that Gibson identified, contact improvisers trained through exercises that defused the primacy of the visual and focused intensively on the perception of touch. Spending many hours learning to sense gravity's effects on motion and momentum, and to develop a porous and sensitized skin that could discriminate subtle shifts in one's own weight and that of another person, contact improvisers purposefully dehabitualized their bodies' tendencies to rely on the visual for orientation. In so doing, a new experience of self was produced in which the "I" was contingent upon and a product of the ongoing contact between the two bodies.

Where the early modern dancers had imbued gravity with the ability to hold the body in dynamic relation between earth and air, gravity for contact improvisers functioned as a medium in which to explore any and all bodily positions and points of contact. Where modernist conceptions of kinesthesia integrated emotion with motion, contact improvisation focused on the physical facts of bony levers, weight transfer across regions of the body, and intensities of speed. These seemingly neutral features of physicality suggested a space for investigation beyond cultural or psychological values. They were analogous to Gibson's neutral terminology for identifying features of one's surroundings, such as stimulation, ambient array, and external invariants, criteria of measurement that rebuffed any cultural or historical specificities.

Thus, both modernist and Gibson's conceptualizations of kinesthesia – as the muscular connection to our deepest feelings, and as the orientor of our senses and sense of identity – were rationalized by distinctive universalist worldviews. Kinesthesia as entwined with the emotions presumed that all humans shared this same connection and that they were all equally moved by the same depictions of human predicament or struggle. Kinesthesia as baseline for evaluating the senses presumed that all humans had equal access to the same conditions for sensing the world. Although physical impairment could cause a person to perceive the world differently, social difference did not. Both conceptions of the kinesthetic imbued dance with a unique capacity for communication; it functioned either to awaken and enliven feelings or to assert the vitality of physicality as separate from the emotions. In the first case, the dancer's body became a vessel for the dance's message and the viewer received that message by being moved by it. In the second, the dancer's body emitted actions to a viewing body that actively sought out their message.

The same year as Gibson's publication, earthlings saw the first pictures of their planet from outer space. Although it had been conceived of as spherical since the time of the Portolan charts, these first images of earth floating in space and the space exploration that made them possible contributed to a new sense of one's orientation on the planet. Ecological theorist and architect R. Buckminster Fuller began to promote a new conception of earth as a spaceship traveling through the universe. In order to focus awareness on the limited resources aboard, he encouraged thinking that confirmed, even in quotidian activities, a sense of earth as spherical and global. Instead of jumping "up," for example, one jumped "out."[120] No longer surveying the world from a static point of view, the subject in this antichorological theory of orientation was located in relation to an earth's center and to the universe.

Concurrent with Gibson's research on kinesthesia, a new national mandate to attend to physical fitness implemented new policies encouraging exercise, especially among youth. In the US the government established the President's Council on Youth Fitness in 1956, responding to studies that America's youth was becoming "soft" due to new comforts in transportation and leisure activities.[121] President-elect John F. Kennedy promoted even greater governmental involvement with fitness when he published a notorious essay in *Sports Illustrated* entitled "The Soft American."[122] Physical vigor, he argued, was "one of America's most precious resources," and its dwindling and softened presence signaled a national security emergency. It was necessary not only for military strength, but also for moral and intellectual vitality. In order to restore vigor, he called upon all Americans to engage with effort and determination in building strength and muscle tone. Specifically referencing the Soviet Union as a powerful adversary, Kennedy proposed that the government now needed to assert leadership in fitness in order to combat communism. Only a decade earlier Alfred Kinsey had published his studies on sexual habits and proclivities among adults, indicating a much greater occurrence of homosexual encounters than previous studies had determined. The specter of the "soft" American undoubtedly summoned up effeminacy and homosexuality as well as general sloth, and these should be addressed by tough and vigilant work.

Kennedy instigated wide-reaching programs in schools and community facilities to promote vigor and health, almost as if resuscitating the muscular Christianity movement of the early twentieth century. As part of this unprecedented involvement by the nation in fitness, girls were to be given equal access to physical education, and all schoolchildren were measured on their abilities in a softball throw, a broad jump, a fifty-yard dash, and a six-hundred yard walk/run. Where the "alternative" movement explorations such as contact improvisation that fleshed out Gibson's theories focused on expanding perception and consciousness, these new initiatives in fitness proposed a physicality to be monitored through testing and regulation, a physicality that played a crucial if limited role in defining citizenship.

With health now defined as a civic right and a government dedicated to preserving that right, fitness became a major cultural preoccupation and the fitness industry burgeoned into a massive educational and commercial venture.[123] The synergistic product of medical, diet, sports, advertising, beauty, and fashion enterprises, fitness was promoted through collective participatory events such as sports and also through individualized training regimens that took place as a highly compartmentalized activity within one's day. With increasing precision, fitness was determined through several kinds of measurement. What began as the length of a jump or throw became a complex matrix of variables much more detailed than Sargent ever could have imagined. These included caloric intake, protein and carbohydrate consumption, proper hydration, and ratio of fat to total body mass; anaerobic threshold and heart rate and pulse at different moments in exertion; number of minutes spent warming up and cooling down, distance and speed walked or run, and correlations between muscle size and strength in relation to light and heavy weight repetitions.[124] Doctors and health advocates encouraged individuals to keep diaries with measurements for exercise performed each day.

Responding to the proliferation of criteria determining health, new fads of exercise were introduced ranging from jogging and speed-walking to aerobics, jazzercise and televised workouts, each claiming to make-over the body efficiently and effectively. Many of these regimens approached the body as an unruly and unresponsive mechanics that would only show improvement through arduous and exhausting repetition. Slogans such as those made popular by Jane

Figure 2.12 A buff and buoyant Jane Fonda promoting her video exercise routines, a series of regimens that were so popular they prompted the widespread purchase of the newly invented video cassette recorders (VCRs)
Photo by Steve Shapiro
Copyright; Steve Shapiro. Corbis
Courtesy of Jane Fonda

Fonda's influential video regimens, "No pain, no gain," and "Go for the burn," signaled the assumption that the acquisition of fitness entailed pushing the body to maximums of exertion.[125] Although the patriotism attached to Kennedy's mandate lessened over the years, the tone and attitude he established for the culture of fitness endured for the rest of the century. Exercise, more a form of work than pleasure, led the body through rigorous exercise regimes. The body's improvement could be measured in terms of the increases in amount of weight lifted, length of time enduring aerobic action, the enhanced flexibility of specific muscle groups, and the reduction of cholesterol in the blood.

As in the early eighteenth century, physical appearance and shape, in particular, became a major preoccupation.[126] Instead of graceful comportment and an erect carriage, however, the new obsession centered on the body's fat – its accretion in certain areas and the resulting lumpy and bloated appearance of the physique.[127] Diet industries alongside fitness promoted one new eating regimen after another, each designed to offer a painless approach to weight loss that relied on the latest discoveries concerning metabolic functioning and nutrient value. Systematic measurement of one's weight was strongly advised. The new diseases of anorexia and bulimia signaled the urgent and obsessive focus on maintaining slimness. As Susan Bordo has argued, these disorders also demonstrated the special pressure exerted on women's bodies by capitalist society in which the contradictory mandates to spend and save bear down on women through stipulation of fashionable appearance both at home in the workplace.[128] Where women needed to control weight in order to conform to standards of appearance, men dieted for heart-attack prevention.[129] In marked contrast to Galenic or eighteenth models of health that focused on balance and integration among all parts of the body, the heart and circulatory system now played a special role in both health and fitness.

The intensive focus on the details of producing fitness, spectacularized in the professional sports industries, also entered dance training where it was implemented to accomplish a very different set of goals. Dancers, now responsible for organizing their own training regimens rather than participating in the choreographer's daily technique class, drew upon anatomical insight to determine the needs of their specific physicalities. As in H'Doubler's time, students explored ranges of movement at each joint, but now, with increased precision and an intensive focus on minute degrees of tension in various muscle fibers. Skinner release technique, Klein-Mahler technique, and body–mind centering, among others, geared students' attention towards an absolute economy of effort by encouraging them to sequence slowly through a joint's motion, or to dwell in specific positions, making tiny adjustments to weight distribution. Iyengar yoga likewise mobilized anatomical insights to imbue the asanas with proper alignment. As in contact improvisation, these meditative investigations yielded an alternative experience of self as no longer commanding the body to act but instead witnessing motion as it unfolded.

These training techniques aligned with a variety of other pursuits oriented around cultivation of the "natural" body that contrasted sharply with mainstream projects of fashioning the body to suit its owner's requirements and desires for a specific identity. The natural body was no longer embraced as an aperture to expanded consciousness as in the 1960s and 70s but as a rejection of consumer society and values. Thus as many pursued the muscles, how to bulk them, dope them and sculpt them, as key elements in assembling one's visual appearance, others emphasized the ongoing information that the musculature provided and worked to expand their sensitivity to that information. Where some amended diet using hi-tech additives to enhance the appearance of the musculature, others relied on purifying fasts to detoxify the body followed by organic, seasonal, and locally produced foods. Where some used plastic surgery, implants, and botox, others explored Ayurvedic healing and herbal remedies. Where some refashioned nature as gymnasium for cross-training and as an alternative to many hours a day in the gym, others sat on a hilltop and practiced breathing. Unlike Mulcaster, who sought to balance self with environment through judicious selections of exercise, these contemporary visions of nature, either as fitness center or as site of solace, used it for self-fulfillment.

Paralleling the self-fashioning at the center of the fitness industry, the definition of kinesthesia transformed once again in the 1990s with work done by Alain Berthoz, among others, on the brain's sense of movement and with the discovery of a new class of brain cells, called "mirror neurons." Building on Gibson's theory of perception as an active engagement with the world, Berthoz approached the external senses as systems rather than channels and as interrelated rather than mutually exclusive.[130] And like him, he saw kinesthesia as playing a central role in orienting and organizing all the senses. He departed from Gibson, however, in two crucial ways: first, he argued that perception was a simulation of action; and second, he did not assume that observers shared a common environment, but instead, that each individual might perceive the world quite differently, based on the kinds of cultural and gendered differences from which their *habitus* was formed. Thus the perceiver no longer performed a "contact improvisation" with the environment, but instead, rehearsed and simulated multiple roles, through one's own actions as well as those of others. In the process of rehearsing these roles, individuals formulated a self, not as an entity that would then perform an action, but rather as performance itself. Like the fitness industry that promised to deliver identity through the repetition of a carefully designed regimen, so too, perception itself allowed the individual to sort through multiple options for every next move.

Synthesizing a large number of experiments on perception and cognition, Berthoz emphasized the anticipatory quality of attention. As one is looking at the armchair, one is already simulating the motions associated with seating oneself in it. As one sees the brake lights on the car ahead, one is already coordinating exactly when and how strongly to apply the brakes. Increasingly, neuroscientists were asserting that perception and action are embedded in each other, arguing that

> cortico-ponto-cerebello-thalamo-cortical loops exist, within which internal simulation of movement can occur completely independent of its actual execution. These loops contain . . . here I do well to

hesitate, like Faust. "Representations" is too vague; "models" is modern but probably vague as well; "images" is too visual; "schema" is the term perhaps most common in the literature; "kinesthetic series" would make Husserl happy.[131]

Through these "kinesthetic series," the brain simulated various movement options in order to choose the best strategy. Thus the cat could catch a mouse, anticipating its future position, because "its neurons are sensitive to the velocity of movement: they do not calculate a velocity."[132] The cat has evolved this capacity as part of its adaptation to and survival in its environment.

Although most cats are similarly talented at catching mice, humans, Berthoz argued, undergo a far more complex perceptual process. They do not necessarily perceive all events in the same way. Where Gibson assumed that all individuals could stand in the same place at different times and be afforded an equal opportunity to explore it,[133] Berthoz emphasized research that shows that "the oculomotor path followed to explore a face is completely different depending on what the observer is thinking: whether she thinks that the individual is rich, sad, or well-coifed, that his ears are protruding, and so on."[134] Pleasure or fear or interest, all influence the tiny motions of the eye, known as saccades, through which visual perception occurs.[135] One's history of engagement with the environment profoundly affected how one sees and consequently what one sees.[136] Berthoz referenced Bourdieu's notion of the *habitus* as a way to theorize these perceptual inclinations.[137] The long-standing features of our cultural as well as physical environment inform the way that we perceive the world.

Strong evidence in support of Berthoz's argument that perception simulates action has been provided with the discovery of mirror neurons, located in several areas of the cortex. These neurons fire when the subject performs an action, and they also fire when the subject sees the action being performed. Thus as we watch someone moving, motor circuits in the brain are activated that do not necessarily result in visible movement but nonetheless rehearse that movement. These recent neurophysiological investigations of kinesthesia support, in part, John Martin's argument about what happens when we see dance. The viewer, watching a dance, is literally dancing along. And yet, Martin's conceptualization of kinesthesia attached the physical feelings of the musculature to universally felt emotions, whereas these findings focus simply on behavior. Although the acts of perceiving and moving may be infused with emotion, what the mirror neurons indicate is the mutuality of sensing and physical action. Whether or not we feel afraid as we watch someone walk along the edge of a precipice, we may well move our arms and legs so as to displace our body's weight to the side of safety.[138] Whether or not we are hoping for victory, we twist and incline as if to exert a magic force over the bowling ball as it rolls towards the pins. And as many scientists have determined, this phenomenon "was present not only during the observation of goal-oriented movements, but also during the observation of meaningless art movements."[139]

Alongside these new theories of kinesthesia as a process of simulation, new digital technologies began radically overhauling people's systems for orienting in the world. Widespread use of the cellphone began to disconnect perceptual systems, creating significant lapses in users' navigational abilities, and in a compensatory strategy, GPS devices were introduced to provide immediate locate-abilities with respect to one's immediate surroundings and even the earth as a whole, replacing the internalized north that chorographers sought to inculcate with real-time positioning. Cellphones disrupt the integration of kinesthetic with aural information by establishing a new privileged contact with another body across an unspecified distance. Where normally, the movement of the body through space produces changes in auditory stimuli as one approaches or distances oneself from a given sound, with the cellphone, locomotion does not alter the register or volume of the voice one hears unless one loses the signal. The disintegration of the voice or interruption of contact with it, however, is largely unpredictable, further enhancing the separation of one's actions from one's perception of the voice. Absorbed in this contact with the voice on the other end, cellphone users typically exhibit a notorious disregard for the loudness of their own voices and the space they are occupying. They slow down unpredictably, stumble into other people or objects, and seldom assist in sustaining the modulated flow of bodies moving through public space. Those who are not talking on their cellphones often seem to adjust for the talkers' insensitivity by giving them extra space within which to execute their unpredictable movements.

Having disoriented themselves while talking on the phone, however, cellphone users could easily dial up Google Earth to reestablish their location using global positioning technology. Developed by the US Department of Defense, the Global Positioning System consists minimally in 24 satellites, four in each of six orbital planes, that emit signals designed to be decoded by a receiver to compute the receiver's position, velocity, and time.[140] Four satellites are required for each reckoning, usually provided in less than a tenth of a second, with an accuracy of 1-10 meters. The computation can be displayed as a set of numbers indicating longitude and latitude, or it can be reconciled with a map that locates the receiver, in motion, with respect to various features, such as roads or buildings, of the landscape. This map continues to unfold on the screen, locating and tracking the receiver as it moves. Not unlike the Portolan charts whose sixteen equidistant points gave mapmakers the stable reference with which to calculate star positions and ground locations, the GPS uses satellites, similarly omniscient, to project each body's motion onto a two-dimensional map for a map-reader who, like those using the Portolan charts, is on the move.

While GPS positions the viewer directly above his or her own body, a new generation of smart phones with Android software developed by Google is using the cellphone's camera to construct a three-dimensional view of one's surroundings including annotated distances to objects that may be obscured by buildings in the foreground.[141] This technology restores the primacy of sight functioning from the head of the viewer as the origin of calculations about location, although it can be used in alternation with the GPS mapping to oscillate between seeing straight ahead and seeing from above. Other software by Google has introduced the possibility of connecting one's own changing location to those of one's friends through a location-aware friend-finding system known as Latitude that delivers updates on the locations of people who subscribe to the service as they move around. Like the architecture of the brain's sense of movement established through the discovery of mirror neurons, these networked and hyperlinked technologies assist the cyber-body in establishing both self and other's orientations.[142]

For readers of Portolan charts, the body not only moved along with the map, but also exchanged substances and forces with its surroundings. The networked body made possible by new digital technologies is similarly hooked into environments both immediate and distant. Zooming into any point on the planet via the simulated spaceship that transports the mapreader in seconds from the earth as a whole to a specified destination, the networked body deploys multiple orienting skills, deterritorializing space with Google Earth's version of the graticule and also surveiling intimately the tops of houses, walking paths, or the alignment of grazing cows, for they, too, have the capacity to determine north and comport themselves accordingly.[143] The networked body pictures itself, not so much as erect and gracefully proportioned but as buff and smiling, as it waves into its phone and snaps a picture of itself to be disseminated via Facebook and YouTube to potentially millions of viewers. Far from the singular and autonomous body that Condillac proposed, or the muscularly dynamic body of early twentieth century modernism, this body draws upon a cyber-kinesthesis to rehearse options for making its way in the world.

3 Empathy

With the announcement of an impending Supreme Court vacancy, President Barack Obama, barely one hundred days in office, confirmed the pledge he had made on the campaign trail: to seek an appointee who had "empathy for peoples' hopes and struggles." Regarding empathy as "an essential ingredient for arriving at just decisions and outcomes," Obama defined the Justice's role, in part, as understanding how laws affect people's daily lives. Arguing for the need to look at the situations of others and what feelings they might provoke, Obama proposed empathy as the capacity to move everyone, regardless of class or privilege, outside of themselves in order to experience events as others might: "Empathy . . . calls us all to task, the conservative and the liberal, the powerful and the powerless, the oppressed and the oppressor. We are all shaken out of our complacency. We are all forced beyond our limited vision."[1]

Obama's assertion of empathy as a criterion for the appointment provoked a firestorm of criticism from Republican and right-wing commentators who expressed outrage at the potential consequences of such a justice's decisions. Equating empathy with partiality, with being "soft," Republicans charged that empathy would lead to rank violations of justice and exacerbate lawlessness. Exercising empathy would inevitably cause the Justice to identify with one side in a case and, further, to succumb to indulgent emotions typical of the feminine psyche. Arguing in response, that empathy does not imply "gooey sentimentalism," supporters of Obama championed empathy as providing the much-needed capacity to question one's certainty about one's own opinions.[2] Where the Republicans envision empathy as a force pulling a Justice into sentimental partiality, Obama and his supporters see it as precisely that quality that preserves impartiality.

Despite Obama's desire for and Republican concerns about the effects of empathy, they may have little choice in the matter. Appearing just a few weeks before Obama's announcement, new research by neuroscientists Antonio Damasio and Mary Helen Immordino-Yang indicates that empathy and the feelings, such as compassion and admiration that it enables, are "hard-wired" in the brain. Immordino-Yang summarizes a wealth of neurological investigation of specific brain sites by claiming:

> Our study shows that we use the feeling of our own body as a platform for knowing how to respond to other people's social and psychological situations. These emotions are visceral, in the most literal sense – they are the biological expression of "do unto others as you would have them do unto you."[3]

Although the brain may be organized to engage empathetically with others, new technologies that engender multitasking, such as cellphone, email, and twitter, may be compromising our ability to exercise empathy. According to Damasio and Immordino-Yang, feelings such as admiration require a lengthy and concentrated assessment of the object under consideration, and these new technologies are encouraging a faster response time, hence the headline of their interview: "Rapid-fire media may confuse our moral compass."

The issues raised in this recent public meditation on empathy – whether empathy entails "stepping outside oneself," or "falling" into sentimental attachment, whether it enhances or compromises acts of evaluation and judgment, and whether it is pan-human, biologically based, available to some or to all – have been examined and debated for centuries even though the term "empathy" is little more than one hundred years old. Like "kinesthesia," empathy came into usage at the end of the nineteenth century. Naming the experience of merging with the object of one's contemplation, it was originally coined in 1873 by the German aesthetician Robert Vischer as *Einfühlung,* and translated into English by Edward Titchener in 1909. Both Vischer and Titchener conceptualized empathy as entailing a strong and vital component of kinesthetic sensation. And both envisioned empathy as an experience undertaken by one's entire subjectivity.

In an effort to analyze the visual experience of seeing a work of art, Vischer distinguished between an initial and immediate apprehension of an object and the potential for a second phase of perception in which the observer moved into the object: "When I observe a stationary object, I can without difficulty place myself within its inner structure, at its centre of gravity. I can think my way into it, mediate its size with my own, stretch and expand, bend and confine myself to it."[4] Through an act of the imagination, but with the help of kinesthetic sensation, the observer was able to enter into and inhabit the other, and experience a consequent contraction, if the object was smaller, or expansion, if the object was larger, of the self. As a result, "the compressed or upward striving, the bent or broken impression of an object fills us with a corresponding mental feeling of oppression, depression, or aspiration, a submissive or shattered state of mind."[5] By sensing the structure of the object and allowing oneself to project into and experience that structure, one would inevitably assume a mental state that was inspired by its composition.[6] In objects or bodies in motion, this composition would include an apprehension of their gravity and momentum and the relation among their parts if differently in motion.

Adapting the Greek term *empatheia*, Titchener introduced Vischer's *Einfühlung* into English in his *Lectures on the Experimental Psychology of the Thought-Processes*. Asserting the ability of kinesthetic sensations to produce images in the mind, Titchener distinguished between a mental nod that signified assent to an argument using the "mind's muscles," and the actual physical action of nodding the head activated by "body's muscles."[7] Kinesthetic as well as other forms of information served as the vehicles for meaning. As a result, he argued "Not only do I see gravity and modesty and pride and courtesy and stateliness, but I feel or act them in the mind's muscles. This is, I suppose, a simple case of empathy, if we may coin that term as a rendering of Einfühlung";[8] Feelings that one experienced in response to observing another person or object were produced through a replication in the mind of the actions of the other. Empathy consisted in the act of reproducing in one's mind the kinesthetic images of the other, images that synthesized physical and emotional experience.

Although they differed in their conceptualization of the mental processes mobilized in the empathic experience, both Vischer and Titchener consistently referenced a strong component of physical engagement. For both, part of what one felt about the experience of the other included what the other's body was doing – the rhythm and intensity of action, and the location of the body in space. And this experience of inhabiting the other profoundly affected the sense of one's own bodily stance, tensility, and dynamism. It affected equally one's emotions. The "bent or broken" structure of the other was experienced as brokenness and also as a "shattered" state of mind. "Gravity," "pride," and "stateliness" were both physical and emotional states.

Although they launched a new kind of inquiry into the experience of feeling, examination of an immediate and responsive feeling of another person's feelings long predates Vischer's and Titchener's investigations.

A very similar sense of being connected to the feelings and actions of others can be found much earlier in English-language history, identified through use of the term "sympathy." In the seventeenth and eighteenth centuries, sympathy referenced a range of physiological and medical phenomena, and it also named the act of feeling what another was feeling throughout a full range of passions. As Adam Smith explained:

> Pity and compassion are words appropriated to signify our fellow-feeling with the sorrow of others. Sympathy, though its meaning was, perhaps, originally the same, may now, however, without much impropriety, be made use of to denote our fellow-feeling with any passion whatever.[9]

In what follows, I trace out a genealogy for the experience of feeling what another is feeling, with special emphasis, following Vischer's and Titchener's analyses, on the physical dimensions of the experience. I also search for the anatomical and medical explanations for sympathy/empathy that were summoned to rationalize its workings. I hope to show that the term "empathy" was neologized, not to express a new capacity for fellow-feeling, but to register a changing experience of physicality that, in turn, influenced *how* one felt another's feelings. As the body acquired a musculature and transformed into a volumetric and dynamic organism, the entire project of inhabiting another's situation or feelings likewise changed. Instead of casting one's self into the position of the other, it became necessary to project one's three-dimensional structure into the energy and action of the other.

As part of tracking the concept of sympathy/empathy, I will pose the question of the power relations inherent between those who feel and those who feel for or with them. The history of sympathy/empathy when placed in parallel with the history of colonization helps to explain how the British evaluated and responded to the foreigners whom they encountered in North American, Asia, and the Pacific. Sympathy/empathy served to establish the grounds on which one human being could be seen as differing from another. It also helped to rationalize how and why they could relate to one another as they did, exercising forms of political and social control, punishment and torture, and enslavement.

Taken unawares by surprising magnetisms

Both sympathy and sensibility were widely invoked throughout the sixteenth and seventeenth centuries to name a transference of feeling between bodies. Entangled within medical and physiological discourses, on the one hand, and social and aesthetic theories on the other, sympathy was connected variously to the concepts of sensitivity and sensibility. Sensibility and sensitivity typically accounted for the capacity to sense something or anything, whereas sympathy entailed a transformation resulting from the tuning of one thing to another. In medical treatises, it was invoked to explain the spontaneous responsiveness of one part of the body to another, or one body to another in, for example, the contraction of contagious diseases. In philosophical texts, it referenced a likemindedness of thought or feeling. More generally, it often referenced agreement, harmony, consonance, and accord.

At the beginning of the eighteenth century, a refined usage of sympathy came into circulation as a concept undergirding and rationalizing the constitution of human society. Like choreography, it circulated into English largely from French sources. Two influential texts, one by rhetorician Bernard Lamy and the other by aesthetician Jean-Baptiste DuBos, outlined the operations of sympathy in cementing relations between humans. Both were concerned to explain the persuasive powers that one person could exert upon another, in Lamy's case through public speaking, and in Dubos's, across a range of presentations that included live events such as gladiatorial combat and rope dancing, as well as artistic renderings of human action in painting and literature.[10]

Lamy identified sympathy as the principle that connected the voice of the speaker to the ears of the listener. The resonance and cadence of the voice and the intervals between breaths as one speaks had the capacity to affect the listener's Animal Spirits. A rough or boisterous sound, for example, would so animate the mind that the muscles would immediately prepare for flight.[11] Speech, being a uniquely human accomplishment, existed in many forms, given the variety of customs, Lamy's word for cultures, extant in the world. The purpose of rhetoric was to improve one's elegant mastery of the specific language in which one wished to converse and the various figures of speech, or tropes. Lamy argued that in order to convince the listener of the passion being represented in the discourse, it was necessary for the orator likewise to feel and not merely represent that passion.[12] In so doing he allied himself with one side of a debate, celebrated most famously in Diderot's *Paradox of Acting*, that acquired greater urgency over the course of the eighteenth century. Such a fervent delivery, Lamy asserted, stimulated the listener in a way that a performance in which the declaimer did not feel the subject never could. This was because sympathy operated on a level prior to or beneath the level of language.

DuBos similarly argued for the fundamentality of sympathy and for its role in enlivening the mind. Arguing that sympathy formed the "very basis of society," because it gave humans the ability to transcend their own self-interests, DuBos described sympathy as a reflex-like responsiveness to others that would help humans to secure one another's assistance or affirmation. Even before knowing the occasion for a person's cries of help, the observer would rush to their side "by a mechanical movement previous to all deliberation." Joy painted on a person's face likewise inspired the sentiment of joy, even before knowing the reason. [13] Like Lamy, DuBos conceptualized sympathy as that which enabled a physical change in response to witnessing another's plight or good fortune. The observer's body would markedly alter, softening or becoming agitated, in response to the image of another body in distress or rage. Also like Lamy, this responsiveness preceded any reflection, occurring immediately and spontaneously upon seeing the other's image.

Influenced by his reading of Locke, DuBos believed that human beings were attracted to especially vivid images of suffering or danger because of the mind's preference for active engagement over lassitude and boredom.[14] The performance of the rope dancer was compelling because of the potential for serious physical injury:

> In proportion as the movements of a rope-dancer are more or less dangerous, the attention of the spectators is raised or abated. If in his dancing between two swords, the heat of his motion should chance to fling him an inch out of the line he is confined to, he becomes instantly a proper object of our curiosity. Put but a couple of sticks, instead of two swords, or let the tumbler stretch his cord only two foot high in the middle of a meadow, the very same leaps and movements as he made before, will be thought no longer worth looking at, and the spectator's attention will terminate with the danger.[15]

Balanced atop the rope, dancers frequently performed complex sequences of steps, relocating the very dances that Feuillet had notated from the floor to the air high above. Viewers might well have relished the class critique implicit in stealing aristocratic dance vocabulary and performing it brilliantly on the rope, however, the ability to perform nobility more perfectly while at the same time showing its precariousness was not what excited viewers, according to DuBos. Rather, the potential that a slight mistake in motion could fling the dancer off the rope and onto the pointed sword lurking below was what captivated them, raising or abating their attention.

Figure 3.1 Two dancers performing on ropes of differing degrees of tension at one of the fair theaters.
Courtesy Bibliotèque Nationale

DuBos was particularly concerned to explicate how a pictorial or literary presentation of suffering or distress could so move the viewer, and he rationalized art's power to affect us as similar to the fascination we feel upon witnessing the suffering of another person. Whether a gladiator's last stand, a rope dancer's potential demise, or a painted depiction of human suffering, viewers enjoyed projecting themselves into those situations while at the same time knowing that they were not actually living those situations. Art thus provided a pleasure free from the actual danger that would be part of real experience. Occasionally, a viewer might be so transported by a performance as to cry out or gesture involuntarily, but this only demonstrated a momentary lapse of awareness of the appropriate conduct in public, for the performance was only a copy of life.[16]

For DuBos the qualities in one's blood, as influenced by properties in the air, in turn affected by the sun and by emanations from the earth, prompted people in different regions to develop with distinctive sets of customs. People living in Sweden and Andalusia, for example, "will differ, when they grow up to the state of manhood, in sense and inclinations . . ."[17] Air, itself, consisted in a mixture of many elements, including small animals, that acted upon the body to alter mood and health. Thus, the "fermentation" responsible for a storm also affected the mind, weighing it down and inhibiting it from proper exercise of imagination. It likewise corrupted the body, aggravating wounds and general distemper.[18] Even though a change in the weather could alter either a person's mental or physical condition, the primary effect of air was upon temperament. Because the organs in the brain decided "the spirit and inclinations of men, more than the bones which determine their stature and force," DuBos considered that all nations manifested more differences in "inclinations and mind than in make and color of body."[19]

Since the differences among peoples primarily resulted from air and temperature acting upon temperament, they could be acquired. For example, various Europeans had taken on the disposition of the natives in the countries where they had settled. Franks settling in the Holy Land had become "pusillanimous and vicious," whereas Portuguese settling in East-Indies were as "effeminate and cowardly" as the natives there.[20] In some countries, such as the southern parts of Europe, Asia, and Africa, people manifested a greater vivacity of spirit that made them more impressionable, so much so, that in the case of the Jews, prohibitions against painting or carving the human figure were necessary, because the people were too "passionately fond of all objects capable of moving them."[21] These gradations in sympathy and one's consequent susceptibility to art all fell along a continuum of difference measured in degrees. Pusillanimous and effeminate, vicious and cowardly were sets of oppositions constructed around greater and lesser amounts combativeness or aggressiveness.

In his emphasis on the importance of air and climate on temperament, DuBos's analysis recalled the work of earlier explications of sympathy, most notably that of Sir Kenelm Digby, whose 1658 publication entitled *A Late Discourse made in a Solemne Assembly by Nobles and Learned Men at Montpellier Touching the Cure of Wounds by the Powder of Sympathy*, was published in several languages and editions.[22] Digby began his treatise with a gripping description of his cure of a friend's infected sword wounds. Placing a Powder of Vitriol in a basin of water, he submerged a garter covered with the patient's blood in it, and the man immediately recovered completely.[23] In the interest of proving that this cure was not the work of demons, Digby set out on a lengthy explanation of the physics through which the cure was accomplished, citing principles of nature as follows: Light was a material, corporal substance, that bounced like a tennis ball. In bouncing, it loosened some of the particles of that on which it was shining.[24] The air was thus full of "atomes (sic) drawn out of their jackets by means of light," ("or they sallied out by the interior natural heat of those bodies"), such that wind was atoms agitated and smells were preponderances of certain kinds of atoms.[25]

Various kinds of forces of attraction – suctional, magnetic, electrical, flaming, and filtrating (as when liquid seeps out of a jar by moving up a cloth draped over it) – drew atoms to one another.[26] Yet these forces of attraction worked more powerfully if the atoms were willing to mingle with the body that drew them together, and that willingness was determined by the extent of their sympathy, or resemblance, one to another. Resemblance depended upon the atoms' mutual heaviness or weightiness, their shared degree of rarity or density, or of shape (square, hexagonal). Atoms that composed any given material shared a resemblance and were strongly attracted to one another. Thus, to cure a burn you must expose it to fire; or to cure bad breath, you could open your mouth inside the privy for a while.[27]

This mutual attraction of atoms to one another was what accounted for the sympathetic response of humans to one another. As Digby observed:

> We see daily, that if a person gaze those who see him gazing are excited to do the same. If one comes perchance to converse with persons that are subject to excess of laughter, one can hardly

forbear laughing, although one doth not know the cause why they laugh.[28]

Although humans would laugh, yawn, or cry upon witnessing these actions in others, their sympathy partook of a larger system of attractions and repulsions governing all the world's atoms. Women and children, because more moist, were most susceptible to this "contagion of the imagination," yet all bodies in the universe responded according to this composition of the forces of attraction.[29]

Digby's analysis synthesized earlier Galenic conceptions of the body with the new focus on the molecular constitution of all matter typical of the microscope-inspired theories of science from his period. He did not rely on the animal spirits or on the humours to explain how or why one body moved in response to another, but instead, identified the atom as the smallest unit of operation responsible for movement. His principles of attraction, however, were not based on mechanical logics; he did not envision atoms as constructing the levers and pulleys that permitted action. Instead, he posited that diverse kinds of matter could be attracted one to another thereby perpetuating Galenic ideas of reciprocal attractions between elements within and outside of the body.

For Digby, sympathy constituted a cosmic magnetism, one that operated at every level and upon every thing in the universe. The various forces of attraction that drew things together enmeshed all beings within a web of causal attractions that helped to account for behavior. Thus throwing a dog's excrement on a fire would cause the dog to become overheated, just as allowing a cow's milk to boil over might infect the udder that had given it.[30] Sympathy thus exerted influence in every direction, binding the body's excretions back to it as well as imprinting one body upon another. Like the court dances that Arbeau had documented, where bodies bound together by the requisites of social propriety were attracted to and repulsed from one another based on their demonstrations of modesty or ostentatious exaggeration, Digby's vision of sympathy charged it with the power continually to transform relations among all things in the world.

The masques presented at the seventeenth century court danced out these reciprocal relations in the form of gracefully evolving configurations, like well coordinated atoms, among groups of dancers. They relocated the court dances that Arbeau had documented onto the stage for presentation to an audience and sequenced the various dances within a narrative of order lost and restored.[31] Their careful displays of cosmic and sovereign harmony were often followed by disruptive interludes, antimasques, in which witches, satyrs, or other foreign or barbaric

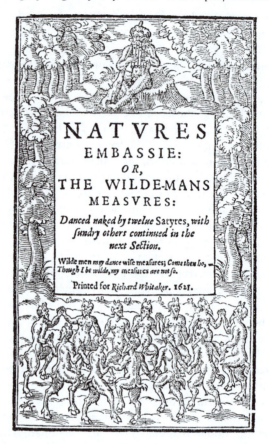

Figure 3.2 The frontispiece from Richard Braithwaite's *Nature's Embassie*, depicting a masque dance for twelve satyrs.
Frontispiece by Richard Braithwaite
Braithwaite, Richard. *Natures Embassie: Or, the Wilde-mans Measures: Danced naked by twelve Satyres, with sundry others*. London. 1621.
Courtesy of The William Andrews Clark Memorial Library, University of California, Los Angeles

creatures embodied the quixotic and dark underworld where chaos reigned. Skiles Howard has shown how the feminine and the exotic other merged in these disorderly outbursts, only to be docilized by a reinstatement of civility and decorous harmony.[32] The masques thus assuaged anxiety over the success of the colonial project and its management of foreigners as well as the ongoing uncertainty over women's roles by resolving in favor of an unchallengeable masculine and royal dominance.

In contrast to Digby's universal forces of attraction and the masque's orchestration of their proper order, sympathy as proposed by DuBos and elaborated by philosopher David Hume and others, served primarily as a human capacity to observe and then register the feelings or others.[33] Hume envisioned sympathy as producing a copy in one's mind of the passions or affections felt by the other.[34] This copy was then converted by the imagination into an impression that exerted itself on both body and mind.[35] Where the masques and court dances emblematized Digby's conception of sympathy as based in cosmic attractions that operated in every direction, the rope dancer illustrated DuBos's and Hume's theories of sympathy by providing a spectacle that the observer would see, copy in the imagination, and then feel. In Digby's sympathy viewers would be subject to the multiple attractions or repulsions of atoms, managed through the dancers' reigning in and harmonizing of the body as they danced and responded to the dancing of those around them. If appropriately moderate, solicitous in their attitudes towards others, and judicious in their responses, they would impel viewers into their mutual indebtedness and prevail over the chaotic forces of otherness. In contrast, DuBos's and Hume's sympathy was based on isolated individuals who viewed the situation of another and assessed that person's relative merits or predicaments.

Whether on the ground or in the air, dancing by the early eighteenth century no longer inculcated in viewers the moral probity alluded to by Elyot and dramatized in the masques. Instead, as the collections of dance notations made evident, it displayed fashion and accomplishment, exerting over viewers a persuasive image of physical dexterity and alacrity. Onstage, in the ballroom, or on the rope, it transmitted an impression of the dancer's carriage and proportion and the buoyancy or stateliness of the steps. Although the rope enhanced these perceptions by featuring the dancer's precarious positioning, the performance, as in other forms of dancing, offered a presentation and demonstration of uprightness and grace, and when undertaken by the most successful dancers, a breathtaking virtuosity. DuBos was particularly concerned with scenes of violence and danger in order to show how the mind was drawn to lively images and how art functioned in society as a copy of life. Not as laudatory in its embodiment of taste and beauty as other forms of dancing, he saw the rope dancer, who appeared most frequently in stalls or makeshift theaters at London's many fairs, as a class of entertainment. Hume, in contrast, focused more on sympathy as the source of the social bonding. He would have envisioned the dancer as an occasion prompting people to experience collectively a spectacle of danger. Both attended to sympathy as a crucial foundation for social experience.

The need to theorize a common ground on which one human recognizes another such as those developed by DuBos and Hume developed along with the growing awareness of cultural difference brought on by colonial expansion. Since first contact in the late sixteenth century, Britons had participated in and been exposed to an escalating number of accounts of massacre and enslavement, grueling torture, abduction, and survival, prompting urgent inquiry into what human beings can and will do to one another. The numbers of people from other lands, bearing their different appearances and customs, expanded dramatically within Britain, heightening awareness of cultural difference.[36] The deleterious effects of intense urbanization were likewise witnessed daily as demonstrations of deprivation, sickness, and general poverty proliferated in the dense space of the city.

Pressured from multiple directions to account for the responsibility of humans towards one another's suffering, philosophers and aestheticians tapped sympathy as a framework within which to evaluate the human condition. Sympathy sutured humans one to another across the breaches of humanity wreaked by slavery and colonization. Similar to chorological and choreographic conceptions of space as a blank geometry within which to place objects or to the botanical classificatory rubrics used to delineate relationships among plants, sympathy served as the common connectivity through which distinctions among individuals emerged. Rather than sharing a cosmic sympathy across species, each individual felt for others who were similarly positioned upon an abstract plane that defined humanity.[37] Like the varieties of dancing collected and categorized according to types and their variations, all humans could now be located on a shared grid symbolizing the world, and taxonomized according to variations measured in terms of degree: more or less civilized; darker or lighter skinned; more or less pusillanimous; with greater or lesser talent in a given pursuit. Sympathy helped to construct that grid and then to connect individuals across it, momentarily melting the lines of difference that held them in their places.

Underlying and permitting this set of claims about humankind was a tacit set of assumptions about who had the right amount of sympathy and who was qualified to make judgments based on sympathetic understanding. Because sympathy was innate but could be cultivated, those with the best responsivity were men of a certain class. Women, as Hume observed, were woefully undereducated, and hence, not likely to be qualified to exercise discernment.[38] Similarly, for DuBos, all people possessed not only the capacity for sympathy but also an inherent ability to fathom the rules governing the relative merit of art.

Nonetheless, those with a certain exposure to the world and its commerce constituted the public upon whom DuBos depended for the determination of excellence and ranking.[39]

Sympathy thus coalesced as a property within the body and among all human bodies that provided the means through which both evaluation and regulation could take place. As a physiological principle, it governed the coordination of all parts of the body and their ability to come into proper coordination. As a human capacity, sympathy enabled everybody, but most especially men of means, to feel another's feelings, thereby serving to coordinate the laws that allowed human society to function effectively. Like the viewers who relished the rope dancer's performance as she served up a spectacle to be evaluated in terms of the degree of danger and likelihood of bodily injury, the discriminating practitioner of sympathy, surveyed and assessed human interaction. No longer imbricated within the mutually constituting sociality of the court dances and the mutual magnetisms of like-minded atoms, the individual spectator emerged as singular yet connected, by discernment, to others through sympathy.

Surveying the scene, nervously

Over the course of the eighteenth century sympathy developed as a theory of connectivity among people increasingly seated in the physiological functioning of the body.[40] By mid century, such a substantial anatomical foundation for sympathy had been documented that the Chevalier de Jaucourt, writing the entry on Sympathy for the *Encyclopédie*, demonstrated how the ability to read and feel emotions in others depended on distinctive sets of nerves. He observed how the eyes, for example, conveyed our passions most vividly, because the fifth pair of nerves to which the eyes were attached, communicated with the brain and its nerve juice was sent into the eyes and imprinted there its diverse motions.[41] Jaucourt acknowledged a generalized usage of the term "sympathy" as the wonderful feeling between two souls who experienced shared feelings, yet he focused on the physiological organization that subtended that communion.

Although the neural structure that supported sympathy was what enabled the mutual experience to occur, humans did not share these feelings by any direct contagion, as Digby had argued, but rather through an act of imagination that allowed one body to transfer him or herself into the situation of another. Adam Smith reminded his readers that even in witnessing public punishment one would never know directly another's pain or joy.[42] Smith who had read DuBos, likewise argued that through an act of imagination the observer could come to feel "all the same torments" as the other person, even becoming "in some measure the same person with him," although the observer's experience would be weaker in extent.[43] Humans had the capacity to feel physically another's pain or joy, but always to a lesser extent because the mind of the observer made a copy of what was witnessed and entered bodily into that imagined copy.

Not a play-acting in the mind, sympathetic reactions entailed a full response of the whole body. Seeing another's arm or leg in jeopardy, we "naturally shrink or draw back our own leg or our own arm."[44] Similarly, "The mob, when they are gazing at a dancer on the slack rope, naturally writhe and twist and balance their own bodies as they see him do, and as they feel that they themselves must do if in his situation."[45] Having made a mental copy of the situation, viewers reacted to the dancer's treacherous and suspenseful relationship to gravity and the potential hazards that might befall her by moving their own bodies as if to avoid falling. Expanding on DuBos's analysis of viewers' responses to the dancer, Smith argued that they would feel every twist and turn. In his treatise *A Theory of Moral Sentiments*, Smith elaborated on this primal capacity to identify physically with another, extending the sympathetic principle to encompass a full range of emotions in relation to the circumstances that generated them.

For Smith, the physical basis of sympathy resided in "fibers" and was elicited, variously, according to their degree of delicacy.[46] In keeping with Jaucourt's analysis of neural reactivity, Smith along with his colleagues in the Edinburgh medical sciences, envisioned the body as governed by a responsivity that they termed the "vital principle."[47] This vital principle explained how the body could receive stimuli and direct the various organs of the body to make the appropriate response without the person's conscious awareness of the process. Where Jaucourt envisioned the nervous system as juice-filled, Smith thought it functioned through the medium of an electric nervous energy.[48] Whether conveyed through fluid or electrical mediums, however, bodily function was no longer constituted by the tubes, spirits, or glands that had been hypothesized in the early century mechanistic model of anatomy, nor was it composed of various atoms drawn towards one another, as in Digby's model. Instead, the body's self-regulating capacity was traced to an inherent sensibility that could be witnessed in the synchronous motions of the eyes or in the secretion of saliva at the sight of a favorite dish.[49] The sights, sounds, tastes, and smells of the world impressed themselves upon the body, and its responses were organized and conveyed through a reactivity, often envisioned as a vibration, that was more immediate and total than a physics of levers and pulleys could ever accomplish.[50]

Like Lamy's description of the orator, the immediacy of this reactivity accounted for the effect that the actor might have upon the viewer, as biologist and acting theorist John Hill explained:

> we feel with the character: we forget that it is a player who speaks, and that it is an imaginary scene which is represented before us; we conceive the hero and the husband betray'd, injur'd, and glorying in his insatiable revenge: we not only see the character thus before our eyes, but we feel with him; we pay an involuntary tribute to the author and the player; we glow with their transports; the very frame and substance of our hearts is shaken as if conscious of the same due to honour and resentment, we swelled and trembled as he did; like strings which are so perfectly concordant, that one being struck, the other answers, tho' distant.[51]

Referring to it as a kind of contagion, Hill relied on the notion of the string's vibration in order to explain the fullness of the viewer's transference into the character's situation. "Glowing," "shaking," "swelling," and "trembling," the audience lived the character's story along with him.[52]

For Smith, it was not simply that one lived the other's experience, since, as he emphasized, we experience only a reduced version of it. Instead, one's sympathetic response depended upon one's ability to read the entire scene in which the other person was enmeshed as it unfolded in time. Apprehending the scene for its narrative, for all the clues signaling the status of its actors and the "general idea of some good or bad fortune that has befallen the person" was essential to understanding the other's plight.[53] Some emotions, such as grief and joy, prompted an immediate transference: "A smiling face is, to everybody that sees it, a cheerful object; as a sorrowful countenance, on the other hand, is a melancholy one."[54] However, more frequently the larger situation in which these feelings were located necessitated additional observation:

> Sympathy, therefore, does not arise so much from the view of the passion, as from that of the situation which excites it. We sometimes feel for another, a passion of which he himself seems to be altogether incapable; because, when we put ourselves in his case, that passion arises in our breast from the imagination, though it does not in his from the reality. We blush for the impudence and

rudeness of another, though he himself appears to have no sense of the impropriety of his own behavior . . ."[55]

The sympathetic response also required time "to picture out in our imagination" exactly why and how the person was experiencing the feelings he or she was feeling.[56]

DuBos had explained the fascination of the rope dancer in terms of the potential to misstep and thereby succumb to the pernicious consequences of a fall. The viewer's sympathy was intensified based on the degree of danger evidenced in the swords pointing upwards or the height of the rope. In contrast, Smith's sympathetic responsiveness was based not only on logics of gravity and force, but also on the social consequences of improper actions. His theory required a reading of the social as well as physical scene. More like Weaver's ballets in which "Vulcan expresses his Admiration; Jealousie; anger; and Despite: And Venus shews neglect; Coquetry; Contempt; and disdain,"[57] Smith's notion of sympathetic feelings developed as a story, a series of tableaux vivantes, unfolding before the viewer's eyes. Like the characters in the ballet, who invited viewers to progress through a danced dialogue built from call and response actions, Smith's sympathy depended upon a reading of the narrative logic as it developed throughout the scene. Concerned that viewers would fail to comprehend how the actions were conveying the story, Weaver had felt it necessary to explain the codes for *The Loves of Mars and Venus*. By mid-century, however, the growing popularity of story ballets and pantomimes confirmed viewers' new facility at reading a danced narrative, perhaps even influencing the way that Smith described sympathy.

For Smith, persons of each rank and profession acquired different characters and manners and differing capacities for sympathy.[58] Sympathy accrued to those in a civilized society who lived in relative comfort and those of better means possessed greater sympathy. Savages, in contrast, necessarily spent their time tending to their own needs with no available time to devote attention to another.[59] As part of their survival strategy, they assumed

> upon all occasions the greatest indifference, and would think themselves degraded if they should ever appear in any respect to be overcome either by love, or grief, or resentment. Their magnanimity and self-command in this respect are almost beyond the conception of Europeans.[60]

Native Americans allowed their parents to arrange their marriages, disdaining to express a preference for one person over another as

Figure 3.3 The frontispiece from John Weaver's publication of the scenario for his *Orpheus & Euridice*.

John Weaver. *The fable of Orpheus and Eurydice, with a dramatick entertainment in dancing thereupon; attempted in imitation of the ancient Greeks and Romans. As perform'd at the Theatre Royal in Drury-Lane.* Written, collected and composed, by John Weaver, dancing-master.

Courtesy of Houghton Library, Harvard University

spouse. If taken prisoner of war, they would undergo unbearable torture with no response, except to curse at their captors while they, in turn, joked at the prisoner's burnings and lacerations.[61] This same contempt of death existed among all savage nations and was, in part, responsible for the enslavement of the African negroes, whose captors, coming from the lowest ranks of European society, could not detect their suffering.[62]

Those of greater wealth and education drew upon a far greater reservoir of sympathy, in part because of their aptitude for impartiality, and in part because sympathy, unlike humanity, required nobility and generosity.[63] As a result, Laura Hinton argues, Smith's sympathetic observer was resolutely gendered as masculine. Although humanity was "the virtue of a woman," generosity occurred as part of a masculine repertoire of feelings and behaviors.[64] Even though it required a certain delicacy of fibers to render one sensible to the scene, thereby mitigating against the robustness of manhood, it remained clearly within the masculine domain to exercise a generous response to what one observed. Both men and women, equally, could read the narrative, as the massive interest on the part of women in the novel throughout this period makes evident. However, the additional compassion required to evaluate the consequences to the persons observed in the scene in which they were situated remained part of a masculine ethics of spectatorship.

Within civilized and relatively affluent society, the viewer's feelings about the scene consisted in a relation of scale or amount, one to another. As for Hume, differences were constituted in terms of amount or degree. Propriety and impropriety, decency and ungracefulness, gratitude and resentment, all formed a reticulated chart of emotions, each related to the next based on degrees of intensity. All individuals were seen as performing for one another, and sympathy functioned, in part, to enhance all people's desire to improve themselves by allowing them to imagine what others thought of them.[65]

Each of the civilized societies boasted a different balance among all the passions and different sets of manners for responding sympathetically to one another, yet these differences consisted in degrees or amounts of vivacity, tendency to weep, sobriety, or animation.[66] Sympathy, more or less available to all, helped to bridge differences among members of different social classes, and to render tolerable the customs of those from other nations. Savage nations, in contrast, revolved around such hyperbolic stoicism that sympathy was nearly extinguished and a reading of the scene impossible. Being "obliged to smother and conceal the appearance of every passion," savages acquired the tendency to dissimulate and conceal the truth.[67] Whereas the behaviors of civilized societies existed along a continuum, the practices of savages approached a degree of otherness so as to make them "almost beyond the conception of Europeans." Since individuals would elicit a sympathetic response from others only if a reading of the scene within which they were situated was possible, the savages seemed almost inhuman. Their scenes were unreadable, not only because the savages dissimulated but also because the intensity of their denial of sympathy created a new kind of difference, one based more on kind than degree.

Smith's elaboration of sympathy as a process of reading the body in its scene occurred at moment in British history when colonial policies were in transition.[68] The unification of Britain itself and its triumphs in the Caribbean and North America combined with the waning of the great Asian empires and successes in India to create a new British identity as a global power. Linda Colley argues that this new dominance provoked excitement but also disorientation in the face of such vast and diverse holdings.[69] Worried about the cost of maintaining control over such distinctive cultures, Britons were also challenged by the need to legitimize their rule. Given their self-proclaimed freedom as citizens, how could they justify to themselves as well as to others their colonial project?[70]

Smith's notion of sympathy as one in which a masculine observer compassionately and impartially read the scene suggested a new foundation on which colonial policies might be developed. Sympathy, no longer merely a shared human capacity, now originated in the neural composition of the body's physical structure, and it operated according to the structures of physical responsivity. This neurologicization of sympathy fleshed out individuals so that they could take on the traits of characters composing a cohesive scene. Not the full-blown psyche of later periods, this subjectivity nonetheless drew people into sympathetic identification through a narrativized logic. According to this logic, individuals would elicit a sympathetic response from others only if a reading of the scene within which they were situated was possible. Those whose scenes were indecipherable slid off the continuum of humanity into a new kind of otherness.

In his 1762 survey of the world's dances, Giovanni-Andrea Gallini, director of dances at the Royal Haymarket Theater, was still able to identify some attributes of humanity displayed by savages dancing. Describing dances from the "Gold Coast" he observed:

> This was called the dancing-season. To this solemnity all came dressed in the best manner, according to their respective ability.

The dance was ridiculous enough; but it served to keep up their agility of body. And amidst all the uncouth barbarism of their gestures and attitudes, nature breaks out into some expressions of joy, or of the passions, that would not be unworthy of an European's observation.[71]

Even with the chaotic tumult of uncouth gesticulations, glimpses of genuine feeling could be seen that could be shared and were worthy of being witnessed by the English observer.

In contrast to this tenuous connection, David Arnold has shown that beginning mid-century, British assessments of India began "to focus on essential characteristics – its timeless and unchanging nature, its long history of invading armies and despotic rulers, the rigidity of its religious and social divisions, the passivity of its Hindu population."[72] Britons noted with increasing alarm the passivity displayed in response to the famine alongside the performances of self-immolation and self-mortification by practicing Hindus. Arnold argues that

In such a sensationalized world of self-imposed suffering, it was hard for Britons to identify with Indians' suffering as if it were their own. . . . Indians were too strange, too perverse in their ways, beliefs, and customs, for Europeans, even in the Age of Enlightenment, to be able to engage with them on the basis of a common humanity and shared sensibilities.[73]

No longer able to read the scenes in which these bodies acted, Britons could justify a new plan of colonial expansion based on the presumption of the inhumanity of those they ruled.

A different kind of essentializing effected Native Americans. Following King Philip's War in 1675, the reports of which probably influenced Smith's description of their savage character, conflicts between British and Native peoples moved further West, and many Natives living in the original colonies were assimilated into, or lived at the margins of English populations. Leading up to the American Revolution, the image of the Native American was utilized by the British as a symbol of the colonies, alternately noble or savage, as it depicted the natural resources and wealth of the land or the willful unruliness of the colonists.[74] By the late eighteenth century, as the Boston Tea Party made evident, Native Americans, even as they were routed off their lands and pushed to the absolute margins of society, were reappropriated by the colonists as vehicle for a new American identity. By the 1820s this image was resuscitated further in the US as a noble but vanishing species whose barbaric treatment by the British proved the good fortune of Americans no longer under colonial rule.[75]

Alterity and domesticity

Smith worked alongside anatomists who continued to explore another notion of sympathy – as a neural phenomenon, governing the ways that all parts of the body communicated with one another. Although the distinctiveness of their approaches was not immediately apparent, the contradictory uses of sympathy were evident even in Smith's own theorization of it. On the one hand, sympathy occurred instantaneously, a product of delicate nerves encountering the vivid feelings and situation of another person. On the other, sympathy resulted from a judicious exercising of interpretive skills available to those with the capacity for generosity of spirit. Over the next hundred years, the disparity between these responses embedded itself in the evolving sciences of medicine and sociology with the result that sympathy as a rubric for explaining humans' responsiveness to one another fell out of use. Like the term "choreography," sympathy's meanings proliferated into vague and also infrequent use. It endured only in the arts, and especially literature, where it took on a refined and specific set of connotation associated with the role and capacity of middle-class women.

In medicine, the nervous system assumed increasing importance in explaining health and well-being, displacing both the role of the humours and mechanical models of equilibrium. Disease continued to be predicated on imbalances within the entire system, however, the nerves played a more central role in creating and transmitting imbalance.[76] Depending upon the degree of delicacy of one's nervous system, the body was more susceptible to certain kinds of illness, and this delicacy, in turn, correlated with one's occupation and degree of means. As physician William Cullen explained, stomach problems, menstrual disorders, colic, hysteria, and gout became the chronic ailments of the wealthy, whereas uncivilized populations and the laboring poor, who were more or less devoid of sensibility, would survive through the body's inherent capacity to regulate itself.[77]

In the nascent social sciences, new techniques of observation and measurement, designed to inculcate complete objectivity, eradicated sympathy from the discourses addressing the nature of humanity. Mary Poovey argues that the abstract and geometric conception of space that came to dominate late seventeenth and early eighteenth century scientific inquiry depended upon a continuous and uniform field subject to mathematical laws. This presumption about space, so vividly expressed in the graticule and effectively mobilized in the early dance notations, was implemented in the early nineteenth century to study society, now constituted as a social body. Its component parts could now be measured and adjusted using protocols of inspecting, aggregating, and managing ever larger segments of the population.[78] By the early nineteenth century, the study of society presumed an organic wholeness in which the social body was recast as a single organism, having both an interior and an exterior and parts with specific functions.[79] Invoking anatomical methodology to examine society, investigators probed the dark recesses of the urban underclasses, recording statistically the features of poverty they witnessed.[80] Authoritative witnesses, grounded in scientific disinterestedness, but willing to enter into the repulsive squalor of urban slums, reduced the objects of their analysis to a passive aggregate.[81]

The same strategies of observation began to inform the study of colonized peoples with the use of physical measurement figuring prominently in the establishment of social, moral, and spiritual inferiority. Beginning with England's first contact with foreign lands and continuing up through the eighteenth century, all humans were seen as originating in a common ancestor, with differences in appearance and custom deriving primarily from distinctive climates and terrains. In 1665 the Royal Society had issued specific guidelines for the observation and classification of "flora, fauna, geology, and Natives and Strangers" in order to assist explorers and colonists with the classification of their experiences. Royal Society guidelines included the following:

> their Stature, Shape, Colour, Features, Strength, Agility, Beauty (or want of it), complexion, Hair, Dyet, Inclination, and Customs that seem not due to Education. As to their Women (besides other things) may be observed their Fruitfulness, or Barrenness; their hard or easy labour, etc. And both in Women and Men must be taken notice of what diseases they are subject to.[82]

Seeking to discover the extent of the effects of climate on physical appearance and capacity, the Royal Society list of traits, those things not "due to education," resembled the kind of inventory of dances that Arbeau had undertaken decades earlier, but with the added specificity of scrutinizing the body's individual parts.

Although microscopy had identified the egg and consequently the possibility for generational transmission of the same traits, climate continued as the preferred explanation for physical differences into the eighteenth century.[83] By that time British who had lived in North America for several generations realized that they had not changed visibly in stature or skin color, although they congratulated themselves on the extent to which their bodies had been "seasoned," like wood, to the American climate.[84] In contrast, Native Americans were beginning to be seen as inferior constitutionally or as non-native, based on their dramatic susceptibility to and death from diseases brought by the colonists who began to invoke their own hardiness in order to justify their authentic American identity, as people who were destined to thrive on that land.[85] The same conceptual process through which Native Americans were uprooted, was also applied to African slaves. Throughout the seventeenth century slaves transported from Africa to the Caribbean retained their African names when entered into plantation lists. By the 1730s, however, the proportion of African names had diminished substantially, with masters' names for slaves often deriving from some perceived physical propensity entering into the records regardless of the slave's family, geographical origin, or social status.[86] Their origin was erased, replaced by a physical trait.

The very term "race" endured throughout the eighteenth century to refer to a tribe, nation, or people regarded as from common stock. Only at the end of the eighteenth century did typologies of race begin to appear that differentiated peoples on the basis of skin color, and even these differences were largely thought to result from climate, nourishment and custom.[87] By the early nineteenth century, however, race was redefined as "any of the major groupings of mankind, having in common distinct physical features or having a similar ethnic background."[88] And these sets of physical differences were seen as responsible for the character of a people. Developing the studies of cranial difference initiated by Dutch physiologist Petrus Camper, naturalist Georges Cuvier argued for three races, defined by specific sets of physical features, in which the development of the nervous system, as indicated by the relative size of the brain, correlated with intelligence and hence with a degree of animality.[89] Cuvier instructed voyagers to seek empirical confirmation of these differences by measuring the size of the cranium, the degree of projection of the muzzle, the width of the cheekbones, and the shape of the eye-sockets.[90] Cuvier's treatise on the animal kingdom was translated and published several times in English, and served as one of the crucial texts with which the influential ethnologist James Cowles Prichard debated.

Convinced of the unity of humankind, Prichard refuted polygenist arguments that humans did not derive from a common ancestor.[91]

Their proposals, based on the assertion of the close proximity of Negroes to the great apes in terms of cranial size and shape, argued for different species or races with different intellectual and social proclivities. Pritchard instead revised earlier theories that had asserted racial difference as a process of degeneration, and he applied the notion of progress to both physical and mental development, proposing that Europeans had progressed from savagery to civilization as well as from black to white skin. Physically the flaring nostrils and cranial narrowness of the Negroes suited them for savagery, although, as Prichard continued to insist, their minds were in no fundamental way different from Europeans, making them good candidates for Christian conversion.

As debates between monogenist and polygenist explanatory models intensified, a common assumption made in both arguments concerned the essential differences, in kind not degree, of the different races. No longer based on the inexplicability of the narratives in which the savages were observed, difference was now measured in terms of anatomical variance.[92] Thus, Gallini, who could not decipher or understand the gestures of the Gold Coast dancers, could nonetheless share with them certain basic features of a common humanity. Blasis' indictment of the *chica* reflected an altogether different basis for assessing difference: the moral values of Negroes resided deep in their anatomy, causing them to perform a dance whose dangerous potential to contaminate lay in the immediate connection between its mobilization of physiognomy and the resulting lascivious feelings and moral impropriety.

Gender likewise came to be defined in terms of anatomical difference, with women's capacity for procreation assuming paramount importance in determining women's roles in society. Ludmila Jordanova has shown how anatomical representations of the female skeleton exaggerated the smallness of the cranium and the expansive girth of the pelvis in order both to reflect and reinforce the conception of woman as mentally inferior and destined for child-bearing.[93] These bone-deep differences affirmed the strategies pursued in physical education regarding the delicacy, even frailty, of woman's physicality, and the consequent need to circumscribe and moderate women's activities.

Dancing in moderation continued to be advocated for women as a healthy pursuit, but only if there was no isolation of parts of the spine or torso. As Blasis warned, women were particularly susceptible to the unseemly effects of the hip-shaking *chica*. They were equally susceptible to over-taxation and over-stimulation of the body's vitality. Social dances, therefore, maintained a firm uprightness, a delicate buoyancy, and a proper distance between partners. Even in the supervised and

Figure 3.4 This parodic depiction of "The Waltz" details the evils of social dancing and the fate that awaits the female dancer.
"The Waltz." An illustration from William Combe's *English Dance of Death*, Plate 52 by Thomas Rowlandson. Watercolor.
Courtesy of the Huntington Library, Art Collections, and Botanical Gardens, San Marino, California

regulated spaces of the ballroom, however, the potential for too much excitement threatened the dancer's stability and status. And worse, it intimated the onset of disease or even death. As one observer noted, the over-crowded conditions and excessive activity produced the same nefarious effects as those witnessed at "the black hole in Calcutta."[94]

As masculine and feminine roles became increasingly polarized, emotions of all kinds and affect in general were relocated into the domestic sphere.[95] The organization of the woman's constitution around reproduction inclined her to self-sacrifice and domestic duties. The excessive delicacy of her nervous system also made her more susceptible to her own feelings and to those of others.[96] Men's capacity for abstract reasoning justified their regulation of social and political economies, whereas women's ability to apprehend aesthetic achievement and to exercise imagination enabled them to interpret the social distress and plight of the less fortunate. Thus sympathy became sequestered within the feminine psyche in the same way that race and gender became specified through bone-deep differences in anatomical structure.

As sympathy was mobilized within this highly delimited arena, it provoked a series of contradictions. The delicacy of women's nerves intimated an instability and an uncontrollability that lurked beneath the domestic serenity that woman was intended to promote within the private sphere.[97] In the same way that dancing had the capacity to improve women through its moderation, but equally, the ability to produce excessive unruliness, so too, the anatomy of sympathy endowed it with a dual potential. As women were invited through literature or in charitable acts to witness the alterity of another's suffering, they both identified and non-identified with their plight. Audrey Jaffe observes that the trope of sympathy across a range of literary projects entailed the "horror" of becoming the other, and hence a "fall" from one's own position, that in turn, provoked a

Figure 3.5 In this illustration of Fanny Ellsler performing *La Cachucha,* it is clearly evident how the geometry of the ballet has infused the Spanish folk form with its emphasis on the linear shaping and proportion of the limbs.
Courtesy of The Lester S. Levy Collection of Sheet Music, Sheridan Libraries, The Johns Hopkins University

loss of identity.[98] Sympathy functioned to produce a double vacillation – between the promotion of charitable feelings and the indulgence in excessive affect, and between confirmation and loss of an essential self. This vacillation, in turn, began to create the conditions under which the modern notion of interiority developed as an autonomous inner self with the same volumetric structure as the physical body.[99]

Although sympathy existed in the domestic sphere, where a woman could fall from her precarious social position by identifying too closely with the plight of another or by dancing too much, it operated less and less as an epistemology of performance viewership. The most powerful character in the Romantic ballet, Giselle, who loved to dance too much and who brilliantly staged the instability of the feminine psyche, largely disappeared from European stages by the 1860s. At the same time, ballet technique mastered and docilized foreign forms, geometrizing the serpentine undulations of the Cachucha and varying the frenzied repetitions of the Tarantella. By the 1850s Victorian suspicions around the impurity and sexuality of dancing prompted a serious decline in the popularity of ballet, causing an end to productions on London's elite stages.[100] When they reappeared in the 1870s as part of music hall and popular theater offerings, they were no longer regarded as serious portraits of romantic narrative or virtuosity, but more as frothy and titillating displays of charming female flesh.[101] The rope dancer's potential fall might exhilarate, enthrall, or titillate viewers, but she did not provoke sympathy as she had at the beginning of the eighteenth century.

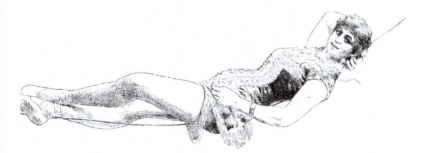

Figure 3.6 Music Hall dancer Oceana Renz reclining on a slack wire.
Hughes Le Roux & Jules Garnier. *Acrobats and Mountebanks*. Translated from the French by A.P. Morton. London: Chapman and Hall, Limited. 1890.

Identifying and emoting

When Vischer and his colleague Theodore Lipps began to apply their new term *Einfühlung*, it referred not to a capacity for fellow-feeling, but rather to the distinctly human ability to move into and feel anything in the observable world. The curve of a line in a painting, the thrust of a building, or the undulations of the sea – all invited the observer to enter into their dynamic state and experience its uniqueness. *Einfühlung* thus shared with Digby's notion of sympathy the capacity for transference across any kind of entity, whether animate or inanimate, yet it differed profoundly from all previous iterations of sympathy in its process of apprehending the other. Rather than receiving a picture of the other and replicating it in one's own mind, the observer now grasped the other through a simultaneous moving into and melding with the substance of the other. Rather than evaluating the circumstances and consequent predicament of the other, the observer expanded into the other, taking on its structure, rhythm, and momentum. In this act, the entire dynamism of the other was replicated within the observer's self. Empathy thus worked to affirm the capacities of a newly constructed interiority whose proclivities for repression, identification, transference, and sublimation were just beginning to be explored and whose defining consciousness could be fathomed only through intensive introspection.[102]

Sympathy continued to function as the compassionate stance that one might feel towards others, particularly those who were suffering and less fortunate. Both Jean Piaget and George Herbert Mead addressed sympathy, not so much as fellow-feeling, but as a vehicle for establishing moral compass. Piaget identified sympathy as an innate capacity but one that needed cultivation in order for the child to move from an "intropathic" assessment of the motivations that guided one's own action to an evaluation of others' intentions based on their observable actions.[103] Mead analyzed sympathy as instrumental in the individual's capacity to take on the "role" of the other person as a means to understanding how they view the world. In both cases, sympathy assisted in achieving judgment and social generosity, but it entailed no physical dimension or experience and it occurred only between human beings.[104]

Empathy, in contrast, was developed by both German and British aestheticians as a theory about the ways that specific features of a painting, sculpture, or building could pull the observer into a direct experiencing of them. Guiding this inquiry was a new fascination with the dynamic vitality of objects – how they expressed within their structure certain movement impulses. Not at all pictorial, art was now perceived as having intensity, momentum, pull, and energy, and also a coherence based on the relative balance or equilibrium among these impulses. At the same time, a new awareness of the experience of the observer, fueled by new discoveries of neuromuscular organization, promoted an introspective analysis of how the observer's physicality responded to objects.[105] Experienced as a volumetric totality, the observer's body was aroused and affected in its entirety by the dynamics of the other. As Stebbins demonstrated in her exercises, and Isadora Duncan and Loie Fuller made evident onstage, the body and the space and objects around it were momentum-filled.

In her efforts to deconstruct the feelings of someone who finds something beautiful, Vernon Lee expanded on the concept of *Einfühlung* by positing a separation between the object being contemplated and its various aspects, which, she argued each evoked sensations to which the observer responded physically. The actual perception of the object culminated in the act of "grasping or taking in" the relations of these various aspects, one to another.[106] Not an act of projection, but instead, of reaching out and grasping, the act of observation involved the viewer physically throughout this process, with movement serving as the source of contact between the observer and the world. Some acts of perception, repeated as they were numerous times, became stored in memory, routinizing inclinations to assess the symmetry or rhythm in what was perceived.[107]

Like Vischer, Lee dissected empathy into an initial stage of the relationship between perceiver and perceived, and a subsequent stage in which an object, such as a mountain, came to be seen as rising. Also like Vischer, Lee argued that such attribution originated in one's own awareness of a kinesthetic responsiveness to the object: "The rising of the mountain is an idea started by the awareness of our own lifting or raising of our eyes, head or neck, and it is an idea containing the awareness of that lifting or raising."[108] Informed by stored and averaged memories of one's physical response to rising, as well as the immediate apprehension of the body's reaction to the visual sensation, the observer would "make the mountain raise itself."[109] Mood and emotion were not directly involved in this process, but were nonetheless implicated in the dynamic conditions established in the relations among parts of the object experienced. This implicit connection was evident in descriptions, such as "lighthearted or languid, futile, gentle, or brutal, inexorable, forgiving, hopeful, despairing, plaintive or proud, vulgar or dignified," that referenced both the structure of the object and one's emotional state in response to it.[110]

John Martin, who had read both Lipps and Lee, took up the role of the emotions in empathetic experience, calling it "metakinesis" and argued for emotional engagement as one of the fundamental components of watching dance.[111] Dance meaning was apprehended through the combination of kinesthetic sympathy, the experience of feeling what another's muscles were doing, with metakinesis, the process through which intention was deduced or inferred from movement:

> Through kinesthesis, any bodily movement arouses a sympathetic reaction in the mind of the spectator. If it is a representational movement, the spectator recognizes it at once because in performing the same action he has utilized the same movement. If it is non-representational, the same process holds true. The maker of the movement has a purpose, an intention, in making the movement; the movement is transferred in effect by kinesthetic sympathy to the muscles of the spectator, and because he is used to associating movement with intention, he arrives by induction at the intention of the particular movement under consideration . . . This thought-conveying quality of movement . . . was called by the Greeks "metakinesis," or the overtones of movement, so to speak.[112]

Taking up the two-part analysis conducted by Lee, Martin first proposed dance as an event that would be replicated at a subliminal level within the viewer's own body.[113] He then asserted that implicit within any movement was an intentionality, a fundamental connection between movement and emotion, that enabled the viewer not only to apprehend the argument of the dance but also to be moved by it.

By 1939 Martin had refined and reorganized his theory of communication through dance, abandoning the terms "metakinesis" and "kinesthetic sympathy" and synthesizing their operations into a single process called "inner mimicry" which took place in the "inner man."[114] As the nucleus of the personality seated in the vital organs with its own independent nervous system, inner man was tucked inside the physical body, able only to communicate but not act upon his desires and needs. Closely connected to the inner nervous system were the movement receptors that reported postural change and also all varieties of motor reactions to objects and events in the surrounding world, whether animate or inanimate. The experience of watching dance depended upon the integration of these two systems, motional and emotional:

> Since we respond muscularly to the strains in architectural masses and the attitudes of rocks, it is plain to be seen that we will respond even more vigorously to the action of a body exactly like our own. We shall cease to be mere spectators and become participants in the movement that is presented to us, and though to all outward

appearances we shall be sitting quietly in our chairs, we shall nevertheless be dancing synthetically with all our musculature. Naturally these motor responses are registered by our movement-sense receptors, and awaken appropriate emotional associations akin to those which have animated the dancer in the first place. It is the dancer's whole function to lead us into imitating his actions with our faculty for inner mimicry in order that we may experience his feelings.[115]

Viewers' bodies, even in their seated stillness, nonetheless felt what the dancing body was feeling – the tensions or expansiveness, the floating or driving momentums that composed the dancer's motion. Then, because such muscular sensations were inextricably linked to emotions, the viewer also apprehended the intentionality and motivation in those movements.

For Lee inner mimicry played a circumscribed role in empathic experience, precipitating the muscular connection to the other, but not imitating it, since imitation could only be based upon a separation of self from other wherein the self would replicate, or mimic, the other's movement. Martin, in contrast, proposed inner mimicry specifically to address the role of dance and the effect that one body's motion would have on another body viewing that motion. For him inner mimicry named the entire process of physically sensing and emotionally feeling the other, and it did not yield up a copy of experience, but the actual experience itself. Both Lee and Martin agreed that empathic connectivity existed prior to and outside the realm of language as a more immediate and mostly subliminal or unconscious experience. And both located its effects as a product of relational perception – how one part of the other was related to other parts in order to produce distinctive kinds of tension, serenity, agitation, or saturation.

In examining the experience of the "mountain rising," for example, Lee argued that any object or event is composed of multiple and complex lines of movement, and the sense of its rising derived not from a simple upward lift, but rather from the relation of its various slopes each of which might rise or descend, spring up or rush down, creating a sense of rhythm. When contemplating the entire range of mountains, this complexity could "seem to perform a dance, [as the peaks] furl and unfurl like waves.[116] Similarly for Martin, any given dance movement consisted in spatial, temporal, and dynamic qualities, that, when taken together, produced a specific effect within the viewer. Watching a dance, these movements accumulated so as to create an evolving connection to the dancer's being.

For Martin the emergence of the new modern dance demanded a new theorization of dance spectatorship, in part because the dance could be composed of what he called "non-representational" movement. Wigman, who Martin had seen in Germany, and many US choreographers such as Graham did not create dances depicting characters engaged in pantomimic gestures telling a story. How, then was it possible for viewers to fathom the significance of what they saw and to garner some assurance as to the choreographer's intention? Eighteenth century philosophers had argued for a spontaneous and mechanical connection between the viewer's perception of and feelings about the dancing body, yet that connection was determined by the logic of the scene – the self-evident cause and effect relationships among the tightrope dancer's instability, the narrowness of the rope, and the extent of the fall. Martin, in contrast, asserted an intrinsic intertwining of muscular action and emotion that prompted viewers to feel the expansive glide of arms sweeping across an arc as magisterial and the erratic puncturing of space by elbows and knees as troubled.

Thus, for Martin, inner mimicry secured the universal capacity of dance to mean the same thing to everyone. Rationalized at a biological level by sense receptors and neural connections, and existing prior to language and culture as a more immediate and spontaneous reactivity, inner mimicry was a fundamental and pan-human process. Underlying the many different patterns of choreography, a common emotional core of experiences united all human kind and communicated itself easily through dance. Such a proposal justified Shawn's and Graham's impersonation of Native Americans, just as it rationalized Helen Tamiris's embodiment of the plight of the Negro.[117] And Martin's claims promised an even broader form of artistic omniscience in which the dancer represented the deepest and most essential qualities of humanity itself.

Eighteenth century theories of sympathy conceptualized bodily movement as yet another, albeit the most fundamental, in a hierarchy of communicative systems. Because of its rudimentary yet powerful eloquence, movement could "speak to all nations of the globe."[118] Martin, in contrast, imagined movement as the transparent vehicle of an inmost, pan-human emotional realm. In the same way that muscular action intrinsically linked to emotion, so, for Martin, the individual psyche replicated the tensile patterns of the universal human condition. Where Smith saw the body necessarily engaging with a system of rules and conventions in order to convey any meaning, Martin presumed that the body spontaneously mapped the contours of the psyche, the veracity of its pronouncements a direct product of its connection to interiority.

For Smith the universality of the tightrope dancer's performance stemmed from the universal applicability of categories such as safety and danger, fortune and misfortune, advantage and disadvantage. Any social encounter, regardless of its distinctive details, could be measured and evaluated in terms of standard hierarchies of worth, merit, and security. Martin, in contrast, focused on individual more than social circumstances in constructing empathy. He dismissed the scene, or more precisely, relocated scene-like properties within the individual dancer's psychic interior. Differentials of status, circumstance, or need were staged within the body. The "dialogues" created in these internal scenes yielded the distinctive movement impulses and qualities from which the dance was composed. The result, a psychological rather than social portrait, impelled viewers into the inner landscape of the danced character. Once there, the viewer felt his or her own version of the emotions summoned up by both choreographer and dancer.

Despite the seeming universalism of Martin's claims, specific cultures and races, in different historical moments, and also men and women embodied distinctive sensitivities to the world around them, based, in part, on their physical differences. Because of the suppleness of their legs, allowing them to sit on the floor, for example, Asians invented different forms of "furniture, clothing, and social practice."[119] Influenced by the writing of Irving Pond, who argued that physical qualities attributed to racial types were equally evident in the types of architecture they produced, Martin endowed different peoples with specific physical proclivities, most evident in their varied embodiments of rhythm.[120] Pond considered architecture to be a static form of dance, enunciating the kinds of rhythmic complexity in dance movement through its configuration of solids and voids.[121] Similar to Horst's analysis of different movement characteristics associated with the movements styles of distinct cultures, Pond identified equivalences between racialized physiognomies and architectural structure based on the sense of rhythm enunciated in each.

In each of his major writings on dance, Martin emphasized rhythm, defining it as the product of dynamic impulses in the muscles and arguing for its existence in any and all movement no matter how erratic or incidental as "the very root of the aesthetic experience."[122] Rhythm played a special role in concert dance as one of the fundamental features of form, along with spatial design and sequence, through which the choreographer crafted an argument. Martin commended La Argentina for the complex rhythmic eloquence of her dancing, but he condemned "the insistent thump, thump, thump of the miserable type of jazz which is dispensed by the neighbor's

Figure 3.7 Illustrations by Irving Pond demonstrating the connections he perceived between physiognomy, architecture, and racial temperament.
Irving Pond. *The Meaning of Architecture.* Boston: Marshall Jones Company, 1918.

radio for a considerable number of hours a day," claiming that it "seriously offends the taste of the more cultivated."[123] Built upon the alternation of silence and accent, with a regularity slightly in excess of the blood's pulse, this rhythm produced a false stimulation well known to primitive man and deliberately used by him to produce frenzy and unconsciousness.[124]

It was the pacing of rhythms over the course of a dance that imbued it with evolving meaning. The choreographer crafted strong moments, indicating a common experience to be shared among all viewers, and between them, a weaker series of intervals in which viewers were allotted time to garner from their personal experience all the details necessary to prepare themselves for the reception of the next essential element. Martin gendered this alternation between sender and receiver as the combination of masculine and feminine.[125] Although he never explicitly assigned specific rhythms to specific races, Martin did apply different criteria of empathic communicability, specifically to black and white bodies, and he also suggested that different ethnicities boasted distinctive rhythms that could be used effectively by the modern dance choreographer to suggest or reinforce a specific choreographic vision.[126]

Thus in his reviews of African-American choreographer Pearl Primus, Martin intimated, although he did not specify criteria for, separate standards based on racial identity. He praised Primus for being "true to herself both racially and as an individual artist," and in a subsequent publication equivocated in describing her within the same paragraph as "the most gifted artist-dancer of her race" and at the same time, as "an outstanding dancer without regard for race."[127] Where Primus was held by Martin to a double standard, Graham was lauded in her work *Primitive Mysteries* for "listening to the potent rhythms of the Indian dance, the pulse of the American landscape, the underlying beat of a humanity resisting destruction."[128] The white, and for Martin racially unmarked, body of Graham could feel free to absorb and draw from the rhythms specific to racially marked peoples, whereas the black body struggled under dual responsibilities to art and to race.

Eighteenth century chorographers and choreographers had swept the land and the dance clear of all defining features in order to replant them along a blank horizontal plane, giving them precise geometric coordinates. Martin claimed for American dance a similar type of origin based on the country's history of "cutting its way through wildernesses, both mental and physical,"[129] in order to found a new conception of society based on an antiauthoritarian embrace of human value rather than archaic traditions. However, where the eighteenth century choreographers located dancing in fundamental principles, Martin asserted the fundamentality of movement itself. Its capacity to invoke an empathic response, based on its kinesthetic and metakinetic make-up, absorbed vast differences into it, transforming culturally specific patterns and practices into pan-human dramatic action.

Graham had visited the Southwest several times in order to draw inspiration from the dancing in ceremonies there. These events, frequently promoted by the railroad companies and other tourist organizations, took place, even as governmental restrictions on Native dance curtailed dance events dramatically. Having been removed to reservations across the Western and Southwestern US, Native Americans were further policed at the beginning of the twentieth century by injunctions against any form of ceremonial dancing, seen by the Bureau of Indian Affairs as wasteful and distracting from meaningful labor. Jacqueline Shea Murphy has detailed the extraordinary contradictions in the policies that would prohibit ceremonial dancing but allow commercial dancing, showing that these policies derived from the government's conception of dance as mere entertainment. Examining how and why Native dancers might nonetheless willingly participate in events such as the Buffalo Bill Cody Wild West Show, Shea Murphy argues that in their conception of dance its efficaciousness could be accomplished, regardless of location, as long as the dancers dedicated themselves to it. Whereas the government officials dismissed dance as entertaining "representation," as a performance that conveyed no impact beyond a momentary diversion, Native dancers believed in their ability to enact the values called into being by dancing every time they performed.

Martin aspired to a form of dance that, even through representation, nonetheless changed people's minds and hearts. The very function of art was based on the need to harmonize the impulses of inner and outer man. Both play and art could effect this conciliation, but art had the further capacity to reach out to others and connect their experiences one to another. Empathy thus functioned for Martin not only to connect people to their surroundings but also to unite them across different registers of representation. In all its inclusiveness, however, Martin's theory persisted in exercising the same kinds of exclusions and double standards that Smith had assumed two centuries earlier. It was, after all, the white, middle-class body that could feel into and for all others.

Mirroring and resonating

Traveling to India in 1971, Yvonne Rainer recorded this description of a solo performance she witnessed depicting the Ramayana's character Nala:

> a once great king doomed to exist as an ordinary man after a serpent sent by a jealous god bites him. . . . I got so involved that I began to mimic Nala's hand gestures. Felt very powerful and quick as though I could actually do it. Now I see what great performance really is in this form. The younger ones wiggle their eyebrows, turn up the corners of their mouths and do a few more things and that's about it. But this guy actually projects "emotion." His cheeks vibrate, he seems about to cry, he looks startled, he looks afraid, he looks puzzled, he looks proud. But all through extremely small changes in particular parts of his face. Watching his face is like watching a map while on LSD. A chart of human feeling. You notice a change and then register the reading. Perhaps it is a lesson. I don't watch most people's faces that closely, but it must all be there. His hands I couldn't read. I simply responded kinetically. I haven't experienced kinetic empathy for years.[130]

For Rainer "kinetic empathy" consisted in an immediate, seemingly spinal-level mimetic capacity. Divorced from and devoid of emotion, kinetic empathy was the capacity to reproduce physical articulation. The face of the Indian dancer projected a chart of human feeling whereas the hands performed a purely kinetic repertoire. Rainer could read the face, finding in its display a carefully crafted representation of a universally recognizable repertoire of emotions. In contrast, the hands did not "mean" anything, yet they elicited a spontaneous response in which Rainer was seemingly able to replicate their complex motions because they moved in such an energizing and charismatic way. The ability to master the dancer's movement, gave her a feeling of power.

In her own dance practice, Rainer worked assiduously to cultivate and valorize a "pure" physicality and to imbue it with its own kind of power and dynamism, in part in order to eschew claims such as those made by Martin of universal sharings of values based in universally shared emotional states. She also worked to undo the organic flow of movement across interconnected parts of the body championed by Stebbins and early modern dancers, and instead, to investigate all parts of the body with egalitarian neutrality. Her use of kinetic empathy may well have reflected this aesthetic agenda, since she clearly demarcated the emotions expressed in the face from the rapid action of the fingers. It may also have commented on a larger transformation in the term "empathy" that had taken place subsequent to Martin's theorization of it.

For aestheticians like Lee and Martin, empathy had remained tied to the kinesthetic responsiveness of the body. However, in the burgeoning fields of psychoanalysis and psychotherapy, empathy was variously developed as the capacity of the therapist to enter into and inhabit the patient's emotional life, with compassion but also objectivity. Sigmund Freud, who had read Lipps, adapted his discussion of Einfühlung to the interactions between analyst and subject, making it the necessary precondition for beginning analysis.[131] He believed that simply by listening in an attentive manner, without seeming to advocate for anyone or to promote any particular point of view, the patient would naturally develop a sense of identification with the analyst that would permit a deeper exchange to begin. Following Freud, empathy developed in psychology as a cognitive understanding of others' feelings, more than a sharing of them.[132] From Theodor Reik to Carl Rogers, empathy assisted the therapist in apprehending the patient's emotional world by allowing the therapist to enter into that world and detect meaning of which the patient might not even be aware.[133]

Alternatively, empathy acquired the status of a "personality variable." Continuing nineteenth century practices of objective quantification of parts of the social body, empathy became something that could be measured in terms of behaviors associated with sociability among students in the classroom, inmates in prison, nurses in hospitals, and so forth. In other studies, empathy was rated in terms of estimations of generosity, selflessness, or friendliness, again using quantitative schemata for determining amounts of feeling.[134] Many of these studies identified the object of empathy as the "target," a nomenclature that intimates a theory of empathy as projection, but one with a specific and measurable velocity. In both therapeutic and sociological branches of psychology, empathy was pursued as an attribute of the psyche in which there was no element of muscular responsiveness. Thus Rainer's need to qualify her empathetic response as kinetic marked the absence of any physicality in the notion of empathy as it was developing in the social sciences and in broad usage.

Only in phenomenology, with the translations into English of Edith Stein's *On the Problem of Empathy* [1917] and Maurice Merleau-Ponty's *The Phenomenology of Perception* [1945] in the 1960s was the physicality of feeling retained.[135] A student of Edmund Husserl's, Stein distinguished between two types of consciousness, the primordial, when one was physically present, and the non-primordial, as in memory, expectation or fancy, where one was not actually located in the same place as the experience one was imagining. Empathy was the non-primordial experience of living in another's world. Empathy could be distinguished from memory because in the latter, one retained a sense of continuity to a past self, whereas in empathy, the two subjects, oneself and the other, remained separate. In contrast to Vischer and Lipps, Stein argued that even in the most complete experience of empathy observer and observed did not fuse. If they did, there would be no recognition of empathy, since self and other would be indistinguishable. Using as example the performance of an acrobat, Stein proposed that rather than participate fully in his motions, the observer underwent a non-primordial experience of those movements in which the observer felt "led, or accompanied, by his movements."[136] For Stein empathy was the bodily experience of feeling connected to the other, while at the same time knowing that one was not experiencing directly the other's movements or feelings. Stein further argued that multiple subjects could experience empathy collectively, creating a distinction between "I" and "you," while also bringing into existence a "we." Rather than a feeling of oneness with others, empathy affirmed difference and connectedness, offering the means of enriching one's own experience.[137]

Although he did not address empathy specifically, Merleau-Ponty in his study of perception similarly grounded apprehension of the other in the physical experience of one's own body. Physicality served as the fundamental medium in which consciousness and world were continually co-produced. Like Gibson, Merleau-Ponty believed that the entire body worked actively to synthesize multiple forms of sensation in order to produce information about the world, and he emphasized the ongoing nature of that process. Whereas Lee launched her analysis of empathy from the position of a self who encountered the world, and who experienced kinesthetic sensations about it, Merleau-Ponty identified the experience of bodiliness as the grounding for all conscious experience. As a result, intention and action were inseparable in others as in oneself. Apprehending another's gestures, it was "as if the other person's intention inhabited my body and mine his."[138]

Specifically connecting the research on mirror neurons to the earlier insights of Stein, Merleau-Ponty, and also Mead, neuroscientist Vittorio Gallese began to develop a neural basis for the human propensity to feel what another is feeling in the late 1990s. His conception of empathy emphasizes not only emotional but also physical sensation, thereby reaffirming empathy's connection to kinesthesia.[139] Gallese argues that mirror neuron networking provides a functional mechanism, what he calls embodied simulation, that sponsors our capacity to share "actions, intentions, feelings, and emotions with others."[140] Because the same neurons fire both when an action is performed and when it is witnessed, we are constantly enacting at a neural level the actions we see around us.

Although the physiological mechanisms underlying this response are not entirely understood, Gallese, along with many others working on mirror neuron functioning, describes the mutuality of observing and acting as a kind of resonance:

> A metaphor that describes well this correspondence between observed and executed biological motions is that of a physical "resonance." It is as if neurons in these motor areas start to "resonate" as soon as the appropriate visual input is presented. This "resonance" does not necessarily produce a movement or an action. It is an internal motor representation of the observed event which, subsequently, may be used for different functions, among which is imitation.[141]

This resonance is responsible for the ability to predict the actions of others, and to know what will result if we move in a certain way. It also accounts for what Gallese calls the "contagious behavior" frequently experienced in daily life, where the observation of an action results in the observer's repetition of it, including behavior such as yawning and laughter.[142] More like the acoustical vibration metaphorized by eighteenth century physiologists to explain sympathy than the suctional or magnetic attractiveness of one set of atoms for another that Digby envisioned, these neural networks activate a profound and immediate connection between one's own body and what one sees in the world.

The resonance that connects bodies does not function according to a logic of cause and effect. Mirror neural processing does not entail seeing something and then responding to it. Rather, the tuning of self and world sets the precondition for a variety of possible responses. As in Gibson's theory of perception as an active engagement with the world, resonance occurs prior to any action, enacting the simulation of multiple next responses. The viewer thus responds to the tightrope dancer's performance, not because of the logic of the scene or because of the feelings of fright that she must feel, but instead, based on the rehearsed simulation of the event of the fall.

Extrapolating from the embodied simulation established through resonance, Gallese proposes that human consciousness begins as a self-other identity, and this shared existence precedes the apprehension of the dichotomy between self and other.[143] Drawing from Merleau-Ponty in order to assert this fundamental intersubjectivity, Gallese speculates on the evolutionary implications of mirror neuron activity, arguing that the ability to sense the physical actions of those around us forms the basis on which socialization and the experience of the social takes place. Although none of this neuromuscular activity registers in consciousness, according to Gallese, it does not exist in opposition to language and culture. Rather, the kinesthetic simulation of others' actions constructs an empathetic connection among all humans who recognize in the actions of others an equivalent intention and goal. Action thus becomes the "a priori" principle that enables social bonding.[144]

Eighteenth century philosophers looked out upon society in its various stages of development and sought to ground moral behavior and actions towards others in fellow-feeling. Gallese, in contrast, argues that sociality itself originates in and depends upon this physicalized empathy. Empathy forms the basis upon which society exists and functions. Prelinguistic and entirely subconscious, neural resonance may or may not leave the kinds of traces in consciousness that Titchener detected. For him, there existed the possibility to train awareness to apprehend the impulses that movement makes in consciousness and to register the distinctive responses that the body adapts when typing a letter to a friend or writing a lecture. In this way, one could dance along with the dance, actually feeling at a subliminal but detectable level, the dancer's movements. Resonance, while experienced as a physical tuning among bodies, most often occurs so immediately as to be unnoticeable.

Focusing on the anticipatory function of mirror neurons, Ivar Hagendoorn proposes that dance's intrinsic appeal lies in its ability to excite viewers' interest in movement's trajectory.[145] Many laboratory studies show that when a person executes a simple task, such as grabbing a cup, the brain of the observer creates movement arcs that it sees itself or others fulfilling. But what if the goal of the movement arc is not obvious? What if the form of movement is exploratory rather than goal-oriented? "Meaningless art movements" as one study terms them, rather than functional?[146] Hagendoorn argues that the viewer completes the movement in advance and then sees the guess confirmed or refuted, leading to added engagement with the movement and increased efforts to predict the next arc correctly.

Where Martin presumed that kinesthetic engagement led to emotional attachment, and Rainer hoped that movement could be enjoyed simply for its physical factuality, Hagendoorn envisions watching a dance as a continual conjecturing of possible arcs and flows. Viewers, like the choreographer, think up the movement and decide how and where the dancer should move next. They do not simply decide where or what to watch, but instead, create versions of the dance as it unfolds in time before them. The process of comparing possible dances with the dance being seen can provoke many feelings and sensations in the viewer, which, according to Hagendoorn, have likely been experienced by the choreographer in the process of making the dance. In this way the choreographer's intention is communicated to the audience. Rather than flesh out a narrative, or convey a deep psychic impulse, Hagendoorn's conception of dance movement emphasizes its physical unpredictability. Like the choreographers he discusses – Forsythe, Balanchine, and Cunningham, his idea of dance, based on the body's articulateness, envisions dance as opening the viewer up to new moves that one can make. The bodies onstage revel in the many directions their moves could take, and viewers read them as malleable indicators of multiple scenarios.

For Gallese the responses of each individual's mirror neural network are based on that person's history of experiences as well as their unique mental capabilities. Where phenomenology grounded its exploration of consciousness in a universal subject, similar to Martin's conception of the individual, Gallese believes in the partiality of perception and simulation: "Every instantiation of mirroring is always a process in which others' behavior is metabolized by and filtered through the observer's idiosyncratic past experiences, capacities, and mental attitudes."[147] Like Berthoz, who noted that each individual's eyes might follow a different path across a face, noticing specific features relevant to the perceiver's own history, so in embodied simulation, we rehearse movement pathways that are specific to our history of moving. Thus the perceiver no longer performs a contact improvisation with the environment, but instead, rehearses and simulates multiple roles, through one's own actions as well as those of others. In the process of rehearsing these roles, individuals formulate a self, not as an entity that will then perform an action, but rather as performance itself.[148] The habitus, as Berthoz identifies it, even as it influences substantially the individualized process of perception, does not "control" our actions. Rather we bring the habitus into being through our actions.

In keeping with Berthoz's hypothesis that the perception of these "meaningless movements" could be culturally specific, scientists have found that viewers trained in a specific form of dance, "dance" along more intensively with that form than with a form they do not know. Studying the mirror neuron responses of ballet and capoeira practitioners, chosen especially because the two forms manifest clearly delineated yet distinctive vocabularies, they noted that those trained in the form they were watching had a significantly greater neural activity.[149] Furthermore, their study showed that what the observers see is not muscle activation, but rather, cultivated action. Many of the movements in both forms such as jumping and turning, for example, involve the use of the same muscles, yet what viewers responded to was the organized interplay of these muscles as it constructs a specific vocabulary of movements. In an uncanny affirmation of Martin's assertion that taking a dance class could help the viewer to enjoy more fully a dance concert, neuroscientists are exploring how perception is profoundly affected by our history of movement practices.

Yet for Martin, empathy remained universally identical for all humans, whereas empathy as extrapolated from these studies is a pan-human, but highly individualized phenomenon, produced through the individually and culturally specific acts of each perceiver, including the full range of movement experiences that any given subject has undergone. It connects humans one to another in ways similar to the networks mobilized for Internet and cellphone use. At the same time, these new technologies, integrated into our physicality, are challenging and transforming our capacity for empathy. The new cyborgian bodies do not connect with one another, feel for one another, by staging and then deciphering pictures of themselves as eighteenth century bodies did. Nor do they sense the tensile relation between core and surface that renders motivation, repression, and emotion corporeal as Martin suggested is possible. Instead, they catch fugitive, flickering glimpses of one another's corporeal status as it transits, blurred into the prosthetic devices that intensify even as they obscure physicality.

N. Katherine Hayles characterizes the informatics of these material conditions as indicative of a paradigm shift from information exchange based on presence-absence to that organized around pattern/randomness.[150] Contrasting the one-to-one relationship between keystroke and letter that typewriter technology provided with the densely encoded layerings of functions that one touch of the computer keyboard provokes, Hayles argues that contemporary bodies are spliced into circuits whose codes reiterate and then suddenly mutate. Not only have we become cyborgs, imbricated within a vast array of prosthetic enhancements to physicality, but we operate by accessing and implementing codes based on the pattern/randomness principle that structure technological and also social life. Traveling along these circuits, identity coalesces around the changing point of view (what Hayles, following cyber-punk author William Gibson, calls the "pov") that the subject exercises as the body moves.

In this world where intimacy, proximity, and even subjectivity are constantly reconfigured, Smith's impartial vantage point for assessing need and dispensing empathy does not exist. Nor is there an opportunity to become engulfed by the dynamic tension of an otherness through "inner mimicry." As public and private collapse onto the site of the individual body, its ability to elicit or impart empathy from others is being relocated into new sets of framing devices. No longer stimulated by the self-evident logic of the scene or by the interiorized dynamics of the human condition, empathy is now entwined with the apparatuses, increasingly digitalized, that hurtle images of bodies from one side of the world to the other. In the fleetingness of these images, are we able adequately to exercise empathetic capacities? This is the concern that, in part, is driving Damasio's current investigations of feelings.

Information, always partial and specific, is synthesized moment by moment from scattered sources. Much of the information is composed of images, reflecting actual events, which can be replayed endlessly, making it possible to review and examine events from different angles. In-formed bodies are pressed to learn not only how to access codes, but also to decipher how the format in which the codes are presented affects their meaning. For example, as the television camera zooms in for a close-up shot of the weeping victim, held for approximately ten seconds, followed by the cut-away to a commercial, the viewer must assess the victim's distress as framed within the close-up/commercial syntax. Or when the Foley generated sound track for the fight scene delivers a drastically enhanced auditory rendering of the battering of flesh, the viewer must fathom the body's damage as conveyed through Foley electronics. And viewers must process codes and their formats while themselves in motion, discriminating between the contexts in which their own movements are responsible for producing difference and those where they are not.

As if in anticipation of these profound alterations in the informatics of empathy, late 1970s break dancers began to investigate a body composed of, and versatile at accessing codes. Like the eighteenth century tightrope dancer, break dancers taunted and triumphed over the destiny of gravity. And like her, they appropriated moves from elsewhere so as to choreograph a commentary on social inequalities. Her *passés* and *cabrioles*, abducted from an aristocratic Baroque dance vocabulary, signaled her mastery over the codes that preserved class difference. Similarly, break dancers' splicing together of vocabularies ranging from those of martial arts to Capoiera to signature moves of pop stars demonstrated their familiarity with the world stage even as their own performances took place on street corners decimated by inner-city poverty. The tightrope dancer's audience, however, followed the clearly unfolding narrative of her transit across the rope, whereas break dance viewers moved quickly from one citation to the next, connecting with a fragment here, an audacious balance there. This versatility with the codes signals dancers' skill at deciphering and responding to the random/pattern organization of the social. Viewers are drawn into their circle of dancing as they are able to sort out and savor the valiant mixing of types of information.

Thirty years after its initial appearances in decimated innercity neighborhoods, hip-hop circulates globally, born on airwaves, tape, and digital media, as an expression of capitalist euphoria at transcending difference. These dancers, multiethnic and multibranded, purvey products with jubilant self-righteousness. Homogenized, sanitized, morphed into generic versions of what were once idiosyncratic and regional innovations, hip-hop reassures viewers as to the vitality of the global market. At the same time, in neighborhoods worldwide, hip-hop has been recuperated as a medium of resistance and empowerment as practitioners invent radical new versions that critique and comment on commercial hip-hop, beaming these along the very same circuits that helped to commodify it. These dancers affirm the local, partial, and contingent construction of empathy as they try out/on various scenarios for moving.

Figure 3.8 Monitor Man from *40 Acres and a Microchip*, choreographed and performed by d. Sabela Grimes
Photographer Hannan Saleh

Figure 3.9 A duet from Dancing Earth's *Of Bodies of Elements*. Created courtesy of the National Dance Project and Santa Fe Art Institute, at the Global Dance Fest of VSA North Fourth Art Center in New Mexico. Choreographer Rulan Tangen. Dancers in this image are Serena Rascon and Nichole Salazar, in costumes by Marama of Aotearoa, Photographer Alejandro Quintana

In contrast to these critical implementations of networking, Native American and other indigenous peoples are mobilizing networks to reinstantiate and reinforce cherished worldviews that have long acknowledged the intimate connection between memory and action. On the web and on the concert stage, these dancers continue to enact, not imitate, their cosmological beliefs. Their actions bring knowledge into being as they did when Winslow, as a colonist in Plymouth, first commented upon them, not as a mastery of diverse codes but as a reaffirmation of their specific locatedness in the world. Dancing celebrates the simultaneity of perception and action that, according to Gallese, provides the basis for creating our social existence.

Smith's empathy had depended upon the separation and sequential progression of perception, feeling, and action. His observer could only exercise a powerful generosity from an immobile and impartial position, having first witnessed and then felt. Rainer, in contrast, delighted in her successful imitation of the unfamiliar and complex motions of the Indian dancer's hand. She apprehended the simultaneity of perception and action, but only felt powerful after that act. Both hip-hop and Native dances suggest radically different and distinctive distributions of power. Hip-hop dancers construct transient communities, hanging-out in virtual and real neighborhoods through the exchange of moves that pronounce and comment upon how they feel. Native dancers connect person to land in order to recycle and redisburse power across the community. Both forms of dancing propose that empathy is imbricated within every action, and each action is simultaneously an act of perception and an act of knowledge production. And these diverse processes of dancing suggest that there are multiple ways of feeling into the world.

4 Choreographing Empathy

I am walking in San Francisco from the Jewish Museum, with its jaunty fusion of early twentieth century façade and twenty-first century blue steel cube, towards the Martin Luther King, Jr. fountain where his eloquent words ring out above the thunderous roar of water – "No, No, we are not satisfied, and we will not be satisfied until justice rolls down like water and righteousness like a mighty stream." A pow-wow is just setting up in the park, and one of the first speakers is criticizing the current commodification of the world captured in the phrase "the earth's precious resources." "The earth is not a resource," he exhorts, "it is a source." The earth is, indeed, in crisis, its precarious balancing of systems of life disrupted, fractured, and probably permanently compromised – the death of a large number of its species accompanied by human famine, genocide, forced migration and a massive population explosion in which a few wealthy individuals consume a grossly disproportionate amount of what the world generates.

As I walk I am thinking about this book – why choreography, kinesthesia, and empathy? Why, even, a book? Here at the end, or at least transformation of print culture, the solidity of the book, that entity I came to love for its permanence and reliability, is transitioning into a minor genre of writing. Is this writing already destined to meet the needs of a vanishing world rather than the one that is approaching?

No, these notions of choreography and empathy are very present in discourses constituting the body politic. As the earth's crisis deepens, the motionality of people and events seems ever more apparent, and choreography has been tapped as a way to identify and analyze the patterns in these motions. As the degree of suffering among the world's impoverished peoples escalates along with the violence wrought by humans upon one another, the capacity for empathy is being debated and reexamined. What has seldom been questioned in these debates, however, is the nature of the body itself that is claiming to feel what another body is feeling. How is its kinesthetic experience constructed, and consequently, what experience of physicality does that body take with it into the experience of empathy? Choreography, whatever its meaning, can provide clues to this specific experience of the physical in the ways that it records or documents movement, and also in the ways that it sets forth principles upon which movement is to be learned and crafted. The notion of empathy then theorizes the potential of one body's kinesthetic organization to infer the experience of another.

As I have tried to demonstrate in the preceding chapters, all three terms have changed radically, yet in tandem, over time. Taken together the three terms flesh out how corporeality is constituted in a given historical and cultural moment. Charting changes in these terms for a small portion of the world, one that wielded exceptional influence over other parts of it, this study endeavors to identify epistemic shifts in the corporeal basis for determining how knowledge is acquired; how desire is configured; on what bases otherness is identified; and how power circulates through and between bodies as they make claims to feel what others are feeling. These shifts in the construction of corporeality enabled a certain view onto the world abroad, one that accompanied, and to some extent facilitated British and subsequently US projects of colonization. Corporeality helped to determine how colonization would undertake to examine the unknown and foreign, and how the body could be cultivated so as to assume a relationship of power over another body. Corporeality likewise participated in articulating the basis for ordering and classifying, and for cultivating an association between land and the feminine in pursuit of mastery and masculine pleasure.[1]

Over the sixteenth and seventeenth centuries, the body began to coalesce as a stilled and singular entity capable of looking out onto the world. Slowly jettisoning its identity as a composite of substances, each with its own disposition and each capable of prompting distinctive behaviors, the body assumed a unified structure whose actions were governed by a coherent set of rules and principles. In its earlier incarnation as an aggregate of humours, the body's health and propriety had been determined in relation to the physical and social landscapes. Striving for a balanced rapport among all its parts, the body had danced or exercised in dialogue with its surroundings in order to achieve and improve upon its social standing. Its capacity for empathic connection to others, governed by laws of magnetic attraction and repulsion, was actualized in the sovereign hierarchies of nobility and order stipulated by the court. As it began to achieve a more individuated identity, this dialogic patterning of interaction and indebtedness, evident in Arbeau's conversation with his dance student and, equally, in the medicinal treatment of the humours, the approach to map-reading required by the Portolan charts, and Digby's notion of atoms' attraction to one another, was replaced with an altogether different logic of the relationship between self and other.

As stationary subjects whose rectitude mattered most, individuals surveyed their surroundings and ventured out into the world to assess its value and meaning in quantitative terms. The observation of the world could likewise be directed towards the interior of the body in order to determine the physical mechanisms underlying its functioning. Knowledge production depended upon sensing, then perceiving, then identifying, and responding to the world. Whether looking out into the world or into the inner workings of the body, differences were noted in terms of degree and then categorized according to sizes and shapes, strengths and weaknesses, talents and deficiencies, and so forth. No longer so rooted in or affected by one's specific habitat, the individual now perambulated across an abstract territory, constituted by mathematical principles and measurements. Land was measured and carved up into portions, and peoples were categorized according to appearance and comportment. Learning to track one's movement across these spaces, through chorographic and choreographic practices, the individual experienced sympathy as the inherent connectivity amongst all humans constructed by their common location within the geometric grid.

Choreography participated in this redefinition of physicality by offering a clear-cut technique for disciplining human movement. It taught dancers how to parse their own motions and classify them in terms of type and degree, and at the same time, to gage their progress across space, conceptualized and pictorialized as a blank plane. Along with cartography, anatomy, botany, and myriad other methods for observing the world, it proposed a system of classification within which all elements could be sorted and ranked. It also promised to establish individual authorship over what had been a shared repertoire of dances. Like maps that identified the boundaries of and established ownership over specific parcels of land, choreography offered copyright for specific sequences of movement. It endowed movement with symbolic substance, promising to secure its permanence.

As physicality was transplanted onto a horizontal geometry, the effort to fathom strangeness and to adjust one's physicality to it transformed into a practice of observation and evaluation based on conformance to presumed standards of comportment. Implementing this bodily disciplining, the British colonial regime could first institute protocols of comportment at home and then proliferate these standards and indexes of behavior to those foreign bodies that it desired to govern abroad. These protocols acquired their persuasive force by standing as the most basic and therefore universal units out of which human behavior is composed. Where first contact had inspired more a sense of wonder and anxiety over cultural differences, once the colonial project gained momentum, it called upon these universal categories and their implicit methods of quantification in order to assert dominance.

By mid-eighteenth century, choreography as a form of analysis and documentation of dances was abandoned as too cumbersome, arcane, and irrelevant to the central features of dancing. Substituting for it were the narrative accounts printed as the programs for the newly minted genre of the story ballet. As a set of principles for categorizing movement, choreography continued to inform and influence the practice of dance technique, however the blank plane on which its dancers' paths had been traced no longer mattered so much as the gestures and actions that embodied the progress of the plot dancers were enacting. An open carriage and gracefully proportioned motions, so cherished at the beginning of the century, were being replaced by a meatier dramatism for which dancers trained using exercises that remedied bodily defects and fortified their command of movement and the story it told. Similarly, in theories of sympathy, the narrative logic of the scene was what propelled viewers into a vibratory fellow-feeling. One observed, almost as if it were a pantomime, the situation of the other and imagined undergoing the same experience. More authentic, because located in the very fibers of the body, sympathy could only operate when the narrative of the scene could be deciphered and fathomed. As a result, otherness began to be constituted in terms of qualities rather than quantities of difference. The behavior of some foreigners was so illogical and incapable of being narrated as to confirm their inhumanity.

Over the course of the nineteenth century, this pictorial and narrativized experience of corporeality eroded, replaced by a more dynamic and three-dimensional sense of one's physicality. The musculature emerged as a central component of one's identity, and with it, the capacity to engage forcefully with the world or, alternatively, to relax in it. As the body began to acquire a more volumetric sense of itself, its relationship to surroundings recalibrated into one governed by flow, intensity, momentum, and inertia. Internally, the psyche functioned similarly, governed by tensile relations between conscious and unconscious desires. Empathy, replacing sympathy, became a process through which one experienced muscularly as well as psychically the dynamics of what was being witnessed.

Choreography commandeered this physicality into expressive action. Issuing from the core of the individual, dance in the early twentieth century began to consist of original movement that testified to the fundamental entwinement of motion and emotion. It communicated its message via the inherent human capacity for what Martin called inner mimicry, the ability of any body to feel muscularly the tension, impulse, and spaciousness of movement and, consequently, to feel the emotional states associated with those movement qualities. Claiming the universality of this process, choreographers were empowered to represent any and all subject positions, regardless of their histories of privilege and prejudice, as participating in a universal human condition. Where earlier the narrative as it unfolded within a given scene indicated the human condition, now the tensile drama progressing through the individual body itself conveyed the human predicament.

As the body acquired muscularity and volume, its evaluation of otherness transformed yet again. Foreignness was no longer measured in terms of degree or kind. The hierarchical evaluations of who was more or less civilized ensured by those forms of assessment were replaced with varieties of almost unfathomable otherness. Exoticized as tantalizing excess, or ungovernable abandon, or dark, unknowable alterity, the foreign was treated as something to be repressed, managed, or ministered to in an effort to salvage some aspect of its humanity. Subsequently, in its subjugated and abject condition, it continued to fuel the imagination of the colonial project by introducing flavors of difference into the universalizing aesthetics of the modern first-world. The dance ethnologist collected and mastered these exotic dances, performing them as windows onto the authentic spirit of a given people.

Now, at the beginning of the twenty-first century, physicality has been overhauled yet again into a cyborgian synthesis of digital and physical matter. Transiting effortlessly between live and virtual worlds, inhabiting monochromatic landscapes that have sprouted up the world over to facilitate global exchange, individuals acquire accoutrements of identity by sculpting and accessorizing their appearance. Continually informed as to our own whereabouts, along with the locations of friends, resources, and consumables, we multitask our way through myriad layers of informatics. The crises facing the earth and its many species bear down on us precipitating a crisis of doubt as to whether we can, in fact, put ourselves in another's shoes and experience their world. And if we could, would that help or hinder Martin Luther King's notion of justice? At the same time, neuroscientists are claiming that empathy is the most fundamental capacity of our minds, foundational to the very way that knowledge is acquired. They argue that we are, prior to establishing an individuated sense of identity, constantly inhabiting the worlds of others, and through mirroring their actions, learning to give shape and significance to our own identity.

In this world of accessorizing identity, there is, superficially at least, no discrimination based on size, shape, skin color, or gender. Having moved "beyond" the need to redress the conditions instigated by colonization, or so the argument goes, we can and should abandon affirmative action policies, feminist critique, and aspirations for government as the insurer of the social body's well-being. Objecting strongly to this argument, this study excavates the genealogies of meanings associated with choreography, kinesthesia, and empathy in order to show how the histories of classification of difference that such meanings encompass bear down upon the present. Nowhere is this more vividly demonstrated than in the dilemmas and predicaments facing contemporary dance artists. In their efforts to make dances, these artists must contend with the problematics established in the ways that choreography, kinesthesia, and empathy have worked together over time to create dominant and dominating sets of assumptions about identity. In what follows I examine how some contemporary artists are recapitulating or working against these dominant conceptions of self, land, gender, and cultural difference.

Grounding and remembering

Alutiiq choreographer Tanya Lukin Linklater is one of a growing number of indigenous American artists who are forging a new genre of expression, one that blends native aesthetic and community values with contemporary dance. Having rarely appeared on the concert stage in the twentieth century, Native artists are increasingly adapting conventions of theatrical dance in order to construct a new form of performance in which to put forth their individual and collective visions of society.[2] These artists form part of a larger indigenous movement that, following centuries of persecution, displacement, and neglect, is reclaiming lands and reasserting native values. In so doing, they are implementing processes of remapping and re-membering that are entirely distinct from Western cartographic and archival practices. As part of that movement, Lukin Linklater's work, *Woman and Water*, endeavors to reroot dancing, to ground it in the world by establishing its location on and connection to the land.[3]

The audience gathers around a woman poised in the shade of a large sycamore tree. She watches them calmly as they settle onto the grass or perch on the edge of a large fountain, and then goes about her work – she cleans the grass of any twigs and leaves, and then unfolds quilt after quilt, placing them on top of one another, scrunching their edges into a roundish perimeter that begins to resemble a bird's nest. Gathering the leaves with delicate embrace, she lines the nest and then settles into a kneel at its edge, emptying box upon box of blackberries into a porcelain colored bowl. Massaging the berries to a paste, she smears the blue liquid on her arms and neck, popping one berry in her mouth.

Rounding her back to balance lower legs on upper arms, she pauses in the yoga posture known as the crow. Then a hand floats upwards; a leg unfurls with immense reach and tenderness. Each part of her body relishing multiple connections between earth and sky ventures away from the nest and into its surrounds. Surging forward she confronts an audience member with her gently inquisitive gaze. Then another and another, each time her visage recalibrates to absorb and reflect the feelings she encounters. Now strutting back and forth in front of the viewers, she puffs her cheeks and buffoons, then drops that persona like a piece of clothing and moves towards the fountain. Swinging arms and torso, she propels herself from land into water, where she explores the knee-deep alternative gravity with sweeping legs and undulating feet.

Figure 4.1 Tanya Lukin Linklater in *Woman and Water* (2006)
Photo courtesy of Center for Performance Studies, UCLA
Photographer unknown

Coming to standing stillness, she beckons to a viewer, summoning her into the water, then enfolding her in a close embrace. She croons a lullaby-like chant, drawing all viewers into the intimate connection between her voice and her partner's ear. Gently disentangling from this embrace, she reaches out to yet another viewer. Four lullabies later, she leaves the water and returns to the bowl and quilts. She begins to distribute them, one by one, to her friends in the fountain and to audience members randomly, until the nest has vanished.

This performance hailed those who had been invited, and also a number of passersby who were willing to pause and observe the action. The site itself, identified by Lukin Linklater as most suitable for the dance, also hailed her, requiring that she adapt actions to its specific size and shape. Veering away from the controlled ambiance of the proscenium, and challenging the proposition that there is a preferred point of view from which to observe the art event, *Woman and Water* asks both dancer and viewers to attend intensively to their specific surroundings. With the surroundings changing the piece itself, it will always be different depending upon where it takes place.

And yet, the dance adheres to certain actions undertaken in a designated order. Lukin Linklater brought the blackberries and quilts with her, even if she used the local leaves and fountain. She orchestrated a sequence of events strongly invoking the elemental constituents of nature – water, earth, and air, in which water serves as the medium through which the self moves from acquiring home and identity, to distributing this wealth on to others. Actions unfold in solemn sequence, performed not ponderously, but with great care. The events summon up the passage from youth to maturity: at first the dancer labors industriously, then prepares herself to explore her environs with curiosity and sensitivity. Stepping into the water, she begins to share what she has learned with others, and then, returning to the nest she worked to create, she redefines its use and value by giving its parts away. Will the quilts go off to perform other services? Will the bowl feed other hungry mouths? Will they engage in the making of other dances? When does *Woman and Water* end?

In its indeterminate ending, and its improvised give and take between action, place, and participants, *Woman and Water* refuses to be assimilated into economies of ownership and commodification. This work does not call out to be discovered in order to move up the hierarchies of avant-garde performance so as to be placed in wider circulation and on larger stages. The piece's ethics, with their commitment to the careful study of place, the taking of time to allow actions to reverberate, shun the entrepreneurial mechanics of concert dance production. In this dance nothing can be bought or owned.[4] Although Lukin Linklater has been commissioned to create and perform the dance, no admission fee is or can be charged. Not the invention of a single author, the dance's narrative braids strands from Alutiiq cosmology just as the movement vocabulary borrows from quotidian and modern repertoires. Lukin Linklater is credited in the program with being the choreographer, yet the dance is performing her as much as she is performing the dance.

By blending designated actions with the unanticipated responses of both participants and a public space, *Woman and Water* resembles the minimalist and conceptual art projects of the 1960s that also called into question the commodification of the art object with its prioritization of object over process. Yet the dance's intent is not to provoke a critique of the status of dance as commodity, or even to confront viewers with the possibility that any series of events might be apprehended as art. It does not aim to assert the experimental and to thereby challenge viewers' conceptions of what art might be. Rather, in its humble and straightforward address, *Woman and Water* offers a proposition about being in time, tuning one's actions to place, and the possibility of strangers coming together to partake in communal gathering. It asks: What if we all spend an hour together, witnessing a dancer's actions, enjoying the breeze and the funny coincidences between her movements and the ambient noise? What if we pause in the harried schedule of our day simply to do this, to notice the grass and trees along with the bodies of fellow viewers, and we allow ourselves to appreciate that we are spending this time together?

Beyond this opportunity to dwell collectively, *Woman and Water* comments on the accretion and dispersal of things as part of life's unfolding. The nest is caringly constructed so as to provide the necessary nurturance for a young being. The body that acquires fortitude from inhabiting it can then expand outwards into the world, exploring its own possibilities for moving and, eventually, sharing its strength and vitality with others. Having served its function, the nest is dismantled and recycled, reinforcing the status of the dance as a process rather than product and also referencing Native practices of potlatch. The narrative floats between the general and the specific, its actions gesturing towards the contours of life from birth to death, while tuning themselves to the unique physiques of each leaf that is gathered and each viewer encountered. By twining these levels of signification, the dance integrates human actions into the natural world as parts of its many cycles.

What does the dancer's body tell us? Clad in a summer sundress, young and long-limbed, she approaches each action with unassuming pragmatism and total dedication. She manifests without pretense the varying degrees of effort required to gather a leaf, unfold a blanket, or hug a person. She is not treading across the geometricized landscape such as the one created by chorographers and early choreographers, its cartographic measurements informing her gait. Trained in vinyasa yoga, several modern dance techniques, and Alaska Native dance, she blends these techniques so as to redefine the relationship between body and gravity developed in classic modern techniques.[5] Those techniques positioned the human as the center of a dynamic and ongoing struggle between gravity and resistance to it, substituting for the horizontal geometric plane an equally universal conception of gravity, as if gravity's downward pull asserts its force equally in all times and places and for all peoples in the same way. Lukin Linklater side-steps the role created by such a conception of gravity in which the dancer is likewise universalized as the locus of gravity's drama. Rather than dramatize her relationship to the earth, she locates each movement in relation to its surroundings, thereby setting up reverberations between human movement and any motion nearby. In this dismantling of the centrality of gravity, she no longer serves as focal point but instead weaves herself into the landscape.

The dance presents a seamless combination of quotidian task, ritualized embrace, and quixotic investigation of space. Especially as Lukin Linklater begins to extend outwards and away from the nest, parts of her body take on birdlike attributes with her arm, wrist, and hand resembling the disjointed articulateness of head, eye, and tail movements, head and torso assuming their angularity and autonomy. Yet this flickering reference to another corporeality does not condense in the body as a sign of temperament or character in the way that Horst theorized. His conception of the aerial, like other styles he analyzed, associated specific movement qualities with personality traits from which a single unified persona could be apprehended. In contrast, Lukin Linklater, even as her demeanor remains constant in its unassuming dedication to each action, inhabits but then leaves behind, each reference to character.

Lukin Linklater refers to her choreographic process as one of "mapping the cosmology onto the performance space and onto the actions of the performers."[6] This mapping, however, in no way implements the cartographic techniques of the European eighteenth century, the very techniques that served colonization in its displacement of native peoples across the Americas. It does not parse actions into small units catalogued according to type. Nor does it privilege an ichnographic apprehension of space. Its bird-like characters, along with all the others, reside within the fabric of the dance rather than soaring apart to survey the whole. The only analog to Lukin Linklater's mapping might be the earlier Portolan charts whose readability presumed that both map-reader and landscape were in flux. In those charts, rhumb lines stabilized the relationship between cosmos and land enabling map-readers to anticipate what they might encounter next and to calibrate where they had come from in relation to where they might be going. Perhaps the choreography of Lukin Linklater's dance functions equivalently, as the framework through which a worldview can be conveyed.

If the choreography helps viewers to contemplate where they have come from and where they might be going, it serves not so much as a repository of knowledge but as an orienting tool for determining and affirming a system of beliefs. The seventeenth century Wampanoag, as described by Winslow, had constructed a repository of historical knowledge based on relating events to the sites at which they occurred. Unlike that practice of oral recitation, Lukin Linklater is transferring, not the specific knowledge about events, but instead, principles for practices of value to her community. Extrapolating from the actions in the dance itself, these principles would include devoting attentiveness to the surrounding landscape; valuing all life; celebrating the uniqueness of each person; and upholding the mandate to generously redistribute wealth.

The Wampanoag history-making that Winslow described bound memory to place. It required the sustained commitment of many members of the community to continually renew and transmit memories of events from generation to generation, and it depended upon the interpersonal exchange that Arbeau found so necessary in describing and teaching the dances he knew. Likewise, Lukin Linklater has shared her dances with her community, seeking their responses to the mapping that she has proposed, using the dance as a vehicle for renewing shared beliefs. In this way the dance catalyzes a re-membering – a way that memory can be recreated and relived. As in Arbeau's treatise, this knowledge is co-produced by student and teacher and mutually dependent upon them. Lukin Linklater commemorates and comments upon this shared production of knowledge in the way that she allows for the specificity of encountering each individual during the dance.

In Arbeau's world of Renaissance nobility, wealth was accumulated or lost during these exchanges as each individual endeavored to perform suitably in dialogue and in dance with each individual encountered. The suitability of one's actions, however, depended upon and was interpreted in terms of the well-known assignations of class and rank. *Woman and Water* presents an altogether different theorization of wealth in which prosperity results from sharing and giving. Although its performance relies on the collective actions of all those sharing the dance, it eschews the hierarchizations that mobilized and motivated Renaissance dancers since it does not conceive of wealth as something to be accumulated and dispensed in order to maintain and increase one's status. Instead, since "nests" are continually built and dismantled, some more slowly and others more quickly, wealth derives from passing along all things useful to the maintenance of the cyclic nature of life.

Also in contrast to the eighteenth century dancing master, who practiced a knowledge that was for sale, this dance cannot be purchased. Any body could undertake to perform its sequence of actions becoming more or less efficacious in tuning self to others and to the landscape. Here, virtuosity does not depend upon acquiring and then surpassing a stipulated set of skills. Lukin Linklater's expertise lies in her ability to remain sensitive to the vicissitudes of breeze through trees and leaves, the milling and settling of people, the distant helicopter, the nearby fountain, and to register these changes in the porousness of her physicality. In this tuning of body to landscape, Lukin Linklater's demonstration of technique resembles the Galenic theory of bodily humours, in which all elements of physicality are enmeshed within and continually attracted to various forces in the environment. Yet, she adds to that protean physicality a vigilant dedication to the task at hand, evincing simultaneously the solemn and the casual. Although it does not shine with the patina that normally identifies the virtuoso, it nonetheless demands extensive and committed training.

Lukin Linklater's practice of choreography specifies a particular constitution of the kinesthetic, one in which body learns to tune itself to others and to the landscape, to explore vigorously, and to give generously and wholeheartedly. It does not attempt to acquire and build up skills anymore than the dance aspires to consolidate and fortify a way of moving. The process of mapping in which Lukin Linklater is involved does not result in the creation of monuments that serve to archive the past. As Jacqueline Shea Murphy has argued, the process of doing something is the archive; the beading of the belt or Bible is not geared towards the production of an attractive object, but towards the commemoration of effort dedicated to a particular task.[7] Thus Lukin Linklater's approach to dancing continually recreates the archive, binding persons to the specific place where the dance occurs, rather than removing objects to a separate establishment for contemplation and evaluation. That which is remembered is a process, rather than a content. Memories are not stored in the body; rather, a process of remembering is cultivated in the body.

Not unlike the first generation of African-American choreographers who attempted to use the modern dance stage as a platform on which to present a synthesis of materials from disparate sources, folk and popular forms, as a way of connecting to and grounding oneself in an Africanist aesthetic, Lukin Linklater remaps and re-members fundamental Alutiiq aesthetics. From the Eurocentric colonial perspective, these works have frequently been received as ritual or ritualistic, as preserving a static and traditional way of life rather than pioneering in the representation of new identities and modern values. Tacitly rejecting this paradigm of ritual and its function, Lukin Linklater disencumbers herself from the mandate to preserve dance while at the same time redoing and rerooting dance so that it will catalyze a reconnection to Alutiiq beliefs as they manifest in the contemporary world.

How is this process shared with the audience? The dance does not acclaim or advertise in any way its existence. It is announced modestly, and offered up to any and all who are willing to commit to being there. Viewers acquire no cultural capital from being in attendance. Nothing in or about the performance promises enlightenment, provocation, or camaraderie. Instead, the dance invites viewers to take the time to attend to their situation of the moment, to look, listen, and register the environment and their collective location within it. As Lukin Linklater summons one viewer after another into the fountain, her embrace enfolds them within a custom of singing. Lukin Linklater chants earnestly, but she is not performing as a fervently feeling individual reaching out to another. Instead, she enacts the long-standing practice of singing as a way of comforting another, and she serves in the capacity of channeling that practice to a given individual. In this way, each embrace extends to and is felt by the entire audience. Not an exclusive shared moment between two individuals, it instantiates a communal and community-making action.

The audience members, however, must willingly engage with the dance's premises and its manner of reaching out to them. Nothing in this dance calls out to the audience to pity the plight or past of Native peoples. The dance does not picture the grievous injustices that nonetheless inform its stance and ask viewers to insert themselves into that world. Nor does the dance depict the Native as the noble and charismatic stoic that Graham envisioned, thereby asking viewers to identify with physical and psychological traits embedded within it. Through its modest address and its blending of the dignified with the casual, the dance systematically refutes these two viewing options, each of which depends upon the assertion of a prior distance and fundamental difference between self and other. Instead, it beckons viewers to meet it by asking them to make an equivalent commitment of time and energy. In their act of attentive participation, they will complete the community that is being proposed. This coming together promises atonement or blessing or some form of transformation, as emblematized by the embraces occurring in the fountain. Yet the more profound and enduring change accomplished in this dance is simply the fact of strangers having come together, and meeting on a new kind of ground where differences are not presumed, even if they might emerge over time.

The dance constructs this new ground through its practice of re-membering, sowing the past into the present in order that it might be regrown. On this ground the ability of one person to feel with another must also be cultivated. The possibility for fellow-feeling exists as a prior given, yet all individuals participating in the dance must continually dedicate themselves to making it happen.

Locating and surveilling

Taking as a given the jacked in and hooked up cyborg body, a number of artists have begun to probe the parameters for dancing established at the interface of the human and the digital. Web dances, motion-capture projects, and telematically collaborative choreography, among other genres of experimentation, all contribute to these explorations, provoking an awareness of ways in which new technologies are constructing new physicalities and abilities to navigate through the world.[8] The two works considered here center on the interface between human and cellphone and also reference GPS positioning. The first, *Call Cutta*, was created by the collective Rimini Protokoll[9] and premiered in Berlin, and the second, entitled *Cell*, was created by the company Headlong Dance Theater in Philadelphia.[10] Each requires viewers themselves to move through a city, thereby destabilizing the static locations from which one typically watches a dance. Similar to *Woman and Water*, they also expand the frame of the performance to include the entire environment in which the viewer is located. However, unlike *Woman and Water*, a performance that dedicates itself to constructing a reciprocal relationship with the natural environment of a given locale, these performances surf a new kind of common ground – the transnational public spaces being established by new digital technologies. Both take individual audience members on an hour long improvised journey, structured by a score of directives issued via the cellphone. Both require new kinds of competence from viewers as they strive to accomplish the instructions and from performers as they adjust the instructions to suit the individual temperaments and abilities of each viewer.

Audience members in *Call Cutta* are issued a cellphone by theater staff at their individually reserved times, and directed outside the theater to wait for a call. When the phone rings, one of ten "performers," identified by name and email address in the program, introduces him or herself and directs the audience member to cross the street and then turn right towards the glass doors of a seemingly abandoned building. Not at all abandoned, the voice explains, this building is one of the main office centers for telecommunications in the city of Berlin. The performer describes the hundreds of workers in small cubicles on the many floors above who are busy processing data, much as she and her colleagues are doing in their home city of Calcutta, the difference being that they are working for Citibank, a transnational finance corporation whereas the Berliners are working for their city and country.

Passing through the building, across an adjacent parking lot, and into a wooded vacant lot, the viewer is pointed towards a group of pictures attached to a tree. Viewers learn that the great uncle of the caller came from India to Berlin to seek Hitler's assistance in his campaign against Gandhi. Nearby, are remnants of train tracks and a loading dock where armaments were shipped to the various war fronts during World War II. Obscured by weeds and small trees, these archaeological remains of a not very distant past seem all the more startling because they are unveiled by a voice from so far away. The performer's geographical remove combines with the intimacy of the cellphone voice and its uncanny connection to Hitler to create a new cybernetic city, one in which the viewer strolls through multiple worlds electronically connected.

Guiding each viewer, performers boast a joking, alluring confidence that asserts an ironic distance from the labor that they typically perform. Satirizing their role as the agent who can sell you anything and make you feel good about the transaction, each performer tries to purvey intimacy through questions about romance and personal preferences, even the possibility of falling in love with a voice on the phone.[11] Crafting a conversation sustained over the entire length of the performance, they blend a chatty spontaneity with the continual directions and confirmation of the viewer's whereabouts. Walking through the backyard of a shabby housing project, the viewer encounters some of the inhabitants, Turkish, judging by their dress, casually conversing as their children play with a ball. The voice directs the viewer to imitate a statue, prompting the audience member to become an actor performing near if not for the Turkish families. Soon, another viewer will arrive to perform a similar choreography. Is this parade of audience members an intrusion on the Turks' semipublic leisure? A voyeuristic exercise of privilege? Who is in control? Who is authorized?

Walking across the bridge, the viewer is asked to wave at the conductor of a train passing below who waves back. Who is in the piece? Who is not? What about the many anonymous shoppers who stroll, with or without purpose, in the shopping mall the viewer has now entered? Here in front of a camera store, performer and viewer finally meet: Waving at the audience member from a television screen, the performer asks the viewer to take a picture with the cellphone, and entreats him/her to "stay in touch" via the email address specified in the program. The audience member is then directed to a bus that shuttles back to the theater.

Blending the anonymity and intimacy that digital technologies make available, *Call Cutta* explores a city and also the new collapse of public and private spaces that cellphones have provoked. Increasingly, individuals, jacked into their globally dispersed contacts, ignore the rituals and protocols that have defined public space. They do not partake in the protocols of civil exchange that defined eighteenth century comportment, nor do they observe the strong opposition between public and domestic spaces that dominated the nineteenth century. Instead, they rely on technologies of surveillance that monitor public behavior to provide the common ground on which they move. Tracked by millions of hidden cameras, today's global citizens, like the viewers in *Call Cutta*, assume that it is possible for someone to know of their whereabouts because of the electronic devices that make up their cyborgian identities. Thus, *Call Cutta*'s audience members obligingly execute instructions given by a voice 5,000 miles away while proclaiming their sexual orientation, or views on love and intimate relationships to an anonymous public of passersby.

This amalgamation of public and private, closeness and estrangement, and the surveillance that holds it intact is also the subject of Headlong Dance Theater's production *Cell*. Headlong's piece begins with an invitation for each audience member to bring their own cellphone to the appointed spot "prepared to walk." When the phone rings, the viewer encounters a voice more mysterious and conspiratorial than those in *Call Cutta*. Asked to turn around and gaze out across the city, the viewer is informed that "all of this is here for you." Then, the viewer is told to begin following a passerby, not too close, but not too far behind. For six or seven minutes, the viewer is contacted repeatedly and asked to follow different people, perhaps crossing multiple streets or even taking the bus for one stop. Then the phone rings again and the voice directs the viewer to a park bench. The caller points out details of activities taking place in the park, however, this time the observations of the caller are repeated, uncannily, by the person sitting next to the viewer on the bench. Who is in the piece? who is not? With eyes obligingly closed, the viewer listens to the woman sitting nearby who sings, then stands up and walks away, then returns.

Now the phone rings again and the viewer receives instructions to walk to the second floor of the nearby bookstore where another performer praises the execution of directions thus far and points the viewer towards the window. From here, the viewer can look down on the park bench where another audience member is being sung to, but now, the viewer at the window can see that when the woman stands up and walks away, she greets another passerby with a semaphoric handshake that entails touching forearms, then clasping hands and crouching before returning to the bench.

When the phone rings again, the viewer is advised to follow the woman wearing a white hat who suddenly pulls out a computer and presents the viewer with a second opportunity to review the performance thus far: a three-minute video starting at the bridge and ending at the store. Then the viewer is directed out the back door and into the alley, where two new performers, a sixty-year-old man clad in business attire and a twenty-year-old woman in casual dress, begin to improvise a walking dance with the viewer, marching side by side or in a line, touching shoulders, skipping or circling around, as the three proceed in tandem down three city blocks.

When the phone rings next, the voice announces that it is time to enter the hive. Directed into a warehouse office, the viewer suddenly comes face to face with the person who has been giving the directions. Surrounded by photos of previous viewers at a desk covered with television screens, the viewer's dispatcher issues the last set of directions. Leaving their contact behind, and entering a theater where a rehearsal is taking place, the viewer is asked to wait and be patient, while three teenage girls make last-minute decisions about the lights for their routine. Then the technician escorts the viewer down a corridor where motion capture images of the viewer collaged with those of previous audience members play on the walls. Eventually arriving in a dance studio, three other dancers now begin to imitate whatever moves the viewer makes. For ten minutes or so, the quartet explores any and all kinds of motions or gestures the viewer offers up. Then the viewer is

Figure 4.2 A moment in *Cell,* restaged in New Haven, Conn., where an audience member is directed by dispatcher Marla Burkholder to look out over the street where the next audience member is engaged in the same dance that the observer in the garage had performed a few minutes earlier.
Photo by Andrew Simonet

led out of the building and issued an invitation to the "cast party" to take place the following week.

Devised by collectives of artists unknown to one another, *Call Cutta* and *Cell* take up uncannily similar issues. Both utilize the city as stage to create a unique experience for each individual audience member. Viewers do not gather together to witness in common a single series of events, but instead perambulate one by one through a changing landscape, guided by cellphone technology as the means for communicating the sequence of activities and for setting the parameters of the mobile theater space. As in *Woman and Water,* the choreography for *Call Cutta* and *Cell* cannot be owned or used for profit, since it exists in the interstices between viewer/performer's responses. As choreography it does not embody and set forth principles for how to move or how to connect movement to feeling. In both performances, however, choreography does establish procedures whereby action will unfold in time, and in its form of address, references to surveillance, and use of improvisation, the choreography for *Call Cutta* and *Cell* produces substantially different experiences for the viewers.

In the kinds of directions given and the ways they converse with the viewers, *Call Cutta* and *Cell* construct two distinct roles for audience members, that of customer and agent respectively. Where *Call Cutta*'s voice issues commands, requests reports, and then expresses approval, *Cell*'s voice hints at a conspiratorial togetherness based on common dedication to the execution of a covert operation. *Call Cutta*'s conversation is sustained, requiring adeptness at mixing small talk with instructions and reports on the viewer's whereabouts. Viewers are coaxed and cajoled into maintaining a civil conversation for over an hour as the voice monitors, processes, and affirms their progress through the piece. *Cell*'s voice, in contrast, contacts the viewer a dozen separate times, always knowing exactly where they are and what is around them, but less interested in conversation than in getting on with the mission. Instructions are quickly given; some encouragement is offered, and then the voice signs off leaving viewers to negotiate the next segment of the score on their own.[12] As a result of the differences in vocal address, the viewers' bodies take on distinctive attitudes of engagement with their surroundings. In *Call Cutta* the body saunter's along, orienting in alternation between features of the environment and the ongoing conversation. In *Cell* the viewer's body reacts to the instructions with wariness and efficiency, ever on the alert for the next call.

Whether as customer or agent, audience members in both performances become intimately tied to and dependent upon their connection to the cellphone voice. This connection overrides any disjunctions and disparities presented as part of the changing landscape through which viewers move. In *Call Cutta*, the bizarre connection between the caller and Hitler, documented so poignantly in the photographs and loading dock hidden in the wooded area of downtown Berlin, does not resonate throughout the piece, but instead, becomes one topos among many, all of similar gravity and intensity, through which the viewer passes. Similarly, *Cell*'s abrupt and tenuous encounters with different performers and the sudden opportunity it presents to reflect on one's own previous actions as another is performing them all flow along, wrapped up in the bond created between viewer and dispatcher. Neither performance is grounded by an underlying proposition or theme. What matters, in both cases, is the medium of the cellphone itself. In both pieces, the cellphone functions as a new form of graticule, deterritorializing all spaces, rendering them all equivalent to one another.

The cellphone not only serves as the mobile theater in and through which the performance unfolds, but it also hosts a complex struggle between improvised and surveilled action. The city offers an extraordinary opportunity to improvise, yet increasingly, the city also surveils its inhabitants, ostensibly to ensure their safety. Cameras in public spaces generate millions of hours of footage documenting events in the street. Citizens are encouraged to scrutinize one another in search of suspicious behavior. The ichnographic perspective articulated in early cartography and played out in the construction of the proscenium itself no longer forms what or how viewing occurs. Instead, surveillance permeates the entirety of public space, and the city assumes the role of giant panopticon. The optical-spatial regime that supported colonialist capitalist modernity has given way to an omniscience constructed through the internalization of surveillance in which each individual watches being watched.[13]

Both *Call Cutta* and *Cell* probe the new intermingling of agency and discipline hosted by these technologies. *Call Cutta*'s voice issues instructions and questions viewers as to their whereabouts, but also affirms in an all knowing way that the viewer has arrived at a particular location, as if the voice were tracking that progress with some system of surveillance such as GPS. Although GPS is not used to track the viewer's location, the call center worker must appear to know where the viewer is at each moment because these workers can never act as though in need of assistance or lacking in information. Although viewers could test the omniscience of the voice by dissimulating or straying from the path, they choose not to in order to remain faithful to the role of audience member. They docilely offer up the necessary information as to their whereabouts, thereby completing the pattern of a technology that is not actually in use.

Cell similarly plays with viewers' expectations concerning systems of surveillance through the labor-intensive procedure of assigning to each viewer a performer/dispatcher who remains out of sight, all the while following the viewer's progress and then calling intermittently to issue new instructions.[14] Because of the looping pathway that all couples follow, performers encounter other viewers while staying invisible to their own partner. They call out to these viewers, "Hey, Buzz," or offer them the code handshake as a way to augment the uncertainty about the identity of performers and pedestrians. These haphazard encounters disrupt both the continuity established with the caller, and the theatricalizing gaze of the viewer onto a pedestrian world. Just when viewers think they are regarding quotidian life as a performance, someone who is passing by reveals him or herself to be a performer. This blurring of art and life reinforces the impression that some overall system of surveillance is informing the whereabouts of all participants.[15]

Both performances obliterate the possibility for a motionless body to survey the world and to consolidate knowledge by storing it in a stilled physicality. Where the proscenium theater constructed a sturdy body, one that could carry the subject from place to place and track the results of that portage through a comparison of motion with sensory change, *Call Cutta* and *Cell* enforce the cyborgian interdependence of body and technology. They build upon Gibson's theory of perception as the product of actively moving in and through the world, yet they insist that viewers be assisted in that process by relying on their connection to the cellphone. In this way they pioneer in reflecting upon the new kinesthesia that is being constructed as bodies and digital technologies implant one another.

In the permeable interface they construct between art and life, both performances implement a flexible conception of choreography, as a kind of scored sequence of events that is nonetheless subject to split-second alterations and last-minute improvised accommodations to an always changing surroundings. By operating within this interface, they also call attention to the daily choreography that has developed around the use of cellphones in public spaces. Walking and talking on their cellphones, viewers also note other pedestrians who are similarly engaged. The hour-long performances offer ample opportunities to reflect on one's own behavior as a cellphone user, the simultaneous experiences of intimacy and obliviousness to the surrounding space that the cellphone entails, and the physical ineptness that results from multitasking.

Both *Call Cutta* and *Cell* also endeavor to query the social and economic functions of this cyborgian body. *Call Cutta* poses the problem of the phone bank worker and *Cell* intermingles commands issued over the cellphone with playful improvised movement conversations. From its opening moments, *Call Cutta* reminds viewers of the political and economic inequalities that are implied in the very job of the phone bank worker. However, as the piece progresses, it succumbs to the effects of deterritorialized space created by cellphone and GPS where all points in space are treated as equal. Beginning with the very promising inquiry into an extraordinarily local set of events

– the uncle, the war, the almost absurdist connections between India and Germany, it proceeds to treat the Turkish tenement, the train conductor, and the anonymous shoppers in the mall as all similarly significant. Rather than considering each place as supporting a local ecology with a distinctive history, it treats all stories as interchangeable. The persona of the call worker and the standard amount of time spent at each location undermine the specificity of each place.

Cell tries to counter this atomization of space by providing multiple occasions for substantial improvised interaction between viewers and performers. Yet all these encounters take place without the cellphone, so that the interstitial territory of cyber-contact and the urban world of human contact remain separated. Two of these experiences of improvising, coming toward the end of the piece, embrace the viewer in a more sustained kind of interaction than any of the earlier contact with the dispatcher. Viewers thus experience an oppositionality between the objectifying world of cellphone surveillance and the "natural" world of dancing that does not allow greater insight into the body as cyborg or the transnational world that it is helping to create.

At the interfaces between art and life, digital and fleshly, where both performances operate, empathy is, at best, immensely precarious. The final image presented in *Call Cutta* of the phone bank caller on a screen in the local camera store waving to the viewer emblematizes the poignancy of outsourced contacts. Do any viewers make an effort to contact her again? After spending over an hour in intimate conversation, the scenic apparition of the person whose voice has inhabited the viewer's ear dramatizes her inaccessibility. Although her voice has felt so close, her calm and confident control over the conversation extinguishes the impulse to imagine her situation. Similarly, because it is a "performance," viewers are not inclined to feel any urgency about events witnessed on the street as they pass by. It is difficult, for example, to feel anything about the impoverished circumstances of the Turks whose picnic they invade. Perhaps most important, the viewer's multitasking kinesthesia, developed during walking, talking, and looking, cannot muster the integrity or purposefulness to project itself into another's world.

Even though *Cell* offers a more sustained opportunity for connection between viewers and dancers, it likewise stages the unlikelihood that empathetic connection can be established. The culture of surveillance that the performance promotes, despite the caring attentiveness that each dispatcher actually devotes to each viewer, gives the impression that every moment of the piece is being impersonally managed. Because the final opportunity to engage with dancers as they imitate the viewer's gestures is preceded by seeing the rehearsal in the adjacent studio, the viewer's own interactions with dancers take on the function of a simulation. Why would the viewer risk becoming engaged with the dancers by attempting to dance with them? The performance suggests that just when a moment of shared intimacy might take place, the cellphone will ring with yet more instructions.

Both performances thus mount a strong critique concerning the viability of empathic engagement within the cyborgian social. They demonstrate, even as they succumb to, the deterritorialized space that the cellphone promotes. How might cellphone technology and the transnational space it constructs be recast so as to provide a non-disembodied period of contact between performer and audience member? How could contact with a cellphone voice not render all experience equivalent? How could a performance be staged on a variegated terrain, dense with memories and associations in some areas, and more sparse in others? Could performer and audience member learn to depend on one another and to solicit candid responses from each other in order to explore mutually the locality of shared experience? What kind of score could be devised to reaffirm and even enhance public protocols of comportment through which individuals rely on and sustain one another? If they do not answer all these questions, *Call Cutta* and *Cell* nonetheless provoke the asking of them.

Engendering and evaluating

Along with the emergence of global stage, artists have initiated a variety of experiments with collaboration across dance forms and traditions. The results of these experiments variously blend, juxtapose, or alternate between distinctive vocabularies of dance in efforts to explore the possibilities for intercultural dialogue. Presented as genuine efforts at egalitarian exchange, these collaborations nonetheless reverberate with the history of colonization and the classifications of the world's dances that resulted from it. The kinds of categorization proposed by Curt Sachs in his *World History of the Dance* and implemented by La Meri continue to inform the reception of intercultural performance. For example, the categories of the traditional and the experimental are frequently implemented as frameworks for producing, booking, and framing dance events. Seen in opposition to one another, traditional dances purvey and reinforce the long-standing customs and values of a people, whereas experimental dances, capable only in "modern" societies, challenge the boundaries of and expectations about concert dance itself.

Exemplary of the new intercultural collaboration, *Pichet Klunchun and Myself* stages a dialogue between two artists, French choreographer Jérôme Bel and Thai classical dancer Pichet Klunchun, who ask each other questions and demonstrate their work to one another as a way of finding out about each other's worlds of dance.[16] Since its premiere in 2004, the duet has toured extensively, garnering adulatory reviews and standing ovations especially across Europe and North America but receiving less positive responses in Korea, Taiwan, Indonesia, and Singapore. Although Thailand was never colonized, it shares with other Asian countries a history of being viewed by the West as both exotic and traditional. Klunchun himself is a classically trained Khon dancer, dedicated to preserving a form of dancing developed over two centuries ago, and Bel is an antitheatrical artist dedicated to challenging the status of dance on the concert stage. Although their collaboration attempts to present an egalitarian exchange of views on dance, it performs the felicitous marriage of two cultures whose histories of privilege, wealth, and access to the global circulation of products and ideas have been markedly different. Tacitly invoking the distinction between "traditional" and "experimental" conceptions of choreography, their dialogue reaffirms and reinvigorates hierarchies of civilization implemented in Europe's colonization of the world. These conceptions of choreography are also gendered such that tradition is aligned with the feminine and experimentation with the masculine, thereby securing for Bel a masculine dominance and superiority in the world of dance.

Pichet Klunchun and Myself does not attempt to fuse or in any way combine classical Thai repertoire with experimental French concert dance, but instead, to present the very first encounters between two artists from very different backgrounds. Whereas *Woman and Water*, *Call Cutta*, and *Cell* all take performance out into the world, blending it with urban life and pedestrian action, *Pichet Klunchun and Myself* reproduces onstage a seemingly spontaneous and pedestrian conversation. The performance begins with Klunchun and Bel entering the stage and seating themselves in two chairs facing one another. Barefoot, and dressed in loose, cropped pants and T-shirt, Klunchun carries a bottle of water. Bel, in jeans, boots, and shirt, glances briefly down at the laptop on the floor beside his chair, before beginning a set of questions to Klunchun. The 90–100 minute performance consists entirely in a mutual interview, conducted informally, first by Bel and then, in the second half, by Klunchun. The conversation proceeds methodically from personal background to training, opportunities to perform and make a living as an artist, and finally, the ways that various subjects might be represented in dance. Each artist, familiar with the answers he will deliver, nonetheless proceeds in a seemingly spontaneous manner, creating a dialogue that is more organized than a typical conversation, yet unpretentiously straightforward and dedicated to the task of finding out about one another.

Audience members learn that Klunchun became a dancer to give thanks to a deity associated with dance after his mother had prayed to it to become pregnant with a boy. Expert in the demon repertoire, Klunchun explains that nowadays he typically performs excerpts of the classical court danced narratives for tourists who book dinner and Thai dance for a given evening. A recent Prime Minister dedicated to modernizing the country, abandoned the classical arts in favor of cha-cha and tango. Klunchun, however, remains dedicated to the project of revitalizing this classical repertoire, one that formed around and in praise of the monarchy, and he intends to demonstrate its value to contemporary Thai culture.

At Bel's request, Klunchun demonstrates various aspects of Khon – basic training exercises, character types, and ways of representing death onstage. Differing positions of arm or hands designating different characters are seen by Bel as almost indistinguishable, however, Klunchun assures him they are enormously different. Scenes of violence and destruction remain opaque to Bel until Klunchun describes the action while dancing it. Once he is initiated into the symbolic system, Bel is better able to follow along, sometimes correctly guessing the meaning of Klunchun's actions. Still, Klunchun must explain to a disbelieving Bel the refusal of the form to represent death onstage.

As part of his explanation, Bel asks Klunchun to teach him some dance. Declining to learn the role of the demon, because he is not in good shape, Bel requests, instead, to be instructed in a phrase from the female repertoire, one of the three other principle character types in Khon. Klunchun then takes him through a phrase, explaining in detail the positions and actions of legs, torso, arms, hands, fingers, and head. Although designed to illustrate the complexities of the form, this pedagogical moment also demonstrates Bel's ability to pick up the movement and execute, at least superficially, a relatively accurate, for the untrained body, version of the phrase. Bel also queries the strenuous, even grotesque, demands placed on the hand when he attempts to reproduce Klunchun's intense curvature of wrist and fingers. Klunchun responds matter-of-factly that the dancer's training constructs analogies between the body and temple architecture. The curves of the hand serve to rechannel the energy back towards the center of the body, so that the dancing establishes a continuous recycling of effort. Klunchun contrasts this aesthetic with the Western propensity to throw energy away in various leaps and extensions of body parts.

Here, for the first time in his interrogation, Bel expresses admiration: "I'm very impressed; this is something I had never thought of before." Up until that moment, Bel alternates most often between silence and skepticism, confusion, disbelief, and perplexity in response to Klunchun's answers and demonstrations. Requesting to be shown a violent scene, for example, Bel initially rejects Klunchun's performance as insufficiently violent until Klunchun decodes it for him. Responding to the idea that death could be signified by a long and exceptionally slow walk across the entire stage, Bel is at a loss to imagine how meaning can be conveyed within the form. Even the "Good luck" that Bel offers in response to Klunchun's expressed desire to vivify Khon for a younger generation betrays an uncomprehending incredulity.

Bel then invites Klunchun to question him, and viewers learn that Bel, although unmarried, has a child. Expressing a desire for children, Klunchun rejects Bel's proposal to bear one out of wedlock. Bel's raised eyebrow and shrug of the shoulders renders Klunchun's response prudish and old fashioned. Asked to demonstrate some dancing, Bel replies with beguiling modesty that he is not a "real" choreographer, nor does he perform. After Klunchun objects that he has shown Bel a great deal, Bel offers one of his favorite scenes: he stands unassumingly gazing out at the audience with interest but no affect. Deploring the society of spectacle in which we are living, Bel explains that such an action is "not a representation." In a second demonstration, Bel uses his computer to play a soundtrack from David Bowie's "Let's Dance" to which he dances with marked absence of energy, commitment, or fervency, thereby exposing the traditional association of rock music with abandoned physical display.

When Klunchun expresses disappointment, Bel retorts that he is not surprised. Advocating for his anti-virtuosity approach, Bel aspires to create more egalitarian relationships using pop music, a form that belongs to everybody. Bel continues by explaining that whereas Klunchun dances about and for a King, Bel's country beheaded theirs two hundred years earlier so as to live in a more egalitarian society. Sponsored by that government, Bel conducts research within the "contemporary arts," producing new works, whose form and content are unforeseen, and whose reception is frequently mixed at best. Nonetheless Bel aspires to make space for viewers to have their own response to life's enduring challenges. He illustrates this invitation by performing a very slow slump to the floor while singing in unison with Roberta Flack's "Killing Me Softly," and then remaining inert for the last verse. Klunchun admits to having been moved by this action since it reminded him of his paralyzed mother's death, and Bel is pleased that his aversion to virtuosity and the quiet and matter-of-fact display of the body lying onstage as the symbol of death have been successful. Having agreed that they are very good viewers, even ideal, of one another's work, Bel reminds Klunchun that he cannot tell him anything. It must be discovered.

In one final example, Bel begins to demonstrate a dance based on the manipulation of pieces of flesh. But when he moves from his ample stomach to take down his pants, Klunchun refuses to view anything further, claiming his culture's standards of aesthetic decency. Bel responds that he has seen considerable nakedness in Bangkok in the bars, but Klunchun explains that these women are working for tourist dollars. At this point, Klunchun and Bel agree to end their conversation.

Although the performance is by and about two male artists, the feminine appears many times, and all of these references to women cast them in highly traditional roles – as mothers, as members of the social whose roles are well established and who take responsibility for grieving for the loss of others, as sex workers, and as roles inhabitable by men when the need or desire arises. Each role locates women in an inferior relationship to men. As mothers their labor is erased, for it is Bel who "has" a child, and Klunchun who became the dancer. As sex workers, they are betraying their country's standards of decency. As theatrical roles, they demand less physically than other character types, or else they serve as vessels easily occupied by the male artists to demonstrate their form's aesthetic proclivities. The fact that these two male artists find so much in common in these archetypally feminine images permits them to establish a tacit familiarity and a tenuous equality to one another. They even perform the feminine together when Bel learns a phrase in its repertoire from Klunchun. The ease with which they move in and out of feminine roles, whether in Khon or lip-synching Roberta Flack, confirms their privilege and superiority.

At the same time, the masculine-feminine binaries operating in the guise of the opposition tradition/experimentation work to place Klunchun in a distinctly inferior position. Klunchun's unquestioning acceptance and pursuit of dancing as a life calling, his devotion to resuscitating an outmoded form, the precise specifications of the form itself with its detailed requirements for roles, stories, and modes of representation – all seem quaint and naïve when compared with Bel's iconoclastic vision. Klunchun's pliability, both in terms of how he has worked to cultivate the body, and also his amenability to explaining and demonstrating his form, signal a willingness to connect to Bel and to the world that Bel's aesthetics, in their guise as pioneering research, disdain. Where Klunchun has dedicated much of his life to the acquisition of technical facility at dancing, Bel has devoted a comparable amount of time to learning and then unlearning how to dance. Where Klunchun can efficiently decode the meanings behind each gesture and phrase in his danced dramas, Bel aspires to create space for the ordinary and the everyday as actions that cannot be decoded because they simply are what they are. Staring straightforwardly at the audience, lying quietly on the stage, Bel claims to eclipse representation by presenting things that cannot mean anything else. Yet even these claims are vivified and fortified by the prior revelations of Klunchun regarding how dance signifies.

Bel stakes his claim to choreographic originality by implementing a distinction between movement caught within representation and movement that occurs outside of it. Asserting a natural sense not unlike that of the early modern dancers a century ago, Bel purposely resists displaying a "trained" body. His physique is not muscular or sculpted or particularly erect. Yet this arduous cultivation of the pedestrian goes unmarked. The labor he puts into fashioning a body that appears to reside outside the boundaries of representation must go unacknowledged in order for the claim that his movement exists outside representation to be persuasive. The early modern dancers used the natural body to assure viewers of its responsiveness to the soul, whereas Bel deploys it to be experimental. Obfuscating his heroic quest for innovation through beguiling ineptness and a willing confession of his lack of competence at dancing and his marginal status as an artist, he secures a prestigious position for himself on the vanguard of the avant-garde. From this position Bel serves, not a monarchy, but rather the "people."

Bel's location beyond representation also depends upon the prior establishment of the mutual interview as the format in which intercultural collaboration will be displayed. The dialogue-as-performance recapitulates Bel's dedication to arranging the "spontaneous" onstage. The two artists have not met, exchanged ideas, and then developed something for presentation. Instead, they re-present onstage their initial encounters and explorations with the same quality of unpretentious straightforwardness that Bel invokes when staring at the audience or lying on the floor as if "dead." Bel has thereby established the representational grounds on which their exchange will take place and then located himself outside that framework as an artist who eschews representation. In so doing, Bel uses the comparison of his own approach with that of Klunchun in order to expose, most humorously, the intentions of his artistic practice in relation to the general workings of contemporary concert dance. However, he also creates for himself a special place of privilege from which to display the brilliance of his artistic vision.

Bel's and Klunchun's performances do not embody any of the standard divisions of labor between the masculine and the feminine staged within Western dance history. They do not articulate a difference based either on degree or kind. Klunchun does not approximate the smaller but otherwise equal version of Bel, as the feminine did in the early eighteenth century. Nor does he appear as the chaotic and unknowable feminine of the nineteenth century, one that increasingly evaded the rational male efforts to capture and contain it. Rather, Bel continually launches his interrogation as the all-knowing arbiter of aesthetic taste, but then turns those same values back on himself in order to ironize his own project. In so doing, he transposes himself onto the feminine as that which is unrepresentable, thereby constructing for himself a soft masculinity. Klunchun complements this stance by asserting a commanding knowledge of his art typically associated with the masculine while at the same time serving as the feminine bearer of tradition.

Throughout the performance, even as he is positioned within this representational system, Klunchun preserves his dignity, integrity, and worldview. He quietly rebuts Bel's dismissal of the different positions of the arm for different characters by asserting their dramatic effectiveness. He likewise rejects Western dance as a practice that throws energy away. And he steadfastly maintains his modesty in the face of invitations to produce a child out of wedlock and to view Bel's naked body. Although located within the apparatus of representation, he nonetheless perseveres in the commitment to his art and his willingness to share it with anyone who expresses interest. He even challenges Bel's theory of representation by continuing to decode, in the same way as he has his own work, Bel's performance of death.

According to Klunchun's aesthetics, the dialogue with Bel places him at no disadvantage nor does it demean his art form or way of life. He never attempts to ingratiate himself or his dance with either Bel or the audience. He presents the facts of his life and dance form with care and confidence. Similarly, for Bel's aesthetics, given the limited amount of time allotted for the two artists to get to know one another, the most honest plan, one preserving the integrity of each practice, would be to present a simulated version of their initial encounter onstage. Yet the collision of these two worldviews and their assimilation into Bel's conception of representation reinvigorate the first-world's heritage of privilege based in colonial histories and the stereotypes that enabled colonization.

Bel has inherited from the history of choreography a conception of dance as a single-authored creation that attempts to present a unique vision to its viewers. He has also assimilated the separation of technical training from the movement vocabulary of which the dance is composed. For Klunchun choreography might be identified in the careful selection of vocabulary from repertoire that portrays specific characters and situations, whereas for Bel choreography must present something never before conceptualized or realized which should challenge the audience's assumptions about viewing dance. For Klunchun choreography and training to become a dancer are part of the same process, whereas for Bel the quest to create something radically new takes place apart from any systematic cultivation of the body.

In this period of increased cultural exchange, a performance such as *Pichet Klunchun and Myself* fulfills the desire to witness a sharing of those differences. Seemingly collegial and egalitarian, the dialogue between the two artists masks over the inequities between their histories as dancers. It suggests that each artist and art form has had equal access to the world stage, whereas the vast majority of funding and visibility for concert dance are generated from within Europe and the US. This inequity in conjunction with the collision between their conceptions of choreography and the feminization of Klunchun others him in a particular way. He is alternately figured as perplexing and unknowable, for persisting in a classical tradition, fascinating and arresting, for displaying such competence at a completely foreign aesthetic system of bodily cultivation, and naïve and unsophisticated, for adhering to old-fashioned values. Within the context of the dialogue between Klunchun and Bel, agreement is reached that for each artist some moments in dance are moving and others are not depending upon the frameworks of representation being enacted and one's understanding of the codes that govern that framework. The performance as a whole, however, makes it impossible to access Klunchun on his own terms. Like the nineteenth century folk dances that fortified the classical ballet, revving it up with a veneer of the exotic, Klunchun can only service Bel's radical artistry.

Following the premiere of *Pichet Klunchun and Myself*, Klunchun created two evening-length works that comment in crucial ways upon his collaboration with Bel.[17] The first, *I Am a Demon* (2006), presents an austere, minimalist excavation of Khon pedagogy. Dedicated to his teacher, the piece begins with basic positions performed in slow motion that emphasize how each part of the body should participate in creating a given shape. It then expands into the regimen of exercises that largely compose the training program, exposing the labor of constructing the powerfully expressive physicality that marks Klunchun's dancing. Following this minimalist exposition, performed wearing only a pair of briefs, Klunchun demonstrates how to wrap and tie the traditional pants worn by the demon character, how to handle a spear in fight sequences, and finally, how to perform a buoyant and light-hearted sequence to music. Alternating between slow motion and extensive repetition of individual exercises, all performed in stark, minimal light, the piece extracts the movement practice from the full costuming and traditional narratives that Khon presents and conducts an anatomy of the form.

The performance is framed by Klunchun directly addressing the audience. At the beginning, he describes his intensive study with his teacher and his feelings of immense loss when the teacher passed away. At the end, Klunchun describes his motivation for creating the piece, explaining that the piece began with the question he posed to himself about how to bring back someone who is gone. Since, as he notes, the only way to see classical Thai dance is to attend a performance in a restaurant for tourists, he created this piece to try to make Khon stronger, to renew it and revitalize its previous meaning and impact. Captivated by the fact that he has, thanks to his intensive training with his teacher, acquired knowledge that is two hundred years old, Klunchun aspires to forge a new vehicle for sharing that corporealized culture so that it might be relevant and inspiring today. *I am a Demon* endeavors to bring back both his teacher and Khon itself.

Much of the piece is performed in silence, adding to the stark focus on the physical acts of lifting the leg, stomping forcefully, lunging, and shifting weight. A recorded interview with Klunchun's teacher occasionally interrupts the rhythm of the repetitions. Speaking Thai, the teacher is translated into English, emphasizing his native language and underscoring the fact that Klunchun is translating Khon for an international audience. Sometimes the speaking is drowned out by the noises generated from the body itself as Klunchun stomps or claps repeatedly. The first use of music occurs over half way into the piece during a blackout following a long, increasingly slow-motion walk across the stage. Although a more elaborate step pattern, with arms and legs carving high through the air, the passage across stage is reminiscent of Klunchun's description to Bel of the representation of death by showing those walking to attend the funeral. In the dark that follows, it is as if viewers are encouraged to imagine the teacher dancing to the faint sounds. The performance concludes with Klunchun dancing, for the first time, an actual sequence of the repertoire to music

Figure 4.3 Pichet Klunchun in *I am a Demon* (2006)
Photographer Edmund Low

at full volume followed by an excerpt from his teacher's interview, projected for the first time on a large screen at the back of the theater. Onscreen the teacher poses a series of questions about the relevance of Khon and the possibility that it could not only survive but also regain its importance within Thai culture.

In his remarks following the performance, Klunchun takes up these questions, admitting the quandary that he and his art face. "They hate me in Bangkok," he confesses, wincing as he reckons with the preference in Thailand for more modern forms of dancing. Looking for ways to promote Khon, both at home and abroad, Klunchun has launched several initiatives to expand awareness of its complex aesthetics. Leveraging his international visibility, achieved in part through his collaboration with Bel, Klunchun can return to Thailand to campaign for traditional and contemporary implementations of Khon while also spreading awareness of the form through international touring.

If *I am a Demon* develops one approach to a contemporary adaptation of Khon, a second work, *About Khon*, in which Bel also participates, presents a closer look at how its aesthetics fit into the classical narratives and staging of Khon. Created in 2008, *About Khon* commences in the same way as *Pichet Klunchun and Myself*, with Bel conducting an even more extensive interview with Klunchun about the nature of Khon. They focus particularly on the ways that it represents events and builds poetic imagery and also on its underlying principles for organizing the body into positions that make possible a recycling of energy out into the limbs and then back into the center of the body. Bel's tone in conducting the interview is noticeably more modest than in *Pichet Klunchun and Myself*, and he seems far more interested in and respectful of Khon. Klunchun then asks him if he would like to learn more and invites Bel to move his chair to the audience where the two continue their conversation as other performers enter playing the roles of the King, his brother, and the monkey. Bel asks questions about the action onstage, and Klunchun explains the characters and their actions until a point in the narrative where he himself must enter as the demon. Performing in his casual shirt and sweat pants alongside the elaborate and glittering costumes of the others, Klunchun executes some of the actions he has explained earlier, giving viewers far greater insight into the way the narrative unfolds onstage while also highlighting the physicality of the movement. By eliminating Bel's own approach to choreography, *About Khon* redresses the imbalance in artistic pursuits that was created in *Pichet Klunchun and Myself*, presenting instead a promotion of and lecture-demonstration about Khon.

Each of Klunchun's pieces proposes a different notion of what choreography is. Both draw upon and adapt traditional elements of Khon, and both are substantially altered and reshaped by the vision of an individual artist, Klunchun himself. In *I am a Demon*, Klunchun has selected and sequenced movements from the classical training regimen, sometimes altering their timing or flow from one into another. However, he presents this innovative sequence, not for the purpose of self-expression, but rather in dedication to the form itself, underscored by his style of dancing that focuses a humble and dedicated concentration on each moment's action. In *About Khon* Klunchun constructs a bricolage of forms, borrowing from his earlier duet with Bel and adapting it to frame an extract from the classical repertoire, itself performed as a mixing of traditionally dressed dancers and Klunchun's rehearsal clad body.

As a result of these different approaches, each piece constructs a different kinesthetic experience. In *I am a Demon* the extensive repetitions of individual steps reference a training procedure that embeds its aesthetics in reflex-quick patternings of muscles and bones.

The repetitions also cry out to the audience, "feel this, feel this," as though Klunchun is endeavoring to share the same bone-deep knowledge his body has assimilated with them. Insofar as viewers can marvel at the precision and specificity of the actions, Klunchun will have succeeded in his desire to share Khon's special way of moving in the world. In *About Khon* Klunchun alternates between a casual pedestrian vocabulary and the fully professional execution of excerpts from the traditional repertoire. Giving viewers an appreciation of the detailed meanings embedded in individual movements, he then reiterates these sequences within the context of the fully staged action. Audience members are thereby summoned from a pedestrian world into Khon's particular physicality and from there into the stories it tells.

Bel's participation in *About Khon* signals an evolution in the cross-cultural dialogue that he and Klunchun have sustained. His willingness to be available as a performer in Klunchun's piece and to deepen his knowledge about Khon suggests that a more egalitarian relationship is possible. Bel and Klunchun came together, not as two classically trained artists dedicated to preserving a historic form, nor as two "experimental" artists invested in forging new forms. They did not decide to interrogate these differences or to stage the politics of intercultural collaboration between West and East. Rather, they determined to keep listening to one another. Taken together, *Pichet Klunchun and Myself, I am a Demon*, and *About Khon* define the contours of a conversation in which two artists can come to empathize with one another and with each other's artistic vision, if given the time and resources to learn from each other.

Downloading and accessorizing

As bodies and digital technologies increasingly permeate and inhabit one another, corporeality is being redefined not only through prosthetic devices such as the cellphone, but also through the pervasiveness of digital images generated by film and photographic cameras and by the ability of those images to circulate globally through multiple genres of the screen. An intensive saturation, especially of images of the feminine, has taken place as advertisements and entertainments from Hollywood to Bollywood travel rapidly across diverse social and entertainment media. Two recent works, one by British choreographer Lea Anderson, and the other by the Japanese performance collective KATHY, each draw upon images from Hollywood films to mount powerful critiques of the contemporary femininity purveyed in this new global exchange of images. [18] They also comment on the mediatization of gender and the imbrication of gender and global consumerism. They show how identity is being constructed not only through the acquisition of accessories to one's physical appearance but also through treating the body itself as an accessory, one that can be altered repeatedly in response to changing fashions and tastes. Taken together they also show how arguments concerning bodily identity resonate with and within a specific cultural surround.

At the beginning of Anderson's *Yippee!!!* the dancers traipse in, exuding a sultry glamour. Their arms poke at space with such earnest ennui. They stare at the audience with a practiced, bored blankness. Striking a statuesque pose, they slouch along in parade, their long mink stoles revealing a glimpse of a shoulder here, of a lower back there. However, any frisson that viewers receive from such a glimpse is dripping with irony, since all the bodies, male and female, are similarly naked – covered only with a translucent unitard that holds delicately in place massive quantities of fake pubic and underarm hair. They glide into ballroom couple poses and swirl gently around the stage. Other dancers pull on fur stockings and saunter in a circle. A more lively group wiggles their way onstage in grid formation, their complex rhythmic gyrations pulsing with fake euphoria.

Each of these scenes is a take-off on filmed production numbers from Broadway-style entertainments. The dancers execute versions of the original choruses and follow their formations onstage, yet they break radically with the gender codes of those early twentieth century productions. Male and female bodies, sometimes indistinguishable with their slicked back hair and similarly muscled physiques, both inhabit the same roles. In scenes where male and female dancers would typically partner one another, men dance with men, women with women, and women with men. In scenes where the traditional chorus line consisted of all female dancers, both male and female dancers engage equally in the same feminine repertoires: broad smiles, mincing steps, gracious displays of the body, and daintily bound gestures.

The performance of such strongly gendered actions by both male and female bodies offers up a powerful representation of the feminine as a gendered construct. Anderson deepens this interrogation of the feminine through her choreographic strategy of faithfully copying sections from film or photographs. Even though the dancers precisely execute eighty-year-old choreography, they lack the accoutrements of the filmic scene that would ensure their reception as realistic actors. Either the movement sequences are not used in their entirety and thereby disrupt with their glaring beginnings and endings. Or they lack the setting that would give them narrative coherence. Or they are cobbled together in an absurd sequence. Or they are repeated excessively such that their staging of exaggerated happiness becomes a most uncomfortable joke.

In all the obsessive repetition that overflows from the performance, what the dancers repeat most is the wiggle. They wiggle as their feet move from side to side in parallel. They wiggle as they skip. They wiggle as they shrug away any intimation of anxiety. Their wiggling is not quite naughty, not at all frenetic. Instead, the body pulls back from completely stretching one way and then the other. As a result, the figures look apathetic, even as they perform cheerfulness. Both the quality of the wiggle and the way it directs motion to one side and then the other signify a profound ambiguity. These dancers can't decide which way to go, and even if they were to decide, so what?

From the beginning, the performance makes a convincing case for its artifice. The main action takes place within a set of lights on movable poles that the dancers rearrange for different sections of the piece. Outside the lights dancers meander among racks of costumes, changing clothes, warming up, and watching the action. At one point, a seeming

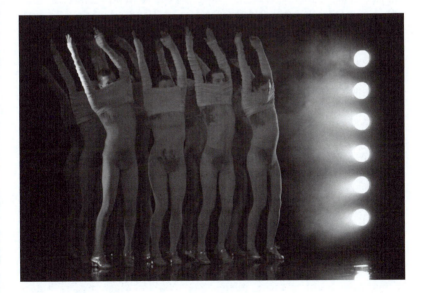

Figure 4.4 The "Wavy Arms" section from *Yippee!!!* (2006)
Photographer Lea Anderson

intermission, the dancers break to drink deeply from bottles of water stored in the open wings. At another, a dancer's fake dentures, enforcing his grotesque smile, pop out, and he fumbles frantically to reinsert them. Throughout, dancers stand in full view awaiting their entrances to the "performance" inside the lights.

As they stand ready to make their entrances, each dancer's body musters all the concentration necessary to make the transition from "off" stage to "on," all the necessary energy that normally would explode with the vitality of dancing. Yet instead, their onstage presence hails the viewer with an unbearable lack of zeal. So soft and subdued, so precisely directed yet fully lackluster, each gesture underscores its own failure to show the audience vigor, excitement, the sheer joy and gusto of engaging with physicality. The driving rhythms of the live band upstage emphasize even further this restrictedness of motion.

How to describe this peculiar quality of restraint? In the history of modern dance, restrained movement has signified an internal struggle in which opposing motivations vie for control over bodily expression as vivified in the choreography of Graham, Humphrey, Anna Sokolow, and many others. Restrained motion is full of tension and drama as the body seems to proclaim simultaneously, "I will," and "I won't." The restraint evident in Anderson's piece, however, does not suggest a willful subject. These rubbery, resilient wigglers never extend themselves fully either towards effortful exertion or lackadaisical relaxation. In part, this inhibited exertion into space reproduces the qualities of effort evident in the production numbers that Anderson has copied. Without the full costumes or bubbly music of the original performances, however, and in contrast to the extreme exertion so prevalent on the concert stage today, these dancers purvey a remarkably fettered physicality.

Anderson's choreographic process of copying and then splicing together movement sequences from other sources also produces an uncanny discontinuity between dancers and their movements. Because of the process of copying the action, the dancers appear to wear the movement. Motions do not originate in the body's interiority, but instead get placed on the body's surface. The bodies execute the next action, as non sequitur as it might be, without any organic flow, any sense of movement's purposefulness.

The second half of the performance turns darker. The happy jumping becomes obsessive, meaningless – a kind of consumer frenzy on display. Now wearing black unitards with silver tap shoes, the dancers' formations become more austere. A "Ballet Masteress"[19] enters wearing a dark fur coat and using a prosthetic foot as a cane. She rehearses the corps, adjusting posture, repositioning the dancers, counting and drilling them, then pronouncing their execution "nice." Anderson's critique of Tiller girls or Rockettes type repetitive movement grinds forward, implementing the tyranny of the eight-count phrase. This nightmarish alternation between emphatic carefreeness and statuesque strutting summons up the underbelly of the beauty industry. In this culture of nip and tuck, women may have more access to athletic pursuits, but there is no gain without pain, and every repetition potentially enhances one's image.

Alternating between grid formations and the parade, the dancers seldom touch one another. Only one couple, adorned with red velvet masks over their noses and mouths, ever sustains physical contact. They perform failed versions of gags, then reappear dancing to the sounds of a tap dance, making reference to an African-American duo such as the Nicholas Brothers on film. Cavorting, buffooning, they counterpoint the vacant monumentality of the larger production numbers. Their brief entre-actes, however, do not offset the alienation of the ensemble numbers. Not the carefully moderated coordination of couples to embody a harmonious cosmos at the Renaissance court, and not the dizzying excitement created in the nineteenth-century ballroom, these dancers display only the drive to display.

For the finale, the dancers return to the ballroom, partnering up with partial tuxedos and strap-on feather boas in a last parade. Their fanciful strutting culminates in a single decorative tableau where all the dancers artfully drape their bodies across the front of the stage. Yet this final image produces no climax, no celebratory exclamation of joy. As if to reassert, once again, the irony of the dance's title, the ending is as lame as the femininity which it celebrates is oppressive.

Where *Yippee!!!* presents a world of science fiction bodies draped with gender codes, KATHY members claim to be directed by an extra-terrestrial, or possibly an American, whose name is Kathy. In the short film *Mission/K* (2002), three dancers cavort through a park-like landscape filmed by a camera whose fish-eye lens represents Kathy's omniscient presence. Sporting shirt-waist dresses and blond page-boys, the dancers glide among vocabularies identifiable as derived from Broadway jazz, ballet, modern, can-can, tap, hula, children's games, and movie musicals – all performed to the effervescent sound-track of Doris Day singing "Good morning" from *Singin' in the Rain*. Unlike Anderson's choreography which cites a homogeneous group of production numbers, KATHY's sequencing selects from diverse genres, both popular and high art. Yet like Anderson's dancers, these women perform every move with a faint but discernible lack of gusto. They flop into arabesque, twirl with groggy abandon, and fall with a clunk; the

Figure 4.5 A still image from KATHY's video *Mission/K*. (2002)
Permission and image courtesy of KATHY

ambivalence in their motion underscored by the black tights that cover their faces, legs dangling as two grotesquely deflated protuberances.

Where Anderson's dancers show a kind of buffness gone awry, endlessly exercising with a mechanical mindlessness, KATHY's dancers seem possessed to perform as instructed while at the same time being overcome with a faint lassitude. Where Anderson's dancers also perform just short of their full-out capability, KATHY's members occasionally demonstrate blatant failure at certain moves: the can-can makes them gasp for breath; the partner fails to catch the dancer as she lurches forward in arabesque. In these failures, the dancers underscore the pretense of their performance. They step into the camera's view, driven to execute a choreography that they show they have not fully mastered. Try as they might, they fail to serve up the requisite virtuosity, or is it that they slyly fail to achieve what is expected of them? *Mission/K*'s ending suggests that perhaps their failures are also part of their tactics to confront the system of surveillance in which they are located.

In contrast to *Yippee!!!*'s finale, a painfully dreary and deflated celebration of glamorousness, *Mission/K*'s dancers conclude their performance with a startling change in energy and direction: they abruptly abandon a swishy phrase of lyrical turns and gallops to march towards and then past the camera, their confident stride a strong reversal with all that has come before. In this exit, KATHY leaves an opening for the possiblity that the laboring dancers might just revolt and walk out of the parameters established by Kathy's all-observing eye. Both performances deconstruct the naturalness of the feminine images they present, however they prompt the viewer towards different conclusions regarding the agency available to both dancers and viewers.

Nobuko Anan argues that KATHY's choreography of ineptness not only ironizes the image of the feminine as the perfect entertainer, but their lack of virtuosity and gusto also signals Japan's inability to "live up to Americanization" in the post-war period, a mastery of American culture that Kathy is demanding.[20] Revealing and commenting on Japan's femininized status in relation to the US, their little-girlness references Japanese citizens' identity as children in relation to US hegemony, stemming from the post-war occupation, but continuing into the present with the coercive demand that Japan assist US forces in Iraq. Analogous to the theory of super-flat launched by artist Murakami Takashi, in which post-war Japan is seen as lacking the maturity, intellectually and ethically, to govern, KATHY displays the infantilization that has suffused US treatment of the Japanese. However, where Murakami focuses exclusively on boys, KATHY's performance introduces a feminist response. Their cut-and-paste sequencing of diverse movement traditions, as in Anderson's choreography, serves to deconstruct the femininity that was put on display in the original versions. As such, it destabilizes Japanese patriarchal assertions concerning an essential femininity, and refuses to return to the patriarchal hierarchies and values governing prewar Japan.[21]

Anderson's critique of the feminine in contemporary British society reacts against postfeminism and the residue of Prime Minister Margaret Thatcher's deregulated, free wheeling economy in which a liberatory consumer culture poses as the equalizer of gender.[22] Her choreography also responds to the rise of commercialization within concert dance, evident in the large-scale and highly popular productions of choreographers such as Matthew Bourne, as well as the drop in state support for the arts resulting from globalization's financial crises. Members of KATHY, in contrast, negotiate between different efforts to reassert Japanese identity, either through a return to traditional patriarchy or a super-flat aesthetics. Both Britain and Japan participate in globalization as advanced industrial and commercial societies, however Japan's history as an occupied country and the sustained hegemony of the US towards Japan create very different contexts for each feminist critique. Anderson's work rejects her own country's postfeminist consumer frenzy, whereas KATHY unsettles traditional Japanese patriarchal values as well as US dominance over its former occupied territory. And where Anderson's critique suggests that there is no exit from the cycle of consumerist delirium that drives women's bodies to spend and save, KATHY's conclusion suggests an opening through which to imagine a future apart from the enduring colonial influence of the US or the paternalistic history of Japan.[23]

Both works elaborate an uncanny physicality – rubbery, pastiched, and pasted onto a malleable perpetual motion machine that is incapable of relaxation because of the relentless pace of trying on and consuming new personas. In neither piece does the body appear as vessel for the expressive subject; it does not house a psyche or personality. Rather, the use of cut-and-paste as a compositional strategy turns the subject–body relationship inside out. Dancers are wearing their identities. Their bodies do not commit to the labor of showing who they are or what they believe in, as in the early modern dances. They do not stage the struggle of embodying a universal predicament. Nor do they casually explore any and all possibilities for moving, as performers committed to making, rather than creating, dances have done. They do not claim an equivalent value for any and all movements. Rather, they display and play with the codes of identity, repeating and recycling movements in order to pose the question of agency – where it is located and how it can be exerted.

Each work redefines choreography as the process, whether undertaken individually as Anderson does or collectively as KATHY does, of carefully identifying and selecting previous instantiations of movement. These are then replicated and spliced to create a new commentary on our contemporary situation. In *Yippee!!!* the movements grind themselves into the viewers' perception of them as if excessive repetition might be the only way to impress their message upon an audience overwhelmed by the deluge of images with which they are confronted on a daily basis. At the same time, the repetition comments on the very physicality that is being promoted in consumer capitalism, fabricated as it is through endless applications of cosmetic enhancements and shored up through grueling regimens of exercise. *Mission/K*, in contrast, builds multiple levels of reflexive commentary into its seemingly carefree exposition of Americana. Far from the sweeping and expansive gestures that Horst had in mind, this version of "Singin' in the Rain" suggests that the only possible exit strategy is to confront the very assumption of omniscient surveillance. Like Dorothy's dog Toto in *The Wizard of Oz*, who cleverly pulls back the curtain to reveal the wizard's terrifying presence to be the product of a few simple machinations, KATHY suggests that the fish-eye might have its own technological limits.

In what ways do these performers call out to viewers? How, if at all, do they encourage viewers to empathize with the action presented onstage and on screen? Rather than invite viewers into their world, *Yippee!!!*'s dancers remain resolutely remote, presenting their pathetic spectacle with fake gusto. They confront viewers with a consumerist wasteland and gender's participation in it, leaving viewers to assess the relevance of the dance's critique to their own lives. *Mission/K*, more light-hearted but no less devastating in its analysis, leads viewers into a space just to the side of the performance, just beyond the sightlines of the camera, but with no clear sense of where to go next. Both dances ruin the standard narratives upon which scopophilic and patriarchal pleasure depend, using startlingly similar choreographic tactics to stage their feminist antagonism. Neither offers a utopic alternative, much less a sense of hope, beyond the critical perspicuity that enabled the imaginative staging of their distinctive yet shared cultural predicaments.

Choreographing empathy

All of these dances push the limits of what has previously been considered choreography. They challenge the conception of choreography as the individual process of creating expressive movement, and, although many of them might qualify as "collaborative," they render that concept so diffuse as to include any artistic undertaking. These dances call for a reconsideration of the partitioning that took place over the eighteenth century between dance-making and the process of learning to dance, asking to what extent the process of forming the body through dancing is intrinsically related to the performance of a given dance. They also expand and alter the boundaries of a dance, asking where and when does the choreography end, and what is included and what is excluded from consideration by the frame and parameters it sets. Each dance elaborates a very different notion of virtuosity, requiring highly distinctive sets of skills for its execution. And each purveys a distinctive vision of the body – what it is and how it is connected to other bodies and to the world.

Woman and Water and *I am a Demon* both make a strong claim for considering choreography as necessarily inclusive of the history of the performer's training and cultivation of expertise at dancing. These dances, especially, draw from and rely on knowledge embedded bone-deep in the dancer's physicality – the product of years of dedicated practice to specific aesthetic and social values. They integrate that knowledge seamlessly into the fabric of the dance, or more precisely, the formation of physicality they have undertaken in learning to dance cannot be separated from other aspects of the performance. It is not simply that other bodies, differently trained, might alter the look and impact of the dances, but instead that the dances could not occur without the prior investments that these performers have made in learning to dance. *About Khon* likewise stages the connectedness of training and performance, but also shows the malleability of the dancer's body as it moves into and out of that trained physicality. Klunchun is casually conversing with Bel and the next moment performing full-out the role of the demon.

Woman and Water, *Call Cutta* and *Cell* all push the boundaries of choreography in a different direction by posing the question of what action is part of the dance and what events are not included in it. They each stage the performance within a field whose frame is not designated, thereby allowing viewers to focus on a wide range of objects and events as part of the performance. By relying so extensively upon audience reaction and interaction, *Call Cutta* and *Cell* also destabilize the score through which the sequence of events is determined. Any viewer could easily derail the score for the performance by dallying or veering off path. Although less reliant on the viewer's cooperation, *Woman and Water* also invites audience participation. All three dances thereby foreground the contract between artist and viewer and the necessity for both to be willing to work together to create a given performance.

Although framed in more traditional formats, by the proscenium and the camera lens, both *Yippee!!!* and *Mission/K* also challenge notions of choreography by transposing and rearranging actions from another medium into dance. *Yippee!!!* extracts actions from film, resequences them, and re-presents them on the live stage framed within a stage, and *Mission/K* selects from filmed and live performances an assortment of actions that are rearranged and then performed live for a camera. Both pose the question of the origin of choreography, and challenge presumptions about its necessary authenticity or newness. By borrowing their content from other sources, especially those from popular culture, and in the case of *Mission/K* by positing the existence of a fictional choreographer who has directed the action, both works call into question the preeminence of the choreographer and the sanctity of his or her vision. They also perturb the aspiration to ownership over movement.

Each dance requires remarkably different sets of skills, at executing predetermined action and at improvising responses to action as it unfolds during the performance. Exercising sensitivity to and connectedness with her surroundings, Lukin Linklater must vigilantly attend to changes in the landscape and the audience. Sourcing her body's groundedness, she must invest in and dedicate herself fully to each action and then let it go as she moves on to the next. Deducing the inclinations of viewers through small changes in their voice or bodily stance, performers in *Call Cutta* and *Cell* must think quickly about how to keep viewers and score for the performance reconciled. They must also mask their role as orchestrators of the viewer's movements by performing as the call center worker or the anonymous pedestrian. Refraining from a dramatic representation of their conversation, Bel and Klunchun must continually reengage with one another so as to conduct a new interview in each performance. In *I am a Demon* and *About Khon* Klunchun must also deconstruct the classical Khon repertoire, performing its fragments with traditional virtuosity and then commenting on that performance in dialog with Bel or the audience. Refraining from individual interpretation of the movements, performers in *Yippee!!!* and *Mission/K* must adhere meticulously to the sequences they have copied. They must show the failing, wiggling, half-baked body in all its fake enthusiasm.

Not only are skill and virtuosity defined and measured differently in each dance, but the very kinesthesis elaborated in their distinctive presentations of the body contrast strongly one with another. Lukin Linklater's body, opening itself continually into porous exchange with earth, air, trees, water, and people, resonates with the vicissitudes of her surroundings. Performers and audience members in *Call Cutta* and *Cell*, whether attached continually or intermittently to their cell phones, enact the cyborgian interdependence of body and machine. In his casual and relaxed attentiveness to Klunchun, Bel performs a close approximation of his pedestrian behavior. In contrast, Klunchun, whether demonstrating a phrase from Khon or drinking from his bottle of water, asserts a highly disciplined erectness, not as in ballet one that strives to levitate, but instead one that is centered equally between earth and air. *Yippee!!!*'s and *Mission/K*'s dancers demonstrate an apathy masked in forced cheerfulness. Taken together, these dancing bodies propose an immense range of kinesthetic experiences, connecting the body to land, to the digital, to popular media, and to culture and history, and through those connections transforming physicality in diverse ways.

In its specificity, the kinesthesis elaborated in each performance summons viewers into a unique kind of empathetic rapport. Lukin Linklater enfolds viewers, one and all, within her embrace, asking them to extend themselves just a step into the simplicity and beauty of what they share on earth. *Call Cutta* and *Cell*, in contrast, provoke an anxiety of physical and psychological orientation as they ask viewers to participate effectively in an almost impossible interface. They leave viewers questioning whether they might have been able to make a more vital connection to those on the other end of the phone. In *Pichet Klunchun and Myself*, Bel, with his witty self-deprecating demeanor, and Klunchun, with his dedicated resolve, invite viewers to savor the richness of intercultural exchange, but only if they are willing to ignore its history of violence. In *I am a Demon* Klunchun fragments his body and practice in order to impress upon viewers the precision and depth of his art's aesthetics. Unlike the wiggly repetitions of *Yippee!!!*, Klunchun invests each repeating movement with full intensity and commitment as if gathering viewers into each step over and over again. In *About Khon* he similarly labors, this time with Bel's assistance, to acclimate viewers to Khon's physicality, inviting them to marvel at the knowledge it embodies. Prompted to partake in the glamorous or playful cheer of *Yippee!!!* and *Mission/K*, viewers are then rebuffed by the underlying ennui and failure exuded in the dancing. Viewers are then left to reflect on their own attraction to and desire for the commodified feminine.

Taken together, these dances show how empathic connections occur in multiple and diverse ways. They foreground the partiality and incompleteness of empathy even as they invite viewers to dance along with them. Most crucially, they demonstrate the many ways in which the dancing body in its kinesthetic specificity formulates an appeal to viewers to be apprehended and felt, encouraging them to participate collectively in discovering the communal basis of their experience. If, as mirror neuron studies have shown, empathy forms the basis upon which knowledge of self and other is generated, these dances enact the process through which that knowledge production takes place. They dramatize how the connectedness among bodies can develop over time. By inviting viewers into a specific experience of what the body is, they also enable us to contemplate how the body is grounded, its function in remembering, its affinity with cultural values, its participation in the construction of gender and sexuality, and the ways in which it is assimilating technologies so as to change the very definition of the human.

Notes

Introduction

1 M. Lisby, Jacqueline H. Barlow, Rebecca C. Burgess, and Rodney Rothstein, "Choreography of the DNA Damage Response Spatiotemporal Relationships among Checkpoint and Repair Proteins," *Cell* 118, no. 6 (2004): 114–25; Allan Pred, "The Choreography of Existence: Comments on Hagerstrand's Time-Geography and Its Usefulness," *Economic Geography* 53, no. 2 (1977); Charis Thompson, *Making Parents: The Ontological Choreography of Reproductive Technologies* (Cambridge, Mass.: MIT Press, 2005).

2 Cynthia Jean Novack, *Sharing the Dance: Contact Improvisation and American Culture* (Madison, Wis.: University of Wisconsin Press, 1990), 114–25.

3 Randy Martin, *Critical Moves: Dance Studies in Theory and Politics* (Durham, N.C.: Duke University Press, 1998).

4 Randy Martin, "Overreading the Promise Land: Toward a Narrative Context in Dance," in *Corporealities: Dancing, Knowledge, Culture, and Power*, ed. Susan Leigh Foster (London: Routledge, 1996), 177–98.

5 Mark Franko, *The Work of Dance: Labor, Movement, and Identity in the 1930s* (Middletown, Conn.: Wesleyan University Press, 2002), 1–2.

6 Thomas DeFrantz, *Dancing Revelations: Alvin Ailey's Embodiment of African American Culture* (Oxford: Oxford University Press, 2004), xvi.

7 André Lepecki, "Choreograpy as Apparatus of Capture," *TDR: The Drama Review* 51, no. 2 (T 194) (2007), 119.

8 Diana Taylor, *The Archive and the Repertoire: Performing Cultural Memory in the Americas* (Durham, N.C: Duke University Press, 2003), 142–43.

9 Susan Leigh Foster, "Choreographies of Gender," *Signs* 24, no. 1 (1998); "Choreographies of Protest," *Theatre Journal* 55, no. 3 (2003). This expanded notion of choreography seems to be one that Andrew Hewitt would also like to deploy in his analysis of nineteenth century literature, comportment, and labor practices. See Andrew Hewitt, *Social Choreography: Ideology as Performance in Dance and Everyday Movement* (Durham, N.C: Duke University Press, 2005).

10 Marta Savigliano, "Worlding Dance and Dancing out There in the World," in *Worlding Dance*, ed. Susan Leigh Foster (London: Palgreave, 2009), 163–90.

11 Jens Richard Giersdorf, "Dance Studies in the International Academy: Genealogy of a Disciplinary Formation," *Dance Research Journal* 41, no. 1 (2009).

12 Anthea Kraut, "Race-Ing Choreographic Copyright," in *Worlding Dance*, ed. Susan Leigh Foster (London: Palgrave Macmillan, 2009), 76–97.

13 John Joseph Martin, *America Dancing: The Background and Personalities of the Modern Dance* (New York: Dodge Publishing, 1936), 117.

14 Dee Reynolds, *Rhythmic Subjects* (Alton, England: Dance Books, 2007). Susan Manning, *Ecstasy and the Demon: Feminism and Nationalism in the Dances of Mary Wigman* (Berkeley: University of California Press, 1993).

15 Deidre Sklar, "Can Bodylore Be Brought to Its Senses?" *Journal of American Folklore* 107, no. 423 (1994): 9–22.

16 Ibid., 14.

17 Randy Martin, "Dance's Diversity: A U.S. Perspective," in *Dance: Transcending Borders*, ed. Urmimala Sarkar Munsi (New Delhi: Tulika Books, 2008), 137.

18 See Lena Hammergren, "The Re-Turn of the Flâneuse," in Susan Leigh Foster, *Corporealities*, 53–69.

19 Sklar, "Bodylore," 14.

20 Two additional fields of inquiry, the history of science and the history of military training, would be important and fruitful additions to this list. Science studies, for example, has analyzed the ways in which objectivity is the product of a particular kind of theory of perception and its implicit conception of the body's involvement in viewing the object of study. Military training could provide valuable insights into the disciplining of the body and the formation of kinesthesia.

1 Choreography

1 See Roland Barthes, *The Responsibility of Forms: Critical Essays on Music, Art, and Representation*, 1st ed. (New York: Hill and Wang, 1985).

2 Johannes van Meurs, *Ioannis Mevrsi Orchestra. Sive, De Saltationibvs Vetervm, Liber Singularis* (Lvgdvni Batavorvm: ex officinâ Godefridi Basson, 1618).

3 Throughout his Preface to *Orchesography*, Weaver argues for the importance of the notation as a means for disseminating dances. Although dancers could benefit from studying Feuillet's systematization of movement, the primary advantage lay in its ability to render more permanent and widely available the work of those who composed dances. John Weaver, *Orchesography; or, the Art of Dancing, by Characters and Demostrative Figures. Wherein the Whole Art Is Explain'd; with Compleat Tables of All Steps Us'd in Dancing, and Rules for the Motions of the Arms, &C. Whereby Any Person (Who Understands Dancing) May of Himself Learn All Manner of Dances* (London: Printed by H. Meere at the Black Fryar in Black Fryar for the author and are to be sold by P. Valliant French bookseller near Catherine Street in the Strand, 1706). In his *An Essay Towards an History of Dancing* (1712), however, he amplifies on notation's benefits, arguing that it would substantially improve the status of dancing, lifting it up from a mere mechanical art to a fine art. Idem, *An Essay Towards an History of Dancing in Which the Whole Art*

and Its Various Excellencies Are in Some Measure Explain'd (London: Printed for Jacob Tonson, 1712), 171–72.

4 Quoted in Rebecca Harris-Warrick and Carol G. Marsh, *Musical Theatre at the Court of Louis Xiv: Le Mariage De La Grosse Cathos*, Cambridge Musical Texts and Monographs (Cambridge, England: Cambridge University Press, 1994), 84.

5 Edmund Fairfax rightfully admonishes scholars to take into account the small range of dance practices that were actually notated with Feuillet's system. See Edmund Fairfax, *The Styles of Eighteenth Century Ballet* (Lanham, Md.: Scarecrow Press, 2003).

6 Weaver, *Orchesography*, 2.

7 The characters on either side of the line frequently resemble the movements they indicate, pictographically designating the ankle, toes, and position and direction of the foot, or else metaphorically suggesting the body's actions, e.g. the sign for lowering the body into a bent knee position is lower than the base line. This iconicity between sign and movement carries over to the dance as a whole in the transparent and unmediated relationship between written and performed dance.

8 Fabritio Caroso, *Nobiltà Di Dame*, ed. with an introduction by Julia Sutton; music transcribed and ed. F. Marian Walker (Oxford: Oxford University Press, [1600] 1986), 162.

9 This is the approach also taken by John Playford, whose book of English country dances was the first collection of documented dances in Britain. See John Playford, *The English Dancing Master or, Plaine and Easie Rules for the Dancing of Country Dances, with the Tune to Each Dance*, ed. Hugh Mellor and Leslie Bridgewater (London: Dance Books, 1984 [1651]).

10 Thoinot Arbeau, *Orchesography*, trans. Mary Stewart Evans (New York: Dover Publications, 1967 [1589]), 15.

11 Ibid., 119.

12 Ibid., 121.

13 As Jean-Noel Laurenti explains: "Thus the notation of an apparently quite simple and very dynamic contretemps balonné . . . requires no less than eight indications: a step forward with the free leg, a sink, a spring, a foot in the air, a second sink and a spring on a half-position sign; the two groups of signs, corresponding to the two movements, are joined by a trait within the frame of the measure." Jean Noël Laurenti, "Feuillet's Thinking," in *Traces of the Dance*, ed. Laurence Louppe (Paris: Editions Dis Voir, 1994), 87.

14 Laurenti provides this example: "Thus the first movement of the contretemps balonné can be isolated and repeated, still on the same leg, while playing on the possible modifications in the course of the free leg: the latter, during the first spring, can beat behind, then in a second spring beat in front, or describe a half-circle in the air; one may also add a half turn to each of the springs." Laurenti, "Feuillet's Thinking," 91.

15 Arbeau's notation was organized along the same lines as John Bulwer's efforts to document all the positions of the arm, hand, and fingers during rhetorical delivery. Like Arbeau, Bulwer simply lists all the actions of the hand along with their corresponding meanings. See John Bulwer, *Chirologia: Or, the Natural Language of the Hand, and Chironomia: Or, the Art of Manual Rhetoric*, Landmarks in Rhetoric and Public Address (Carbondale: Southern Illinois University Press, [1654] 1974).

16 Although initially more interested in determining how plants gained their nutrition, whether from processes in the leaves or in the roots, the Royal Academy of Sciences came to be preoccupied with classification through the work of its member scientist Tournefort. One of the principal sources used by Linnaeus in conceptualizing his taxonomy, Tournefort identified twenty-two classes of plants, seventeen of which were herbs and five were trees, all based on the corolla (the whorl of leaves forming the inner envelope of) the flower. These included labiates, rosaceous, umbelliferous, lilac, papilionaceous. See Joseph Pitton de Tournefort, *Eléments De Botanique, Ou, Méthode Pour Connoître Les Plantes* (Paris: De l'Imprimerie royale, 1694).

17 Feuillet also differed from Tournefort's and Linnaeus's systems in one crucial respect: their taxonomies proposed classes of plants based on a key characteristic. This naming procedure was intended to assist with the collection and classification of the world's plants, whose fundamental conformity to one class or another might not be immediately apparent. Feuillet's system, in contrast, asserted risings and sinkings, etc. as the basic principles underlying all movements, but it then used these principles to notate and then proliferate standard types of steps already in circulation within French dance practice and pedagogy, including *coupés, chassées,* and so forth. Where debate arose as to whether and how to name seemingly new classes of plants in botany, no such controversy ever arose in dance, at least not in the eighteenth century. For more on Linnaeus's and other early botanists' attempts to establish taxonomic procedures of naming, see Londa L. Schiebinger, *Plants and Empire: Colonial Bioprospecting in the Atlantic World* (Cambridge, Mass.: Harvard University Press, 2004).

18 Lisbet Koerner argues that Linnaeus specifically chose Latin nomenclature, much as Feuillet used value-free iconographic symbols, to signify an extra-national context for his enterprise. See Lisbet Koerner, "Carl Linnaeus in His Time and Place," in *Cultures of Natural History*, ed. Nicholas Jardine, James A. Second, Emma Spary (Cambridge, England: Cambridge University Press, 1996), 147–52.

19 Laurenti, "Feillet's Thinking" 87.

20 Quoted in Richard Ralph, *The Life and Works of John Weaver: An Account of His Life, Writings and Theatrical Productions, with an Annotated Reprint of His Complete Publications* (New York: Dance Horizons, 1985), 34–35.

21 Linda Tomko notes that many of the dances were performed for the highest-ranking person in attendance who sat at the "top" of the room. Sometimes indicated in the notations as "The Presence," this person enjoyed the best view of the action. See Linda J. Tomko, "Mr. Isaac's *the Pastorall* and Issues Of "Party"," in *Dance, Spectacle, and the Body Politic, 1250–1750*, ed. Jennifer Nevile (Bloomington: Indiana University Press, 2008), 249.

22 Paul Carter, *The Road to Botany Bay: An Exploration of Landscape and History*, 1st American ed. (New York: Knopf: Distributed by Random House, 1988), 22.

23 Skiles Howard argues that earlier court dance forms had prepared for this by moving the body out and through space, and by emphasizing its awareness of coordinated spatial placements of all bodies. Skiles Howard,

The Politics of Courtly Dancing in Early Modern England (Amherst: University of Massachusetts Press, 1998), 112–15.

24 P. Siris, *The Art of Dancing, Demonstrated by Characters and Figures;...Done From the French of Monsieur Feuillet* (London: Printed for the author, 1706). John Essex, *For the Furthur Improvement of Dancing, a Treatis of Chorography ...Translated from the French of Monsr Feuillet* (London: Sold by I. Walsh and P. Randall, I. Hare, I. Culen, and by the author, 1710). E. Pemberton, *An Essay for the Further Improvement of Dancing* (London: Printed, and sold by J. Walsh, J. Hare, and at the author's, 1711).

25 Ralph, *Life and Works of John Weaver*, 101. Moira Goff believes over one hundred lived and worked in London between 1700 and 1735, and she derives this figure, in part, from the lists of subscribers to the various collections of notated dances published during this period. Moira Goff, "Dancing-Masters in Early Eighteenth-Century London," *Early Music* 26, no. 2 (May, 1998).

26 Engelhardt describes how Dancing Masters, usually middle-class men, used the expanding popularity of dance and the equation of high rank with graceful comportment to improve their own status. Molly Engelhardt, *Dancing out of Line: Ballrooms, Ballets, and Mobility in Victorian Fiction and Culture* (Athens, Ohio: Ohio University Press, 2009), 27–39.

27 As Jennifer Nevile has demonstrated in her analysis of fifteenth-century courtesy and dance literature, the distance among bodies was key to relative nobility. Jennifer Nevile, *The Eloquent Body: Dance and Humanist Culture in Fifteenth-Century Italy* (Bloomington: Indiana University Press, 2004).

28 Caroso, *Nobiltà Di Dame*, 164.

29 Citing the 1586 courtesy manual of Stefano Guazzo, Franko notes that social intercourse is dominated by the desire to conserve and increase one's means. As justification, Franko points to Guazzo's observation: "As a wise man was asked why nature has given us two ears and only one tongue he replied because we should hear more than we speak. That answer gave me reason to attribute income to the ears and expenditure to the tongue." Silence, and by extension, stillness, prompt the accumulation of income because they please others and dispose others favorably toward the listener. Franko argues that this drive to acquire financial gain is retroactively mitigated by the use of health metaphors, so that the materiality of the argument is attenuated by the drive for well-being. Again he quotes Guazzo, "Let us say that the solitary man is sick, as we have indicated, I propose that he engage in conversation for his health so that for a good period of time the income of the house is greater than the expenditure." Income is acquired through the practice of silent and sympathetic attention in which "one avoids a harsh expression in the eyes, twisting the body, a frowning seriousness, looking around." Yet, speaking can also be used to acquire wealth. Guazzo notes: "well-received words bring profit to the listener and honor to the speaker. And just as different sorts of money come out of a purse, some gold, some silver and some copper, so sentences issue from the mouth and other words of more or less value." See Mark Franko, *The Dancing Body in Renaissance Choreography (C. 1416–1589)* (Birmingham, Ala.: Summa Publications, 1986), 72–75.

Guazzo was translated into English in 1581. See Stefano Guazzo, *The Civile Conversation of M. Steffan Guazzo Written First in Italian . . .* trans. George Pettie (imprinted at London: By Richard Watkins, 1581).

30 Thomas Elyot, *The Book Named the Governor*, ed. S. E. Lehmberg, 2d ed. (New York: Dutton, 1962 [1531]), 76.

31 According to Franko, "movement performs the proof of goodness which both dissimulates the clandestine appeal to the emotions of the first proof and yields the 'profit' of power over others: glory," Franko, *Dancing Body*, 76–77.

32 Howard, *Politics of Courtly Dancing*, 17, 50–51.

33 Yet, unlike botanists, choreographers were not so interested in collecting the world's dances as in distributing the latest innovations to those who were removed from centers of fashion. According to Staffan Muller-Wille, plant collectors could come from all nations and backgrounds and embrace diverse opinions on political and even botanical issues, but they were all "disciplined" (my term) by the names given to plants. The names were like coins, immutable – the basic form and substance upon which exchange could occur; each species was like a different coin, whose fundamental composition could never be contested after it had been named. Only the botanist could determine if the plant was indeed new or not. He concludes: "By this simple mechanism, the realm of botanical 'goods' was fragmented into a coherent classification of mutually exclusive "spheres of exchange," encompassing universally reproducible, alienable (as duplicates), and thus universally exchangeable plants of a certain, distinguished kind." Staffan Müller-Wille, "Nature as Marketplace: The Political Economy of Linnaean Botany," in *Oeconomies in the Age of Newton*, ed. Margaret Schabas and Neil De Marchi (Durham, N.C.: Duke University Press, 2003), 161.

34 John Law, *Money and Trade Considered with a Proposal for Supplying the Nation with Money* (Edinburgh: Printed by the heirs and successors of Andrew Anderson, 1705), 97.

35 Soame Jenyns, *The Art of Dancing: A Poem in Three Cantos*, ed. Anne Cottis (London: Dance Books [1729] 1978), 31.

36 Quoted in Karen Ordahl Kupperman, *Indians and English: Facing Off in Early America* (Ithaca, N.Y.: Cornell University Press, 2000), 91.

37 Through an in-depth reading of a notated version of a specific dance by Mr. Isaac using Fuillet's system, Linda Tomko shows how the choreography in the name of the dance, its choice of vocabulary, and its floor path proferred a commentary on the politics shaping the last portion of Queen Anne's reign. See Tomko, "Mr. Isaac's *the Pastorall.*"

38 Anon., "No, 88," in *The Tatler*, ed. with an introduction and notes by Donald F. Bond (Oxford: Clarendon Press, [1709] 1987), 57.

39 *The Tatler*, Tuesday, November 1, 1709, 57.

40 Ibid., 58.

41 Paper money signifying public credit was seen, according J. G. A. Pocock, as a sign of both corruption and dependence. According to Pocock, the central concern in political thought from 1688–1776 revolved around whether a government founded in patronage, public debt and the professionalization of the armed forces was fundamentally corrupt. If one wanted to practice a virtuous life, one's personal autonomy was necessarily

based on ownership of property, and thus the function of property was to confer independence and autonomy. But this moral structure became outmoded at the beginning of the eighteenth century because it became possible to pay for substitutes (in the form of a professional army) to protect one's rights. And as antidote to this corrupting influence, the study of manners replaced conceptions of innate virtue. J. G. A. Pocock, *Virtue, Commerce, and History: Essays on Political Thought and History, Chiefly in the Eighteenth Century* (Cambridge: Cambridge University Press, 1985). The newly emerging credit system, named Lady Credit by DeFoe, Addison and others, signified a future that can only be sought passionately and inconstantly. As Pocock and also Laura Brown have shown, Lady Credit embodied fantasy, passion, and dynamic change, quite distinct from Renaissance conceptions of Fortuna, Occasione, or Fantasia. Laura Brown, *Fables of Modernity: Literature and Culture in the English Eighteenth Century* (Ithaca, N.Y.: Cornell University Press, 2001), 95–131.

42 Joseph Addison, Richard Steele and others, *The Spectator*, ed. with notes by Donald F. Bond (Oxford: Clarendon Press [1711–12] 1965), March 3, 1711, pp. 16–17.

43 Jean Georges Noverre, *Letters on Dancing and Ballets*, trans. Cyril W. Beaumont from the rev. edition published in St. Petersburg (Brooklyn, N.Y.: Dance Horizons [1803] 1966), 132–42.

44 For an overview of Weaver's place within general dance production during the period, see Jennifer Thorpe, "Dance in the London Theaters C. 1700–1750," in Nevile, *Dance, Spectacle*, 136–52.

45 John Weaver, *The Loves of Mars and Venus* (London: W. Mears, 1717), 20.

46 Ibid., 20–21.

47 Bulwer, *Chirologia*, 177.

48 See Joseph R. Roach, *The Player's Passion: Studies in the Science of Acting*, Theater-Theory/Text/Performance (Ann Arbor: University of Michigan Press, 1993).

49 Sandra Noll Hammond, "International Elements of Dance Training in the Late Eigtheenth Century," in *The Grotesque Dancer on the Eighteenth-Century Stage*, ed. Rebecca Harris-Warrick and Bruce Alan Brown (Madison, Wis.: University of Wisconsin Press, 2005), 109–50.

50 Noverre, *Letters on Dancing and Ballets*, 12, 56, 36, and 38, respectively.

51 Carlo Blasis, *The Code of Terpsichore: A Practical and Historical Treatise, on the Ballet, Dancing, and Pantomime: With a Complete Theory of the Art of Dancing: Intended as Well for the Instruction of Amateurs as the Use of Professional Persons*, trans. R. Barton (London: James Bulcock, 1828), 64.

52 "Enchainements in dancing are very numerous. Every good dancer has his peculiar mode of combining his periods, steps, etc. Form, therefore, a style of your own, as originality is the chief means to procure yourself distinction. By copying others you may, perhaps, sometimes excel; but the absence of novelty will, unquestionably, deprive you of attraction." Ibid., 53.

53 Ten years later, Arthur St. Léon aspired to construct from this explication of bodily positionings a new kind of notation system which he published as *Sténochorégraphie* (1852) Capable of documenting only a short solo, the system placed in sequence geometric figures representing the positions

in the dance, using lines similar to those in Blasis's drawings. Reading the figures horizontally across the page, they almost make visible the motions of a dancer who, for example, lifts the leg and circles it from side to back. See Arthur Saint-Léon and Flavia Pappacena, *La Sténochorégraphie 1852*, Facsimile reprint ed. (Lucca: Libreria Musicale Italiana, 2006). For additional perspectives on Blasis's drawings and their significance in terms of suggesting a new mechanics of grace, see Gabriele Brandstetter, "The Code of Terpsichore: The Dance Theory of Carlo Blasis, Mechanics as the Matrix of Grace," *Topoi* 24 (2005): 67–79.

54　Blasis, *Code of Terpsichore*, 18–33.

55　For a lucid analysis of Hegel's and other nineteenth century aesthetician's attitudes towards dance, see Francis Edward Sparshott, *Off the Ground: First Steps to a Philosophical Consideration of the Dance* (Princeton, N.J.: Princeton University Press, 1988).

56　For example, Theophile Gautier rarely uses the term at all, but when he does it references multiple functions. Writing in 1858, he refers to "Taglioni, Elssler, Cerrito, and Carlotta Grisi, not to mention their own ballerinas, [as] a young choreographic army graduate from their ballet school, one of the best run in the world, agile, supple, marvelously disciplined, and with talents already fully formed that lack only stage experience, which will come with time." Théophile Gautier, "Gautier on Dance," in *Théophile Gautier*, trans. and ed. Ivor Forbes Guest (London: Dance Books, 1986), 293. In the same review, he describes Mme. Petipa as "delicate, pretty, light, and worthy to be admitted to that family of distinguished choreographers." Ibid. Both these uses of the term "choreography" seem to emphasize the ability to dance more than prowess at making dances. Yet, earlier in the same year he states, "the author of a ballet scenario is almost a stranger to his work, the credit belonging entirely to the choreographer, the composer and the designer." Ibid., 281. Gautier also frequently refers to the act of composing dance as "writing for the legs." Ivor Guest notes that a short-lived ballet school was established at Her Majesty's Theater, one of whose teachers, Emile Petit, was called "Master of the English School of Choreography" in 1858. Guest also notes that the term "choreography" enjoyed a broader usage, one that principally concerned the organization and teaching of dance classes. Ivor Guest, *Ballet in Leicester Square: The Alhambra and the Empire, 1860–1915* (London: Dance Books, 1992), 3.

In 1878 the anonymous reviewer for the *New York Times* uses the term ambiguously to refer either to the teaching of dance or the ability to compose dances when he describes the French as "a nation of dancing-masters, but whatever their capacities for instruction in choreography, they are fearful and wonderful as performers." "A Dull Season in Paris," *New York Times*, March 17, 1878, 6. Four years later, a reviewer uses the term to refer to the teaching of dancing: "M. Perrin is a Professor of choreography, who, aided and supplemented by his son Charles, makes something like 100,000f. annually by teaching young people how to trip properly he light fantastic." "Scenes from Paris Life," *New York Times*, March 7, 1882, 7. Another review from 1882 uses choreography to ambiguously in describing the performance as one that provides viewers "an opportunity of judging for themselves that symphonic music is not adapted to choreography." "Gay Parisian Topics," *New York Times*, April 2, 1882, 3. And still another review from the same year refers to the dancers as "choreographists." "A Play to Run Six Months," *New York Times* 1882, October 30, 5. And in 1914, Troy Kinney is described as a "student of choreography", explaining that "choreography, or the art of dancing" is enjoying a renaissance with the "modern dance craze." "Modern Dances Held to Mean a Modern Renaissance," *New York Times*, May 3, 1914, SM5.

In *The Times* of London the term "choreography" similarly references all aspects of dancing, such as in the report of a lawsuit brought by two young pupils who had been instructed "in the higher branches of the choreographic art," which entailed learning to dance and also learning to perform on stage and on tour. "High Court of Justice," *The Times*, August 6, 1890, 2. Choreography also references dance in relation to the other arts, as when the reviewer of a production for the King of Siam praised the "choreographic ability of Mme. Maury" alongside the voices of Mme. Heglou and Mme. Delmas. "The King of Siam," *The Times*, September 17, 1897, 19.

57 Martha Graham, *Blood Memory*, 1st ed. (New York: Doubleday, 1991), 236.

58 A large number of reviews in *the Times* of London implemented choreography in order to discuss the new approach to ballet demonstrated in the Ballets Russes productions presented there beginning in 1911. One reviewer praised the Russians for having developed technique to the "highest point" such that they had also been able to develop the "art for which that technique exists, namely, the conveyance of choreographic ideas." "The Russian Ballet," *The Times*, June 24, 1911, 6. In another review comparing *Le Sacre du Printemps* with *L'Après-midi d'un Faune* and *Jeux*, the critic noted the difference between these works' use of music and earlier ballets, such as *Les Sylphides*, whose "choreography [was] fitted to music originally written for another purpose." "The Fusion of Music and Dancing," *The Times*, July 26, 1913, 11. Similarly, when the Ballets Russes toured to the US in 1913, it precipitated a new use of the term. In 1913, Nijinsky is identified as responsible for the choreography of *Sacre du Printemps*. "New Ballet Puzzles," *New York Times*, July 12, 1913, 4. Choreography as the art of creating a dance continues to gain momentum in the press, with its use extending to other theaters, such as the music halls, producing other kinds of dance entertainments.

59 F. B. Moore, "Glorified Ballet Art," *New York Times*, December 24, 1916, III1.

60 Such as *The Jeweled Tree*, premiering in 1926 begin to include mention of the choreographer, in this case, Chester Hale (Display Ad 112, X3).

61 Choreographer's dances were seen as original. However, as much as artists endeavored to secure patents for their work, they only succeeded in 1946, ironically through the process of notating a dance and registering that notation as a kind of publication. In this way, the eighteenth century version of the term returned to assist in authenticating originality. See Anthea Kraut, "Race-Ing Choreographic Copyright," in *Worlding Dance*, ed. Susan Leigh Foster (London: Palgrave Macmillan, 2009) , 76–97.

62 John Joseph Martin, *The Modern Dance* (New York: A. S. Barnes, 1933), 79.

63 Ibid., 81.

64 Ibid., 84.

65 After several years of diligently expanding the physical education curriculum into dance, H'Doubler saw her program awarded the first BA in Dance within Physical Education in the US in 1926 using the creative process of dancing and dance-making as rationale for including dance in the university curriculum. For an analysis of H'Doubler's life and work, see Janice Ross, *Moving Lessons: Margaret H'doubler and the Beginning of Dance in American Education* (Madison, Wis.: University of Wisconsin Press, 2000).

66 Margaret Newell H'Doubler, *The Dance and Its Place in Education* (New York: Harcourt, Brace and Company, 1925), 11.

67 Margaret Newell H'Doubler, *Rhythmic Form and Analysis* (Madison, Wis.: J. M. Rider, 1932), 1.

68 H'Doubler, *Dance and Its Place*, 172.

69 Students could enroll in a General Workshop that included courses in dance composition, music analysis, history and criticism, and stagecraft. Bennington also offered a Workshop Program that consisted of a Technique course taught by Martha Graham and a Choreography course in which she created and rehearsed a new work. For the next several years, the workshop program was directed by different artists, Doris Humphrey and Charles Weidman in 1936, and Hanya Holm in 1937. In 1936 Charles Weidman led a Men's Workshop where he developed *Quest*, and Doris Humphrey presided over a Women's Workshop where she created *With My Red Fires*. And in 1937 Hanya Holm, a student of Mary Wigman's, developed *Trend*.

70 This division of the artistic process into technique, composition, and repertoire – a course in which a faculty member developed a new work – formed the basis of a majority of dance curricula across the US in subsequent decades. Janet Soares argues that the need on the part of dance educators attending Bennington for material to teach in their home programs of dance prompted the accelerated formation of the techniques of Graham, Humphrey-Weidman, and Holm. See Janet Mansfield Soares, *Martha Hill and the Making of American Dance* (Middletown, Conn.: Wesleyan University Press, 2009), 57.

71 The complicated and contradictory notions of technique that proliferated during this period are beyond the scope of this study. For John Martin, technique encompassed mastery of the form of dance composition, as well as mastery of the body as the artist's instrument. See Martin, *Modern Dance*, 62–88. Technique might resemble the vocabulary of the choreographer's dances, while nonetheless standing as a training program distinct from an actual dance. Graham technique, for example, emerged only slowly over time from being the preparatory exercises for a specific dance to a standardized regimen of discreet exercises. In Germany, "technique" class remained focused on movement principles, an approach passed on through Holm to Nikolais, who focused his classes on improvisational assignments. See Alice J. Halpern, *The Technique of Martha Graham* (Pennington, N.J.: Society of Dance History Scholars at Princeton Periodicals, 1991).

72 Janet Soares notes that the project of teaching composition was entirely new and had only been recently developed by Graham and Louis Horst

who taught his first course in the subject at the New York City Neighborhood Playhouse in 1929. See Soares, *Martha Hill*, 54.

73 In addition to "Earth Primitive," Horst identified "Air Primitive," "Archaic," "Medieval," Introspection," "Jazz," Americana," and Impressionism" as styles informing the Modern.

74 Louis Horst and Carroll Russell, *Modern Dance Forms in Relation to the Other Modern Arts* (Brooklyn, N.Y.: Dance Horizons, 1977), 61.

75 Ibid., 63.

76 Ibid., 111.

77 Ibid. 126.

78 This program was co-directed by Hill and Horst. See Sali Ann Kriegsman, *Modern Dance in America – the Bennington Years* (Boston, Mass.: G. K. Hall, 1981), 236–37.

79 The intensive personal investment in each dance was reconfirmed when the choreographer performed in the dance, most often in the leading role. Dancing Masters of the eighteenth and nineteenth centuries might put in an appearance as a soloist, or even in some cases the leading man, yet the plot of the ballet did not issue from their personal experiences, nor did it aspire to fuse the personal with the universal. Only with Fokine's and Nijinsky's radical new scenarios did ballet begin to approach the testimonial fervency of modern dance. The fact that the originator of movement and story issued from the person onstage performing them certified the sincerity and authenticity of the dance's message.

80 Doris Humphrey, *The Art of Making Dances* (New York: Rinehart, 1959), 18.

81 Susan Manning, *Modern Dance, Negro Dance: Race in Motion* (Minneapolis: University of Minnesota Press, 2004), 115–78. See also Gay Morris, *A Game for Dancers: Performing Modernism in the Postwar Years, 1945–1960* (Middletown, Conn.: Wesleyan University Press, 2006).

82 Morris, *Game for Dancers*, 114–46.

83 See Dee Reynolds discussion of Martha Graham's affinity with southwestern culture and the borrowings from the Penitente sect of New Mexico that she implemented in *Primitive Mysteries*. Dee Reynolds, *Rhythmic Subjects* (Alton, England: Dance Books, 2007), 110–36.

84 Russell Meriwether Hughes, *Total Education in Ethnic Dance* (New York: M. Dekker, 1977), 1–2. A somewhat different definition of "ethnic dance" was proposed in the encyclopedia of physical education, amassed from an extensive set of sources in the 1970s that suggests La Meri's influence: "[ethnic dance consists of] the indigenous dance arts of a race which have come to be recognized as the classical theater form of the art." In this categorization, ethnic dance differs from folk dance because it is staged and also because folk dance "is designed for participation by members of the community. However, when folk dance is choreographically transposed for theater presentation, it may be conceived to be ethnic dance." The author cites as examples Japanese Noh, Kabuki, and Hawaiian Meles. M. Frances Dougherty, "'Theater Forms,'" in *Encyclopedia of Physical Education, Fitness, and Sports*, ed. Rueben B. Frost (Reading Mass: Addison-Wesley Publishing, 1977), 697.

85 Her presentations obfuscated any indigenous attributions of artistic contributions that might have been made over the years' by various

masters of the forms. They also eliminated any opportunities for improvisation, especially in the exchange between dancer and musician, by transcribing and notating all the distinctive musical forms for a soloist or small group that accompanied her dancing.

86 Curt Sachs, *World History of the Dance*, trans. Bessie Schönberg (New York: W. W. Norton, 1937), 3.

87 Russell Meriwether Hughes, *Dance Composition, the Basic Elements* (Lee, Mass.: Jacob's Pillow Dance Festival, 1965). Although she distinguished between ethnic, ballet, and modern forms, La Meri did not intend to exclude the world's dances from the domain of choreographic practice. Her 1965 publication, *Dance Composition*, was intended for students versed in any form of dance. Blending together François Delsarte's analysis of the meanings inherent in areas of the body and types of motion, the dramatic analysis of narrative, and a semiotics of the stage space, La Meri put forward the universalism of the modernist aesthetic: a dance should be about the eternal elements of the human condition; the principles of movement – its dynamics, design, and development – were universally recognizable. As illustration, she included discussion of various forms, "Chinese," "Japanese," "Javanese," "Bharata Natyam," or "Flamenco," that exemplified most vividly these principles. Many Flamenco dances as well as Kathak and Barata Natyam items, for example, embodied an ascending peak form of dramatic design in which the dancer attained climaxes of increasing intensity over the course of the dance. Alternatively, the ability to present contrasting dynamics within a single body was achieved in "flamenco, with its slow-moving sensuous arms set above the staccato jab of heels," 65. Other examples included the steady, slow-motion dynamics of the Javanese dance, where "the wrist suddenly moved with staccato force to send the scarf ballooning in a soft curve," or Burmese dance, where the smooth curves of the arms and upper torso contrasted the bright, rhythmic bounce in the knees," 65.

88 Ibid.,142.

89 Ibid.

90 Ibid.

91 Ibid.,143.

92 Nagrin began using "Directed by" when the Workgroup premiered in 1972. See Christena L. Schlundt, *Daniel Nagrin: A Chronicle of His Professional Career* (Berkeley: University of California Press, 1997).

93 Stephanie Jordan, *Striding Out: Aspects of Contemporary and New Dance in Britain* (London: Dance Books, 1992), 13–34.

94 For example, *Terrain*, 1963, was listed as choreographed by Yvonne Rainer, with lighting by Rauschenberg, whereas *The Mind is a Muscle*, 1968, was listed as by Yvonne Rainer as was *Continuous Project – Altered Daily*, 1970, by Yvonne Rainer.

95 Sally Banes, *Democracy's Body: Judson Dance Theater, 1962–1964* (Ann Arbor, Mich.: UMI Research Press, 1983), 8.

96 Ibid., 11.

97 Judith Dunn, quoted in Banes, *Democracy's Body*, 16.

98 Yutian Wong, *Choreographing Asian America* (Middletown, Conn.: Wesleyan University Press, 2010), 110–36.

99 Shobana Jeyasingh, "Getting Off the Orient Express," *Dance Theatre Journal* 8, no. 2 (1990).

100 David Gere and Dance Critics Association (US), *Looking Out: Perspectives on Dance and Criticism in a Multicultural World* (New York Schirmer Books, 1995).

101 Here I make reference to David Gordon's company, which, perhaps in commenting on this shift, he named "The Pick Up Company."

102 Humphrey, *Art of Making Dances*, 132.

103 American Dance Festival course offerings brochure, summer 1991, p. 3.

104 By 1996 ADF had sent teachers to Zaire, Venezuela, South Africa, Russia, Argentina, India, Ghana, Czechoslovakia, Korea, Ecuador, Uruguay, Estonia, Poland, Indonesia, Paraguay, the Philippines, Mozambique, Chile, Romania, Brazil, Lithuania, Panama, and Latvia. "Linkages" is the ADF term for the network of relationships with programs worldwide that it developed and sponsored. For a full list of exchanges cultivated through linkages with these countries, see the ADF website.

2 Kinesthesia

1 Quoted in E. G. Jones, "The Development of the 'Muscular Sense' Concept During the Nineteenth Century and the Work of H. Charlton Bastian," *Journal of the History of Medicine and Allied Sciences* 27, no. 3 (July 1972): 72.

2 See Edward G. Boring, *Sensation and Perception in the History of Experimental Psychology* (New York: D. Appleton-Century, 1942).

3 See Jones, "Development," for an excellent overview of Bastian's work.

4 James Jerome Gibson, *The Senses Considered as Perceptual Systems* (Boston: Houghton Mifflin, 1966). Titchener's *A Text-Book of Psychology* (New York: Macmillan, 1909) had included the vestibular as part of what contributed to the kinesthetic, but Gibson's new theorization of kinesthesia placed far greater emphasis on the integrative capacity of kinesthetic information to draw from a variety of sensory sources.

5 See Londa Scheibinger, "Skeletons in the Closet: The First Illustrations of the Female Skeleton in Eighteenth Century Anatomy," *Representations* 14 (1986). See also Thomas Walter Laqueur, *Making Sex: Body and Gender from the Greeks to Freud* (Cambridge, Mass.: Harvard University Press, 1992).

6 Denis E. Cosgrove, *Geography and Vision: Seeing, Imagining and Representing the World* (London: Palgrave Macmillan, 2008), 93.

7 John Essex, *For the Furthur Improvement of Dancing, a Treatis of Chorography* . . . Translated from the French of Monsr Feuillet. London: sold by I. Walsh and P. Randall, I. Hare, I. Culen, and by ye author, 1710, preface.

8 For a more detailed history of changes in cartographic technology that accompanied changes in British politics, see Robert J. Mayhew, *Enlightenment Geography: The Political Languages of British Geography, 1650–1850* (New York: St. Martin's Press, 2000). For an examination of cartography's participation in Spanish colonization and in the formation of the civil subject, see John M. Headley, "Geography and Empire in the Late Renaissance: Botero's Assignment, Western Universalism, and the

232 Choreographing empathy: kinesthesia in performance

Civilizing Process," *Renaissance Quarterly* 53, no. 4 (2000). And for an overview of cartography's relationship to the administration of government, see David Buisseret, ed., *Monarchs, Ministers, and Maps: The Emergence of Cartography as a Tool of Government in Early Modern Europe* (Chicago: University of Chicago Press, 1992).'

9 See Kenneth Olwig, *Landscape, Nature, and the Body Politic: From Britain's Renaissance to America's New World* (Madison, Wis.: University of Wisconsin Press, 2002), 117–18.

10 *The Compleat Geographer or, the Chorography and Topography of All the Known Parts of the Earth. To Which Is Premis'd an Introduction to Geography, and a Natural History of the Earth and the Elements. . . . To Which Are Added Maps of Every Country. Wherein the descriptions of Asia, Africa and America are compos'd anew*, third edition (London: Awnsham and John Churchill; and Timothy Childe, 1709), 25.

11 For an extended analysis of the ichnographic point of view, see Jonathan Crary, *Techniques of the Observer: On Vision and Modernity in the Nineteenth Century* (Cambridge, Mass.: MIT Press, 1990).

12 Kenneth Olwig argues that the early landscape paintings implemented the same ichnographic perspective as the chorographies. He writes: "These paintings, particularly those of Joachim Patiner, often placed the viewer in a position high above the land, like a map reader, thus making it possible for the painting to encompass whole districts . . . Since the Greek root *choros* in chorography means 'land' (in the sense of country), and since these (choro)graphic depictions were representations of lands, or landscapes, it was natural for such paintings to be termed 'landscape' pictures in the Germanic languages . . . Though these cosmographies may have been intended to mirror the provinces of a Rome-inspired universal empire, they inadvertently also helped stimulate a countervailing local awareness of the historical particularity of the provinces' place identity as countries." Olwig, *Landscape, Nature*, 36.

13 *Compleat Geographer*, 242.

14 By the 1709 version of *The Compleat Geographer*, the boundaries of the various counties throughout the British Isles were familiar and no geometric coordinates were given. For all the other regions and countries of the world, however, the four-part prescription of boundaries, climate and soil, government, and customs was standard. Ibid.

15 Olwig, *Landscape, Nature*.

16 For extensive analysis of the theory of the humours, see Owsei Temkin, *Galenism: Rise and Decline of a Medical Philosophy*, Cornell Publications in the History of Science (Ithaca, N.Y.: Cornell University Press, 1973). See also Michael Carl Schoenfeldt, *Bodies and Selves in Early Modern England: Physiology and Inwardness in Spenser, Shakespeare, Herbert, and Milton*, Cambridge Studies in Renaissance Literature and Culture (Cambridge, England: Cambridge University Press, 1999).

17 Specifically, hot, dry, cold, and wet; fire, air, earth, water; and infancy, youth, adulthood, and old age. For more on Galenic theories of corporeality, see Roy Porter, *Flesh in the Age of Reason* (London: Allen Lane, 2003).

18 Travel was seen as an "initiatic experience of the world, which enabled one to collect, so to speak, the characteristic qualities of different peoples. To this medical theory of the humours, was added a theory of climates,

whereby the conviction that specific values were inherent to specific regions of the world was reinforced. The traveler gathered as he passed through, intent on completing the circle of all the virtues." Normand Doiron and Gillian Lane-Mercier, "Travel Essays," in *Literature of Travel and Exploration, an Encyclopedia*, ed. Jennifer Speake (New York: Taylor and Francis, 2003), 1193.

19 Andrew Wear, "Explorations in Renaissance Writings on the Practice of Medicine," in *The Medical Renaissance of the Sixteenth Century*, ed. A. Wear, R .K. French and I. M. Lonie (Cambridge, England: Cambridge University Press, 1985), 118–45.

20 Wear notes a large number of divergent explanations for dizziness and vertigo including the following: "Vapours from bile or phlegm originating in the stomach or in the womb, could rise up and affect the animal spirits within the brain." Alternatively, dizziness would arise "in bibulous men and in those who frequently cleansed their heads in the sun. According to Gariopontus when the head was heated its veins opened up and haemorrhoids in it would be inflated." "Avicenna thought that the vapours in the brain were given a sort of momentum so that they continued moving in the brain even after the motion had stopped." However, "for Arnaldus De Villanova, vertigo was a revolution of the spirit in front of the eyes or an enveloping of the brain whereby the spirit of vision was impeded . . . Smoke was formed from material in the stomach and coming up to the optic nerve it closed it up. This blockage in the optic nerve produced a change in the essence of the animal spirits and the interactions of smoky vapor and the animal spirits produced a circular motion in the optic nerve just as when two winds of equal force create a whirlwind." Additionally, "for Leonhard Fuchs, the primary affliction of the brain came by sympathy producing vaporous exhalations which drove the animal spirits round." Ibid., 129–34.

21 For much more on the microscope and its relationship to theories of acting, see Joseph Roach, "The Artificial Eye: Augustan Theater and the Empire of the Visible," in *The Performance of Power: Theatrical Discourse and Politics*, ed. Sue-Ellen Case and Janelle Reinelt (Iowa City: University of Iowa, 1991), 131–45.

22 In 1628 William Harvey announced his discovery that blood did not ebb and flow around the body, but instead, was contained within a single system, with the heart as a pump that circulated it. Marcello Malpighi in 1661 and subsequently Antonie Van Leeuwenhoek from 1674 to 1683 worked with a microscope to identify capillaries and corpuscles respectively.

23 Marian Fournier notes this explanation by Hooke of his method: "As in Geometry, wrote Hooke, the most natural way of beginning is from a Mathematical *point*; so is the same method in observation and *Natural history* the most genuine, simple, and instructive." Accordingly the first observation is that of a point (of a needle), the second of a line (the edge of a razor), which is followed by several planes (pieces of woven material) and spatial objects (particles of sand and minerals), and finally by a series of vegetable and animal objects." Marian Fournier, *The Fabric of Life: Microscopy in the Seventeenth Century* (Baltimore: Johns Hopkins University Press, 1996), 34.

24 Ibid., 54.

25 Ibid., 34.

26 Porter, *Flesh*, 51. Arguing that new anatomy resulted in new metaphors and new conceptions of the self, Porter continues: "As the fluids (humours) declined in prominence by contrast to the solids (organs), the guts, belly and bowels (those humoural containers) lost their ancient importance as referents for one's self and its feelings, to be replaced in polite thinking by the head, the brain, and the nervous system." Ibid., 60.

27 See Fournier, *Fabric of Life*.

28 See Jonathan Sawday, *The Body Emblazoned: Dissection and the Human Body in Renaissance Culture* (London: Routledge, 1995). Sawday further hints at the connection between the anatomy theaters and the colonization of America and Africa, arguing that similar principles of investigation are operating in both arenas.

29 Étienne Bonnot de Condillac, *Condillac's Treatise on the Sensations*, trans. Margaret Geraldine Spooner Carr (London: Favil Press, [1754] 1930), 75.

30 Ibid.

31 Condillac explains that only in this way can cognition develop and can the statue become aware "that it *has* a body which moves." Ibid. 78, emphasis added

32 Condillac explains: "The self of a child, concentrated in its soul, would never be able to regard the different parts of its body as so many parts of itself. Nature would appear to have only one means of making the child know its body, and this is to make it perceive its sensations, not as modifications of its soul, but as modifications of the organs which are their occasional causes. Therefore the self in place of being concentrated in the soul must become extended, must be spread out and repeated in some way in all the parts of its body." Ibid., 82–83.

33 Derrida comments on this particular form of knowledge production in his analysis of Condillac. See Jacques Derrida, *The Archeology of the Frivolous: Reading Condillac* (Pittsburgh: Duquesne University Press, 1980). See also Isabel Knight, *The Geometric Spirit: The Abbé De Condillac and the French Enlightenment* (New Haven: Yale University Press, 1968).

34 Thomas Chase, "An Account of What Happened to Mr. Thomas Chase, at Lisbon, in the Great Earthquake: Written by Himself, in a Letter to His Mother, Dated the 31st of December," in *The Lisbon Earthquake of 1755: Some British Eye-Witness Accounts*, ed. Judite Nozes (Lisbon: British Historical Society of Portugal, 1987), 34.

35 Ibid., 41–42.

36 Ibid., 44.

37 For additional accounts of the Lisbon quake, see Nozes, *Lisbon Earthquake of 1755*. Rose Macaulay, *They Went to Portugal* (London: Jonathan Cape, 1946). l'Abbé de Magalhaens, *Lettre Écrite Aux Auteurs Du Journal Étranger Du Moi D'avril* (n.p., 1760).

38 Quoted in Robert F. Marx, *Pirate Port: The Story of the Sunken City of Port Royal* (Cleveland: World Publishing, 1967), 14. Marx provides no publishing details for the original text. The same text is summarized in Shower, who claims that it was originally published in the *Gazette* of Thursday, August 18, 1693. John Shower, *Practical Reflections on the*

Earthquakes That Have Happened in Europe and America, but Chiefly in the Islands of Jamaica, England, Sicily, Malta, &C. With a Particular and Historical Account of Them, and Divers Other Earthquakes (London: Printed and sold at the following pamphlet shops, Cook, James, and Kingman; Cooper; Robinson, 1750). For additional accounts of the Port Royal quake, see *An Account of the Late Terrible Earthquake in Sicily; with Most of Its Particulars* (London: Printed for Richard Baldwin, 1693); and Thomas Doolittle, *Earthquakes Explained and Practically Improved* (London: John Salusbury, 1693).

39 The exact description by an anonymous minister is as follows: "it threw down most of the Houses, Churches, Sugar and Indigo Works, Mills and Bridges, throughout the Whole Island, that it tore the Rocks and Mountains (others tell us that it leveled some Mountains, and reduced them to Plains) that it destroyed some whole Plantations and threw them into the sea." Shower, *Practical Reflections*, 2.

40 Although more focused on the body of a single witness, this description by a British Merchant likewise emphasizes the actions of buildings and earth and sea, more than those of other humans: "Betwixt eleven and twelve at noon, I being at a tavern, we felt the house shake and saw the bricks begin to rise in the floor, and at the same instant heard one in the street cry, 'An earthquake!' Immediately we ran out of the house, where we saw all people with lifted up hands begging God's assistance. We continued running up the street whilst on either side of us we saw the houses, some swallowed up, others thrown on heaps; the sand in the streets rise like the waves of the sea, lifting up all persons that stood upon it and immediately dropping into pits; and at the same instant a flood of water breaking in and rolling those poor souls over and over; some catching hold of beams and rafters of houses, others were found in the sand that appeared when the water was drained away, with their legs and arms out. The small piece of ground whereon sixteen or eighteen of us stood (praised be to God) did not sink. Marx, *Pirate Port*, 16.

41 In one of many treatises appearing at the end of the seventeenth century that shunned interpretations based solely on divine cause, Thomas Doolittle proposes that quakes conform to one of the following categories: "inclining – when the earth is caused to incline one way; lifting up – when the earth lifts straight up and back down; earthquakes that cause chasms, chinks, or openings in the earth; earthquakes that by force break their way out of the earths bowels; earthquakes which by one motion, inforcing or thrusting, overthrow, overturn whatsoever they come upon, or rush against; earthquakes that make the earth incline one way and then another; and those that come with a great noise, roaring, and bellowing." Doolittle, *Earthquakes Explained*, 58–59.

42 French Minister J. D. R., *The Earth Twice Shaken Wonderfully*, trans. Edward Locke (London: Sion's College, 1693/4), 3.

43 For more on the conceptions of space that these maps helped to construct, see Jonathan Crary, *Techniques of the Observer: On Vision and Modernity in the Nineteenth Century* (Cambridge, Mass.: MIT Press, 1990).

44 Denis E. Cosgrove, *Apollo's Eye: A Cartographic Genealogy of the Earth in the Western Imagination* (Baltimore: Johns Hopkins University Press, 2001).

45 John Goss, *The Mapmaker's Art: A History of Cartography* (London: Studio Editions, 1993).
46 Cosgrove explains that chorographic maps "disconnected the mapped from its coordinate geographical position and emphasized its qualitative characteristics of *locus*." Cosgrove, *Apollo's Eye*, 93; *Geography and Vision*. Examining the representation of foreign peoples on sixteenth- and seventeenth-century maps, Valerie Traub argues that the decorative framing performed by the bodies situated along the "geometrically proportioned graticule . . . offers them for comparative viewing and potential categorization." See Valerie Traub, "Mapping the Global Body," in *Early Modern Visual Culture*, ed. Peter Erickson and Clark Hulse (Philadelphia: University of Pennsylvania Press, 2000), 57.
47 Cosgrove, *Apollo's Eye*, 104–5.
48 Ibid.
49 Matthew Edney argues that the graticule's projection of the earth onto the two-dimensional page is the cartographic equivalent of the table in an herbarium on which plants can be arranged and rearranged in conceptual knowledge spaces. In each case the perambulations of the collector/observer are replaced by the static and enduring perspective afforded by absolute principles. See Matthew H. Edney, *Mapping an Empire: The Geographical Construction of British India, 1765–1843* (Delhi: Oxford University Press, 1999). Edney describes the mapmaker's body in these terms: "The geographer looks outwards; he might incidentally insert his presence into his text, but he constituted himself through his rhetoric as an autonomous observing machine. Mechanistic vision and the archive's spatial framework together established a clear-cut relationship between the geographer and the land: the geographer stands in a privileged position outside of the landscape, looking in. . . . He divorces himself from the landscape. He moves through the landscape but he is never part of it." Ibid, 74. See also Matthew H. Edney, "Bringing India to Hand," in *The Global Eighteenth Century*, ed. Felicity A. Nussbaum (Baltimore: Johns Hopkins University Press, 2003), 65–78.
50 Andrew Wear discusses sixteenth and seventeenth century conceptions of the relationship of health to living conditions in Wear, "Explorations in Renaissance Writings."
51 Thomas Elyot, *The Book Named the Governor*, ed. S. E. Lehmberg (New York: Dutton, 1962 [1531]), 59.
52 As Georges Vigarello observes: "during the sixteenth century the body is represented as a massive whole of 'flesh' and 'bone' whose firmness and hardness are enhanced by exercise, rather than as an interplay of levers operated by muscles. . . . Exercise acts through a global process of purification of humours and strengthening by drying, where the more precise and directed dynamics of the muscles do not appear to be central." Georges Vigarello, "The Upward Training of the Body from the Age of Chivalry to Courtly Civility," in *Fragments for a History of the Human Body, Part Two*, ed. Michel Feher Jonathan Crary, Hal Foster, Sanford Kwinter (Cambridge, Mass.: MIT Press, 1989), 167.
53 Richard Mulcaster, *Positions Concerning the Training up of Children*, ed. William Barker (Toronto, Ont.: University of Toronto Press, [1581] 1994), 63.

54 Ibid., 59.

55 Ibid.

56 Reinforcing this theory of exercise's benefits to the humours, Menestrier argued that dancing is useful in moderating four dangerous passions: fear, melancholia, rage and joy. See Claude-François Menestrier, *Des Ballets Anciens Et Modernes Selon Les Regles Du Theatre* (Paris: Chez R. Guignard, 1682).

57 Mulcaster, *Positions*.

58 Ibid.

59 Andrew Wear, "Making Sense of Health and the Environment in Early Modern England," in *Medicine in Society: Historical Essays*, ed. Andrew Wear (Cambridge, England: Cambridge University Press, 1992), 119–48.

60 John Locke, *The Educational Writings of John Locke. A Critical Edition with Introduction and Notes by James Axtell* (Cambridge, England: University Press, 1968), 239.

61 Ibid., 246.

62 Ibid., 310.

63 About this shift Vigarello writes: "Previously it [uprightness] had been based on a mystique of proportion, an ethics of propriety and the threat of a physical evil (a lump). But now, the body was no longer seen as a microcosm, a simple reduplicating of the universe, playing out through its resemblance to the whole set of its relations. Uprightness and physical posture no longer had to reflect figures and proportions given elsewhere . . . [Now] one must exhibit proper deportment in order to put on a good front and to avoid ridicule." Vigarello, "The Upward Training of the Body from the Age of Chivalry to Courtly Civility," 183.

64 Ibid., 178.

65 See, for example, Kristina Straub's discussion of the eighteenth century as the century of spectacle in Kristina Straub, *Sexual Suspects, Eighteenth-Century Players and Sexual Ideology* (Princeton, N.J.: Princeton University Press, 1992), 3–23.

66 Vigarello, "Upward Training," 155–68.

67 Andry's *L'Orthopédi* was translated from the French in 1743. According to Leonard Peltier, *L'Orthopédie* derived from the Greek, meaning "straight child." He notes that the frontispiece to the book *haec est regula recti* means "this is the rule for straightness." Leonard F. Peltier, *Orthopedics: A History and Iconography*, Norman Orthopedic Series, no. 3 (San Francisco: Norman Publishing, 1993).

68 Nicolas Andry de Bois-Regard, *Orthopædia or, the Art of Correcting and Preventing Deformities in Children: . . . To Which Is Added, a Defence of the Orthopædia, by Way of Supplement, by the Author. Translated from the French of M. Andry, . . . In Two Volumes. Illustrated with Cuts* (London: Printed for A. Millar, 1743), 75.

69 The corset had emerged in the mid sixteenth century as postural corrective often made of iron that imposed straightness. Vigarello warns that these corsets should be distinguished from the whalebone corsets that appeared at the same time, but that were used for fashion – to assist in creating the proper shape for a dress, rather than as a corrective for malformed bodies. Vigarello, "Upward Training," 175.

70 Vigarello also notes the usefulness of massage in encouraging uprightness, a preoccupation among those concerned with children's care and education, that should be attained early in life, while the bone's are still wet and moldable. Massage to create properly aligned vertebrae is followed by swaddling to contain the infant's body in the proper shape. Ibid., 168–73.

71 Andry de Bois-Regard, *Orthopædia*.

72 The only exception to this occurs when Andry is explaining how to treat the problem of uniform thickness throughout the body. He advises that "jumping makes the body form three Angles, which open and shut, and are of very great service in giving it a free Shape. The first Angle is that which the fore part of the Body makes near the Haunches, where it is joined with the thighs; the second is that at the Joints of the thighs with the Legs behind; and the third is that which the Legs form with the Bone's of the Feet forwards. One cannot conceive how much those Flexions and Extensions frequently repeated contribute to give the head, Back, and the Extremities a free easy Air," and he later adds that this kind of repetition "makes the nourishing Juices circulate through the whole Substance of the Leg." Ibid.,138–39, 148.

73 Jean Georges Noverre, *Letters on Dancing and Ballets*, trans. Cyril W. Beaumont from the rev. and enl. edition published in St. Petersburg (Brooklyn, N.Y.: Dance Horizons, [1803] 1966), 118–19.

74 Erasmus Darwin, *A Plan for the Conduct of Female Education in Boarding Schools* (New York: S. R. Publishers, [1797] 1968), 69.

75 Ibid., 69.

76 In describing the impact of the work of eighteenth century biologist John Hunter, Stephen J. Cross argues that the visible structures of parts of the body came to be replaced by their identification as instrumental of a given function. Lungs, for example, were no longer "identified and *classified* as a visible, tangible presence, but only as the instrument of an ineffable non-existent – as an 'organ of breathing.' A concept must now serve where a name, a character, had before, and only a whole theory of functions, a discourse separate from, indeed constitutive of its objects, will serve to organize the forms that had previously, as it were organized themselves in their immediate being." Stephen J. Cross, "John Hunter, the Animal Oeconomy, and Late Eighteenth Century Physiological Discourse," in *Studies in the History of Biology* (Baltimore: Johns Hopkins Press, 1981), 1–110. Although Cross is addressing the work of one scientist in particular, the argument is more broadly applicable. The new awareness of muscles' function conforms to this paradigm shift.

77 Nancy Armstrong, "The Rise of the Domestic Woman," in *The Ideology of Conduct: Essays on Literature and the History of Sexuality*, ed. Nancy Armstrong and Leonard Tennenhouse (New York: Methuen, 1987), 96–141.

78 Ibid.,116–20.

79 James Mercer Garnett, *Seven Lectures on Female Education, Inscribed to Mrs. Garnett's Pupils, at Elm-Wood, Essex County* (Richmond: T. W. White, 1824).

80 For a detailed analysis of the various ailments potentially provoked by dancing, see Molly Engelhardt, "Seed of Discontent: Dancing Manias and

Medical Inquiry in Nineteenth-Century British Literature and Culture," *Victorian Literature and Culture* 35 (2007).

81 In addition to Walker's texts, see, for example, Catharine Macaulay, *Letters on Education*, Revolution and Romanticism, 1789–1834 (Oxford, England: Woodstock Books, [1790] 1994).; Hannah More, *Strictures on Female Education*, Revolution and Romanticism, 1789–1834 (Oxford, England: Woodstock Books, [1799] 1995); and Alexander Walker, *Woman Physiologically Considered as to Mind, Morals, Marriage, Matrimonial Slavery, Infidelity and Divorce*, 2d ed. (London: A. H. Baily, 1840).

82 Donald Walker, *Exercises for Ladies Calculated to Preserve and Improve Beauty, and to Prevent and Correct Personal Defect, Inseparable from Constrained or Careless Habits: Founded on Physiological Principles* (London: T. Hurst, 1836).

83 Donald Walker and John William Carleton, *Walker's Manly Exercises; Containing Rowing, Sailing, Riding, Driving, Racing, Hunting, Shooting, and Other Manly Sports*, 10th ed., Bohn's Illustrated Library (London: H. G. Bohn, 1857).

84 Walker, *Exercises for Ladies*, 68.

85 Walker also expanded in even greater detail on alignment, explaining that "the larger the base of support the greatest solidity in standing." Preferred alignment placed heels in line, knees straight, arms hanging by the body, elbows turned in, belly drawn in, and breast advanced, with the body "stretched as much as possible" by raising the back of the head. Ibid., 70.

86 See James Douglas Haasum, *Ling's System. Swedish Gymnastics* (London: Librairie Hachette, 1885).

87 Jennifer Hargreaves, *Sporting Females: Critical Issues in the History and Sociology of Women's Sports* (London: Routledge, 1994). By 1882, Herbert Spencer criticizes gymnastics for its boring repetitiousness, arguing that women deserve more and better access to the spontaneous and natural play activities that boys enjoy. See Herbert Spencer, "The Dynamics of Exclusion," in *Education: Intellectual, Moral, and Physical* (London: Appleton, 1882), 252–58.

88 "The more completely a youth learns to depend in his actions upon his own merits, to endure physical pain, to rely upon the inner conviction of his own strength in all times of danger, to deal with every momentary contingency, not in haste but with deliberation, the closer he will approach the standard of the man and true warrior." Quoted in Carl Diem, "Per Henrik Ling; on the Occasion of the One Hundredth Anniversary of His Death," http://www.la84foundation.org/OlympicInformationCenter/OlympicReview/1939/ORUE5/ORUE5b.pdf.

89 Peter C. McIntosh, *Sport in Society* (London: C. A. Watts, 1963).

90 For further perspectives on muscular Christianity, especially as it developed in the literary works of Charles Kingsley, George MacDonald Curdie, and others, see Donald E. Hall, *Muscular Christianity: Embodying the Victorian Age* (Cambridge, England: Cambridge University Press, 1994). See also Neal Garnham, "Both Praying and Playing: 'Muscular Christianity' And the YMCA in North-East County Durham," *Journal of Social History* 35, no. 2 (2001).

91 Armstrong writes: "So conceived, self-regulation became a form of labor that was superior to labor. Self-regulation alone gave a woman authority

over the field of domestic objects and personnel where her supervision constituted a form of value in its own right and was therefore capable of enhancing the value of other people and things." Nancy Armstrong and Leonard Tennenhouse, *The Ideology of Conduct: Essays on Literature and the History of Sexuality*, Essays in Literature and Society (New York: Methuen, 1987), 120.

92 James C. Whorton, *Crusaders for Fitness: The History of American Health Reformers* (Princeton, N.J.: Princeton University Press, 1982).

93 See Janice Ross, *Moving Lessons: Margaret H'doubler and the Beginning of Dance in American Education* (Madison, Wis.: University of Wisconsin Press, 2000), 58.

94 These are enumerated at the end of his illustrated volume, 77. For each exercise the specific muscles affected are listed. See Dudley Allen Sargent, *Handbook of Developing Exercises* (Cambridge: n.p., 1897).

95 Ruyter asserts that 80 percent of the practitioners were women, mostly middle class and well educated. Men involved in teaching the system focused primarily on its use in oratory whereas women cultivated its application to pantomimes and presentations of posing. See Nancy Lee Chalfa Ruyter, *Reformers and Visionaries: The Americanization of the Art of Dance* (New York: Dance Horizons, 1979).

96 See, for example, J. W. Shoemaker, *Delsartean Pantomimes, with Recital and Musical Accompaniment: Designed for Home, School, and Church Entertainments* (Philadelphia: Penn Publishing, 1919). In this collection of pantomimes, the poems to be recited are parsed line by line, annotated with specific instructions for weight change and bodily position and momentum as well as arm, hand, and eye movements.

97 Stebbins, *Delsarte System of Dramatic Expression*, 277.

98 Ibid., 177.

99 Ibid.

100 Genevieve Stebbins, *The Genevieve Stebbins System of Physical Training* (New York: E. S. Werner, 1898), 33–34. Stebbins prefaced her instructions on how to relax by commending Arab merchants on caravans who, needing to continue to travel, paused for twenty minutes of relaxation, and then resumed their journey refreshed.

101 Ruyter identifies this as one of Stebbins' specific contribution to Delsarte's system. See Nancy Lee Chalfa Ruyter, "The Intellectual World of Genevieve Stebbins," *Dance Chronicle* 11, no. 3 (1988): 382.

102 Stebbins, *Genevieve Stebbins System*, 39.

103 Stebbins, *Delsarte System of Dramatic Expression*, 98.

104 See Whorton, *Crusaders for Fitness*, 287.

105 Ibid., 289–90.

106 For a good overview of the exercise and working conditions in the early twentieth century urban US, see Hillel Schwartz, "Torque: The New Kinaesthetic of the Twentieth Century," in *Incorporations*, ed. Jonathan Crary and Sanford Kwinter (Cambridge, Mass..: MIT Press, 1992), 70–127.

107 The term was introduced at a series of lectures at Yale University in 1904 and then published in Charles Scott Sherrington, *The Integrative Action of the Nervous System* (New Haven: Yale University Press, 1906).

108 See Edward Bradford Titchener, *A Textbook of Psychology (1910)*, History of Psychology Series (Delmar, N.Y.: Scholars' Facsimiles & Reprints, 1980), 160–82.

109 Titchener, *Lectures*, 178.

110 Ibid.,180.

111 See Titchener, *Textbook of Psychology*, 367.

112 Margaret H'Doubler, *The Dance* (New York: Harcourt, Brace, 1925), 81–82.

113 It is unusual that Martin would have included the vestibular system as part of the kinesthetic, but he could have learned this from Martha Hill, director of Bennington, who, according to Martin, had also studied medical gymnastics. See John Joseph Martin, *America Dancing; the Background and Personalities of the Modern Dance* (New York: Dodge Publishing, 1936), 110–78.

114 Ibid., 112.

115 Ibid., 113.

116 Ibid., 109.

117 Gibson's theory of "kinesthesis" departs radically from conventional explanations of the term. For example, Howard and Templeton's *Human Spatial Orientation*, published in the same year as Gibson's study, defines kinesthesis as sensory information originating in muscle and joint organs that yield "discrimination of the positions and movements of body parts based on information other than visual, auditory, or verbal." Ibid., 72. For an overview of Gibson's contributions to the study of perception, see Edward S. Reed, *James J. Gibson and the Psychology of Perception* (New Haven: Yale University Press, 1988).

118 "There are many kinds of movement that need to be registered. There is articular kinesthesis for the body framework, vestibular kinesthesis for the movements of the skull, cutaneous kinesthesis for movement of the skin relative to what it touches, and visual kinesthesis for perspective transformations of the field of view." Gibson, *Senses Considered as Perceptual Systems*, 111.

119 Cynthia Jean Novack, *Sharing the Dance: Contact Improvisation and American Culture* (Madison, Wis.: University of Wisconsin Press, 1990).

120 Fuller comments: "I think your words 'up' and 'down' are meaningless. Which direction is 'up'? Which is 'down'? Are people in China upside down? Which star should one's head be pointing at to be identified as 'up' . . . ?" Buckminster Fuller, *Synergetics Dictionary*, vol. 2 (New York: Garland Publishing, 1986), 285.

121 Inaugurated by President Eisenhower in 1956 and expanded dramatically under Kennedy and Johnson, the President's Council on Physical Fitness implemented various programs designed to encourage and award achievement in physical accomplishment. The terms "soft American" and "vigor" were used by Kennedy in two famous publications from the time of his election and his first year in office. See fitness.gov/50thanniversary.

122 John F. Kennedy, "The Soft American", *Sports Illustrated*, December 26, 1960, pp. 14–17.

123 For a detailed exploration of the fitness industry, see Jennifer Smith Maguire, *Fit for Consumption: Sociology and the Business of Fitness* (London: Routledge, 2008).

124 Exemplary of this detailed discrimination in aspects of exercise, Gatorade was developed in the 1960s, specifically to enhance the intake of liquids into the muscles through its high levels of potassium.

125 Fonda's 1982 workout video sold over seventeen million copies, encouraging many Americans to purchase their first ever video-recording device.

126 Jennifer Maguire argues that even earlier in the twentieth century physical fitness becomes both a personal problem and project, one that focuses on individuation and personal improvement. She contrasts this conception of individuation with the earlier idea of self-improvement as reflected in a stronger and better society. See Maguire, *Fit for Consumption*.

127 For a detailed exploration of fat in contemporary US culture, see Laura S. Sims, *The Politics of Fat: Food and Nutrition Policy in America* (Armonk, N.Y.: M. E. Sharpe, 1998).

128 See Susan Bordo, *Unbearable Weight: Feminism, Western Culture, and the Body* (Berkeley: University of California Press, 1993).

129 Only recently have studies of women's heart health been undertaken, showing that they are at equivalent risk for heart attacks and strokes.

130 Alain Berthoz, *The Brain's Sense of Movement*, Perspectives in Cognitive Neuroscience (Cambridge, Mass.: Harvard University Press, 2000), 58.

131 Ibid., 164.

132 Ibid., 22–23.

133 James Jerome Gibson, *The Ecological Approach to Visual Perception* (Boston: Houghton Mifflin, 1979), 43.

134 Berthoz, *Brain's Sense of Movement*, 196.

135 Ibid., 201.

136 Ibid., 221.

137 Ibid., 187–88.

138 Wolfgang Prinz, "Experimental Approaches to Imitation," in *The Imitative Mind: Development, Evolution, and Brain Bases*, ed. Andrew N. Meltzoff and Wolfgang Prinz, Cambridge Studies in Cognitive Perceptual Development (Cambridge, England: Cambridge University Press, 2002), 155–57.

139 Giocomo Rizzolatti et al., "From Mirror Neurons to Imitation: Facts and Speculations," in *The Imitative Mind: Development, Evolution, and Brain Bases*, ed. Andrew N. Meltzoff and Wolfgang Prinz, Cambridge Studies in Cognitive Perceptual Development (Cambridge, England: Cambridge University Press, 2002), 256.

140 Peter H. Dana, "The Geographer's Craft Project," http://www.colorado.edu/geography/gcraft/notes/gps/gps.html.

141 Steve Caps, " "How Long Will It Be Before You Come out of the Subway and You Hold up Your Screen to Get a Better View of What You're Looking at in the Physical World?", *New York Times*, February 17, 2009.

142 I am indebted to Harmony Bench for her research on mirror neurons, and her insight that the metaphor of the "network," so pervasive in contemporary culture, likewise pervades neuroscientists' theorization of mirror neurons.

143 The research, led by Professor at the University of Duisberg-Essen Professor Hynek Burda, used Google Earth images of cows worldwide in order to determine their marked tendency to orient along a north–south axis. See Nell Greenfield Boyce, "Moo North: Cows Sense Earth's Magnetism," http://www.npr.org/templates/story/story.php?storyId=93956323.

3 Empathy

1 Barack Obama, *The Audacity of Hope: Thoughts on Reclaiming the American Dream* (New York: Random House, 2008), 82.

2 Dahlia Lithwick expanded on empathy in this way: "judging requires acts of judgment beyond the mechanical application of law to facts and . . . it's best for judges to know when the mechanical act of deciding cases gives way to ideology and personal preference. Empathy isn't sloppy sentiment. It's not ideology. It's just a check against the smug certainty that everyone else is sloppy and sentimental while you yourself are a flawless constitutional microcomputer." Dahlia Lithwick, "Once More, without Feeling: The Gop's Misguided and Confused Campaign against Judicial Empathy," http://www.slate.com/id/2218103/pagenum/all/.

3 Antonio Damasio and Mary Helen Immordino-Yang, "Tweet This: Rapid-Fire Media May Confuse Our Moral Compass," http://www.physorg.com/news158864256.html.

4 Robert Vischer, Harry Francis Mallgrave, and Eleftherios Ikonomou, "On the Optical Sense of Form: A Contribution to Aesthetics," in *Empathy, Form, and Space: Problems in German Aesthetics, 1873–1893* (Santa Monica, Calif.: Getty Center for the History of Art and the Humanities; distributed by the University of Chicago Press, 1994), 104.

5 Ibid.,104–5.

6 According to David Krasner, this process entailed three stages: sensory or immediate feeling; a kinesthetic or physical response, and a deepening awareness of the object by the viewer that resulted in empathy. David Krasner, "Empathy and Theater," in *Staging Philosophy: Intersections of Theater, Performance, and Philosophy*, ed. David Krasner and David Z. Saltz (Ann Arbor, Mich.: University of Michigan Press, 2006), 255–77.

7 Edward Bradford Titchener, *Lectures on the Experimental Psychology of the Thought-Processes* (New York: Macmillan, 1909), 21.

8 Ibid.

9 Adam Smith, *The Theory of Moral Sentiments*, Great Books in Philosophy (Amherst, N.Y.: Prometheus Books, [1759] 2000), 5.

10 Although DuBos was not translated into English until 1748, there is strong evidence that his text, originally published in 1719, was widely read as part of the general cultural exchange occurring between England and France.

11 Lamy writes: "To search into the Causes of this marvelous sympathy betwixt Numbers and our Soul, and how they come to have that power and efficacy upon our Passions, we must know that the motions of the Mind, do follow the motions of the Animal Spirits; as those Spirits are slow or quick, calm or turbulent, the Mind is affected with different passions: the Animal Spirits, their resistance is but small; and their levity is the cause that the last unusual motion determines them; the least motion of a sound puts them in agitation. Our Body is so dispos'd, that a rough and boisterous sound forcing our Spirits into the Muscles, disposes it to flight, and begets an aversion, in the same manner as a frightful object beget horror by the eye." Bernard Lamy and Pierre Nicole, *The Art of Speaking: Written in French by Messieurs Du Port Royal: In Persuance of a Former Treatise, Intituled, the Art of Thinking. Rendred into English,*

The second, corrected ed. (London: Printed for W. Taylor; and H. Clements, 1708), 184–85.

12 Ibid., 77.

13 DuBos explains: "Nature, for this reason, has thought proper to form us in such a manner, as the agitation of whatever approaches us should have the power of impelling us, to the end, that those, who have need of our indulgence or succour, may, with greater facility, persuade us. Thus their emotion alone is sufficient to soften us; whereby they obtain what they could never compass by dint of argument or conviction. We are moved by the tears of a stranger, even before we are apprized of the subject of his weeping. The cries of a man, to whom we have no other relation than the common one of humanity, make us fly instantly to his assistance, by a mechanical movement previous to all deliberation. A person that accosts us with joy painted on his countenance, excites in us a like sentiment of joy, even before we know the subject of his contentment." Abbé DuBos, *Critical Reflections on Poetry, Painting and Music with an Inquiry into the Rise and Progress of the Theatrical Entertainments of the Ancients. Translated into English by Thomas Nugent, Gent. From the Fifth Edition Revised, Corrected, and Inlarged by the Author* (London: Printed for John Nourse, 1748), 32–33. DuBos described the tendency to become increasingly self-interested as one grows older in these terms: "Nature has thought proper to implant this quick and easy sensibility in man as the very basis of society. Self-love generally degenerates into an immoderate fondness of one's own person; and, in proportion, as men advance in years, renders them too much attached to their present and future interests, and too inflexible towards one another, when they enter deliberately upon any resolution. It was therefore necessary, that man should be easily drawn out of this situation." Ibid., 32.

14 For a discussion of DuBos's role in aesthetic theory of the period, see Marian Hobson, *The Object of Art: The Theory of Illusion in Eighteenth-Century France*, Cambridge Studies in French (Cambridge, England: Cambridge University Press, 1982).

15 DuBos, *Critical Reflections*, 11–12.

16 DuBos writes: "The most that can happen is, that a young person of a very tender disposition, may be so transported with a pleasure which is yet novel to him, that his emotion and surprize [sic] will make him fall into some exclamation or involuntary gestures; which indicate, that he does not actually reflect on the external behavior he should observe in a public assembly. But he will quickly return to himself, and become sensible of his momentary absence of mind: For 'tis not true, that he fancied during his extasy, he saw Roderigue and Chimene. He only was touched in almost as lively a manner as he would have been, had he really seen Roderigue at the feet of his mistress after he had killed her father." Ibid., 350–51

17 Ibid., 177.

18 "The fermentation which prepares a storm, operates not only on our minds, insomuch as to render us heavy, and debar us from thinking with our wonted liberty of imagination; but moreover it corrupts even our provisions. It is sufficient to alter the state of a distemper or a wound for the worse . . ." Ibid.,180–81.

19 Ibid., 189.

20 Ibid., 200–201.
21 "Those objects have always made a great impression on mankind, especially in countries where they have a very great vivacity of spirit, as in the most southern parts of Europe, and the opposite parts of Asia and Afric [*sic*]. We need only recollect the prohibition made by the tables of the law to the Jews, to paint or carve any human figure; the impression made thereby, was too great for a people naturally inclinable to grow passionately fond of all objects capable of moving them." Ibid., 30.
22 According to Sir William Osler, this work's popularity is attested to by the fact that it enjoyed 5 editions in English, 17 in French, 3 in Latin, 5 in Dutch, and 16 in German. Sir William Osler, *Sir Kenelm Digby's Powder of Sympathy* (Los Angeles: Plantin Press, 1972), 3.
23 Kenelm Digby, *A Late Discourse Made in a Solemne Assembly of Nobles and Learned Men at Montpellier in France Touching the Cure of Wounds by the Powder of Sympathy: With Instructions How to Make the Said Powder: Whereby Many Other Secrets of Nature Are Unfolded*, trans. R. White (London: Printed for R. Lownes and T. Davies, 1658). Elizabeth Hedrick has shown persuasively the many flaws in Digby's claims, both chronological and social and I am not concerned with the veracity of his claims, but instead with how his rationale for the effectiveness of the powder illustrates prevailing ideas about sympathy. See Elizabeth Hedrick, "Romancing the Salve: Sir Kenelm Digby and the Powder of Sympathy," *British Journal for the History of Science* 41, no. 2 (2008). Intriguingly, Digby commences his explanation with a Spanish proverb: "Let the miracle be done, though Mahomet do it." And he identifies the origin of powder as having been given to him by a religious Carmelite who had traveled to India, Persia, and China.
24 Digby, *Late Discourse*, 19–21.
25 Ibid., 44.
26 Ibid., 53–54.
27 Ibid., 64–80.
28 Ibid., 93.
29 Ibid.
30 Ibid., 96.
31 For a detailed discussion of individual masques and the dances in them see Barbara Ravelhofer, *The Early Stuart Masque: Dance, Costume, and Music* (Oxford: Oxford University Press, 2006).
32 Skiles Howard, *The Politics of Courtly Dancing in Early Modern England* (Amherst: University of Massachusetts Press, 1998), 110–32.
33 Hume writes: "No quality of human nature is more remarkable, both in itself and in its consequences, than the propensity we have to sympathize with others, and to receive by communication their inclinations and sentiments, however different from, or even contrary to our own." David Hume, *A Treatise of Human Nature Being an Attempt to Introduce the Experimental Method of Reasoning into Moral Subjects*, vol. 2 (London: Printed for John Noon, 1739), 72–73.
34 Hume continues: "'Tis indeed evident, that when we sympathize with the passions and sentiments of others, these movements appear at first in *our* mind as mere ideas, and are conceiv'd to belong to another person, as we conceive any other matter of fact. 'Tis also evident, that the ideas of the

affections of others are converted into the very impressions they represent, and that the passions arise in conformity to the images we form of them." Ibid., 78. For further explanation of the use of DuBos by Hume, Adam Smith, and others, see David Fate Norton, *The Cambridge Companion to Hume* (Cambridge, England: Cambridge University Press, 1993), 260–62.

35 Hume, *Treatise of Human Nature*, 269.

36 As Roxann Wheeler demonstrates, skin color was not the attribute defining or even signaling cultural difference. In line with DuBos's observations that temperament rather than constitution were responsible for difference, Wheeler shows that other markers, especially religion along with manners and comportment were utilized to determine difference. Only in the 1770s, did skin color become the defining factor in identifying otherness. Roxann Wheeler, *The Complexion of Race: Categories of Difference in Eighteenth-Century British Culture* (Philadelphia: University of Pennsylvania Press, 2000).

37 Asserting that sympathy operated through the responsiveness of the humours, Hume emphasized the need for contiguity between people in order for sympathy to work. It operated in degrees depending upon geographical proximity and relation through blood. Thus, people from good families but limited circumstances often moved away from their family thereby diminishing sympathy through distance, and avoiding any judgment upon them. Hume, *Treatise of Human Nature*, 73–76.

38 For a profile of Hume's attitude towards women, see Kathryn Temple, "'Manly Composition': Hume and the History of England," in *Feminist Interpretations of David Hume*, ed. Anne Jaap Jacobson (University Park, Pa.: Pennsylvania State University Press, 2000). See also Christine Battersby, "An Enquiry Concerning the Humean Woman," *Philosophy* 56, no. 217 (1981), 263–82.

39 For an analysis of DuBos's ideas on the public and who was included in that discerning body, see Francis X. J. Coleman, *The Aesthetic Thought of the French Enlightenment* (Pittsburgh: University of Pittsburgh Press, 1971), 77–80. Matthew Craske expands on the notion of the public as part of the evolution of eighteenth century art and its institutions. See Matthew Craske, *Art in Europe, 1700–1830: A History of the Visual Arts in an Era of Unprecedented Urban Economic Growth* (Oxford, England: Oxford University Press, 1997).

40 Joseph R. Roach, *The Player's Passion: Studies in the Science of Acting* (Newark: University of Delaware Press, 1985); G. J. Barker-Benfield, *The Culture of Sensibility: Sex and Society in Eighteenth-Century Britain* (Chicago: University of Chicago Press, 1996).

41 "Les yeux nous marquent les passions, parce que la cinquième paire qui se répand dans l'oil, communiqué avec les nerfs viscere: dès qu'il y a quelque grande agitation dans le cerveau, le suc nerveux qui est envoyé dans les nerfs des yeux, y imprime divers mouvemens." Chevalier de Jaucourt, "Entry on Sympathy," in *Encyclopédie, Ou Dictionnaire Raisonné Dessciences, Des Arts Et Des Métiers* (Paris: Briasson, 1762–72), 220–28.

42 Smith, *Theory of Moral Sentiments*, 3–4.

43 "By the imagination, we place ourselves in his situation, we conceive ourselves enduring all the same torments, we enter as it were into his body, and become in some measure the same person with him, and thence

form some idea of his sensations, and even feel something which, though weaker in degree, is not altogether unlike them." Ibid., 4.

44 Ibid.

45 Ibid.

46 Those with more delicate fibers could feel the "sores and ulcers" of beggars on the streets. Even robust men, looking upon sore eyes, would feel their soreness, since the eyes were, even "in the strongest man more delicate than any other part of the body is in the weakest." Ibid., 5. According the Philippe Fontaine, this ability to feel, even to much lesser extent, the pain of the other, distinguishes Smith's conception of sympathy from that of Hume who envisioned it as a more generalized spread of feeling. See Philippe Fontaine, "Identification and Economic Behavior: Sympathy and Empathy in Historical Perspective," *Economics and Philosophy* 13 (1997): 265.

47 For a comprehensive overview of the displacement of mechanistic theories of physiology by vitalistic assumptions, see Theodore M. Brown, "From Mechanism to Vitalism in Eighteenth-Century English Physiology," *Journal of the History of Biology* 7, no. 2 (1974).

48 Evelyn Forget, "Evocations of Sympathy: Sympathetic Imagery in Eighteenth-Century Social Theory and Physiology," in *Oeconomies in the Age of Newton*, ed. Margaret Schabas and Neil De Marchi (Durham, N.C.: Duke University Press, 2003), 291.

49 Ibid., 292.

50 Some scientists attempted to explain the phenomenon using the metaphor of acoustic vibration. Sensations resonated through the body like the motion of a string that had been plucked, allowing the viewer to retain an impression of an object even after it has been removed. For a fuller explanation of the ramifications of vibration theories, see Roach, *Player's Passion*, 102–4.

51 John Hill, *The Actor: A Treatise on the Art of Playing* (London: R. Griffiths, 1750), 10.

52 For additional perspectives on how the passions were to be performed as part of polite discourse, see Paul Goring, *The Rhetoric of Sensibility in Eighteenth-Century Culture* (Cambridge, England: Cambridge University Press, 2005).

53 Smith, *Theory of Moral Sentiments*, 6.

54 Ibid.

55 Ibid., 7.

56 Ibid., 16.

57 John Weaver, *The Loves of Mars and Venus* (London: W. Mears, 1717), 20.

58 Smith explains: "The objects with which men in the different professions and states of life are conversant being very different, and habituating them to very different passions, naturally form in them very different characters and manners. We expect in each rank and profession a degree of those manners which, experience has taught us, belonged to it." Ibid., 292.

59 Ibid.

60 Ibid., 298.

61 Smith's descriptions of native practices are particularly vivid and detailed. In his analysis of their stoicism can be found the basis upon which the

subsequent distinction between "shame" and "guilt" cultures was proposed in anthropology.

62 Smith, *Theory of Moral Sentiments*, 299–300.

63 The model of the impartial viewer that Smith developed was ambiguously singular or plural, however, it was a person of affluent means. As literary historian David Marshall explains, Smith's observer might function as casual bystander, an abstracted ideal of a neutral person, or a pre-Freudian theorization of the super-ego. This observer could also signify the will of the people or the ideal implementation of the social code. Marshall describes the impartial observer as "alternatively characterized as an ideal observer, an ordinary innocent bystander, the voice of the people, an omniscient deity, the normative values of society, a relativistic social code, absolute standards, the personification of conscience, the internalization of social repression, the superego, and simply a hypothetical, abstract third person." David Marshall, *The Figure of Theater: Shaftesbury, Defoe, Adam Smith, and George Eliot* (New York: Columbia University Press, 1986), 167.

64 Laura Hinton, *The Perverse Gaze of Sympathy: Sadomasochistic Sentiments from Clarissa to Rescue 911*, Suny Series in Feminist Criticism and Theory (Albany: State University of New York Press, 1999), 27.

65 As Marshall explains, each member of Smith's society was performing for all others: "We are actors not just because we appear before spectators played by ourselves, but also because we personate ourselves in different parts, persons, and characters. The self is theatricalized in its relation to others and in its self-conscious relation to itself; but it also enters the theater because 'the person whom I properly call myself' must be an actor who can dramatize or represent to himself the spectacle of self-division in which the self personates two different persons who try to play each other's parts, change positions, and identify with each other." Marshall, *Figure of Theater*, 175–76.

66 Smith, *Theory of Moral Sentiments*, 301.

67 Ibid., 302.

68 British historians identify mid-century as the beginning of a second phase of British colonial expansion. As Linda Colley has shown, prior to 1750 British do not imagine themselves to hold the kind of power over others that they come to acquire during that moment. Linda Colley, *Britons: Forging the Nation, 1707–1837* (New Haven: Yale University Press, 1992), 105.

69 Colley writes: "To those used to being at the center of things, then, but also to those below them, the prospects in 1763 were exhilarating but also frighteningly wide open. Indeed, it is not too much to say that from this point on until the American Revolution and beyond, the British were in the grip of collective agoraphobia, captivated by, but also adrift and at odds in a vast empire abroad and a new political world at home which few of them properly understood. It was a time of raised expectations, disorientation and anxiety in which demands for change on the one hand, and denunciations of change on the other, came from the peripheries of the political nation, from the peripheries of Great Britain itself and from the peripheries of empire as well." Ibid.

70 Colley explains: "Most Britons, though, were more worried about the immediate challenges of extended empire. The prewar empire had been sufficiently informal and sufficiently cheap for Parliament to claim authority over it without having to concern itself too much about what this authority entailed. The post-war empire necessitated a much greater investment in administrative machinery and military force. This build-up of control had to be paid for, either by British taxpayers or by their colonists. But new levels of control also had to legitimized. In what terms could a people who claimed to be uniquely free justify their massively extended dominion to others and to themselves?" Ibid., 102.

71 Giovanni-Andrea Gallini, *A Treatise on the Art of Dancing* (London: R. and J. Dodsley, in Pall Mall; T. Becket, in the Strand; and W. Nicoll, in St. Paul's Church-Yard, 1762), 214.

72 David Arnold, "Hunger in the Garden of Plenty: The Bengal Famine of 1770," in *Dreadful Visitations: Confronting Natural Catastrophe in the Age of Enlightenment*, ed. Alessa Johns (New York: Routledge, 1999), 88–89.

73 Ibid., 97–98.

74 Philip Joseph Deloria, *Playing Indian* (New Haven Conn.: Yale University Press, 1998), 28–32.

75 According to Jill Lepore, the popularity of a play entitled *Metamora* (1828) documents the changing attitudes towards Native Americans as variously constituted in northern and southern regions of the United States. The play, so popular that it fueled dozens of similar productions and even parodies throughout the 1830s and 40s recast the Native American as heroic, exhibiting a virile masculinity in defending their lands, but also as a vanishing species. Lepore argues that the early nineteenth century witnessed a complete overhaul of the image of the Native American in order to use Native American heritage to envision America as a country with a unique culture and its own ancestral past, rather than a minor version of England, but this reimagining of the Indian needed to be based on their absence from society. At the end of the play the Indian warrior dies, symbolizing the end of Indian peoples. Yet *Metamora* was only popular in New England where native peoples had largely been assimilated, and most New Englanders assumed that there were no Indians left alive there. Georgia audiences, in contrast, deplored the play because of the vigorous and active presence of the Cherokee nation nearby. The policy of removal of Indians to western lands was devised in response to their autonomy and "civilized" development. Jill Lepore, *The Name of War: King Philip's War and the Origins of American Identity* (New York: Vintage Books, 1999), 194–226.

76 For a good overview of medical inquiry into the nervous system in the nineteenth and twentieth centuries, see Erwin. H. Ackerknecht, "The History of the Discovery of the Vegetative (Autonomic) Nervous System," *Medical History* January 18, no. 1 (1974).

77 Physician William Cullen observed that in cases where "men were doomed to employments pernicious to their health" yet necessary to society as a whole, then it became society's responsibility to care for them in disease and old age." Rosalie Stott, "Health and Virtue: Or, How to Keep out of Harm's Way: Lectures on Pathology and Therapeutics by William Cullen Circa 1770," *Medical History* 31 (1987). Cullen continues: "Happily

their manner of life and even their hardships are the best means of preserving their health. It is true that this is not universal and many men are doomed to employments more or less directly pernicious to health, but it is necessary for the good of the whole society, and the only compensation the society can make to them is taking the greatest care of them, in disease and old age." Stott, "Health and Virtue: Or, How to Keep out of Harm's Way: Lectures on Pathology and Therapeutics by William Cullen Circa 1770," 140. Both Stott and Risse argue that Cullen's work is typical of a shift that occurred in the latter half of the eighteenth century towards treating the nervous system of patients as the central cause of ailments. See G. B. Risse, "Cullen, the Seasoned Clinician: Organization and Strategies of a Successful Medical Practice in the Eighteenth Century," in *William Cullen and the Eighteenth-Century Medical World*, ed. J. P. S. Ferguson A. Doig, I. A. Milne and R. Passmore (Edinburgh: Edinburgh University Press, 1993), 135–51. See also Alexander Monro, *Observations on the Structure and Functions of the Nervous System Illustrated with Tables. By Alexander Monro* (Edinburgh: Printed for, and sold by, William Creech; and Joseph Johnson, London, 1783).

78 Mary Poovey, *Making a Social Body: British Cultural Formation, 1830–1864* (Chicago: University of Chicago Press, 1995), 28–31.

79 Ibid., 78–79.

80 Ibid.,73–97.

81 Ibid., 74.

82 Quoted in Alexander Butchart, *The Anatomy of Power: European Constructions of the African Body* (London, England: Zed Books, 1998), 51.

83 Joyce E. Chaplin, "Natural Philosophy and an Early Racial Idiom in North America: Comparing English and Indian Bodies," *William and Mary Quarterly* 54, no. 1 (1997): 237.

84 Ibid., 242–45.

85 Ibid., 243–52.

86 See Londa L. Schiebinger, *Plants and Empire: Colonial Bioprospecting in the Atlantic World* (Cambridge, Mass.: Harvard University Press, 2004), 195–96.

87 See Bronwen Douglas, "Climate to Crania: Science and the Racialization of Human Difference," in *Foreign Bodies: Oceania and the Science of Race 1750–1940*, ed. Chris Ballard and Bronwen Douglas (Canberra, Australia: ANU E Press, 2008), 33–99.

88 Oxford English Dictionary, quoted in Ibid., 34.

89 Ibid., 41.

90 Ibid. 46.

91 For a lucid account of the full complexities of Prichard's argument, see George Stocking, "From Chronology to Ethnology: James Cowles Prichard and British Anthropology, 1800–1850," in *Researches into the Physical History of Man*, ed. James Cowles Prichard (Chicago: University of Chicago Press, 1973), ix–cx.

92 For some, like Prichard, the divergences in human character could nonetheless by bridged through moral and spiritual instruction. In the same way that the poor and criminal could be improved through assiduous training and care, so, too, the savages could, with much effort, be brought

towards, if not into, civilization. Still, the poor of the civilized world merited a sympathy that the savages, because of their constitutional differences, often did not elicit or merit.

93 Ludmilla J. Jordanova, *Nature Displayed: Gender, Science, and Medicine, 1760–1820: Essays* (London: Longman, 1999).

94 Quoted in Molly Engelhardt, *Dancing out of Line: Ballrooms, Ballets, and Mobility in Victorian Fiction and Culture* (Athens, Ohio: Ohio University Press, 2009), 117. For more on the relationship between dance and disease and death, see Engelhardt, *Dancing out of Line: Ballrooms, Ballets, and Mobility in Victorian Fiction and Culture*, 112–39.

95 As the Victorian social body became established, governed by the logic of organic functionalism in which each segment of society played its designated role and contributed to its specific purpose, male and female roles became increasingly polarized. Throughout the eighteenth century, middle-class men consolidated their social position in two ways – through marriage to an important family and through participation in clubs and coffee house conversations. By the 1830s, middle-class men could achieve social standing only through their affiliation with domesticity, through the wives and households which they were obliged to support. At the same time, women were completely eradicated from the public sphere, even as they provided the means though which men achieved stature and prosperity. Their ability to connect one to another and to the social body came through literature and through acts of domestic nurturance and social charity. See Poovey, *Making a Social Body*, 125–26.

96 See ibid.,124.

97 See Ann Cvetkovich, *Mixed Feelings: Feminism, Mass Culture, and Victorian Sensationalism* (New Brunswick, N.J.: Rutgers University Press, 1992), 6.

98 Audrey Jaffe, *Scenes of Sympathy: Identity and Representation in Victorian Fiction* (Ithaca, N.Y.: Cornell University Press, 2000), 18.

99 Ironically, sympathy also resulted in the possibility for middle-class women to enter the public sphere even as they were being prohibited from it. Through church or governmental institutions, women were inadvertently able to qualify for work that was classified as an extension of their domestic duties. In the highly specialized capacities of care-giver and educator, women began to exert influence on treatment of the poor at home and the colonized abroad. Although their voices were strongly contained and curtailed, the momentum garnered by their duties as sympathy givers helped to fortify the persuasiveness of both abolitionist and feminist agendas. Poovey writes: "Because the metaphor of the social body highlighted intimate bodily processes and championed the feminized epistemology of sympathy, its proponents inadvertently reinforced women's claims to be naturally suited to work that could be seen as an extension of domestic offices. Poovey, *Making a Social Body*, 43.

100 Alexandra Carter, *Dance and Dancers in the Victorian and Edwarian Music Hall Ballet* (Aldershot, England: Ashgate, 2005), 12–14.

101 Ivor Guest notes that one reason for the decline was the absence of an enduring dance school. A school had been established at Her Majesty's theater, but its function was primarily to provide *corps de ballet* support for foreign principal dancers who toured to London and staged their

work. Ivor Guest, *Ballet in Leicester Square: The Alhambra and the Empire, 1860–1915* (London: Dance Books, 1992), 5. When ballet was relocated to the music halls, Guest explains that "The emphasis on pageantry and spectacle relegated the *corps de ballet* to the level of a chorus, employed more often than not as a background rather than an integral part of the choreography. Although they performed with impressive precision, their evolutions were usually comparatively simple, and the technical skill required of them was limited." Ibid., 7.

102 Here are I am referring to concepts such as Freud's four drives which, I would argue, partake in the new construction of interiority that accompanied the new experience of physicality.

103 Jean Piaget, *The Moral Judgement of the Child* (London: Kegan Paul, 1932), 180.

104 George Herbert Mead and Charles W. Morris, *Mind, Self & Society from the Standpoint of a Social Behaviorist* (Chicago, Ill.: The University of Chicago Press, 1934), 300–302.

105 Consider this description by Vernon Lee: "Empathy . . . is due not only to the movements which we are actually making in the course of shape-perception, to present movements with their various modes of speed, intensity and facility and their accompanying intentions; it is due at least as much to our accumulated and averaged past experience of movements of the same kind, also with *their* cognate various modes of speed, intensity, facility, and *their* accompanying intentions. And being thus residual averaged, and essential, this empathic movement, this movement attributed to the lines of a shape, is not clogged and inhibited by whatever clogs and inhibits each separate concrete experience of the kind; still less is it overshadowed in our awareness by the *result* which we foresee as goal of our real active proceedings. . . . Thus, in themselves and apart from their aims, our bodily movements are never interesting except inasmuch as requiring new and difficult adjustments, or again as producing perceptible repercussions in our circulatory, breathing and balancing apparatus . . . Yet every movement which we accomplish implies a change in our debit and credit of vital economy, a change in our balance of bodily and mental expenditure and replenishment." Vernon Lee, *The Beautiful; an Introduction to Psychological Aesthetics* (Cambridge, England: Cambridge University Press, 1913), 72–73.

106 Lee writes: "Etymologically, and literally, perception means the act of grasping or taking in, and also the result of that action. But when we thus perceive a shape, what is it precisely that we grasp or take in?"; "And it is this making up of shapes, this grasping or taking in of their constituent relations, which is an active process on our part, and one which we can either perform or not perform." Ibid., 30–31.

107 Ibid., 35–49.

108 Ibid., 64.

109 Lee continues "and which Titchener has translated from the German Einfuhlung as empathy." Ibid., 66.

110 Ibid., 80.

111 Martin cites Theodor Lipps as recording his motor identification of the function of a column, which appeared "to rise from the earth and resist the load laid upon it." John Joseph Martin, *America Dancing; the*

Background and Personalities of the Modern Dance (New York: Dodge Publishing, 1936), 119. He also references Vernon Lee in England as someone working on the empathy. Ibid., 146.

112 John Joseph Martin, *The Modern Dance* (New York: A. S. Barnes, 1933), 85.

113 This would take place through muscular contractions so slight that the viewer would not directly feel them: "Psychologists have discovered changes in the postural condition of the muscles in response even to shapes, though there is no outward movement of any kind." John Joseph Martin, *Introduction to the Dance* (New York,: W. W. Norton, 1939), 49.

114 Dee Reynolds surmises that Martin derived his concept of "inner mimicry" from Lipps's work. See Dee Reynolds, *Rhythmic Subjects* (Alton, England: Dance Books, 2007), 47.

115 Martin, *Introduction to the Dance*, 53.

116 Lee, *Beautiful*, 79.

117 Focusing on the production of danced spirituals by both white and black choreographers, dance historian Susan Manning argues that the universal subjectivity of the white dancing body prevails until the 1940s. After World War II modern dance choreographers integrate their companies, allowing both white and black bodies to represent the concerns of the dance. At the same time, a number of African-American choreographers come to prominence, yet they are burdened in their fame by the presumption that they will undertake choreographic projects that specifically address African-American themes and values. Pearl Primus's *Strange Fruit*, Alvin Ailey's *Revelations*, and Donald McKayle's *Rainbow Round My Shoulder*, canonical works in the African-American dance tradition, all portray life in the South and provide vivid images African-American community. See Susan Manning, "Danced Spirituals," in *Of the Presence of the Body: Essays on Dance and Performance Theory*, ed. André Lepecki (Middletown, Conn.: Wesleyan University Press, 2004), 82–96.

118 Jean Georges Noverre, *Letters on Dancing and Ballets*, trans. Cyril W. Beaumont from the rev. and enl. edition published in St. Petersburg (Brooklyn, N.Y.: Dance Horizons, [1803] 1966), 16.

119 Martin, *Introduction to the Dance*, 97.

120 Hillel Schwarcz argues that rhythm became the single most identifiable attribute of primitive cultures within anthropological studies of the late nineteenth and early twentieth century. It likewise became a preoccupation in psychological studies of learning and cognition. Hillel Schwartz, "Torque: The New Kinaesthetic of the Twentieth Century," in *Incorporations*, ed. Jonathan Crary and Sanford Kwinter (Cambridge, Mass.: MIT Press, 1992), 81–82.

121 Irving Pond, *The Meaning of Architecture* (Boston: Marshall Jones Company, 1918), 133–46.

122 Martin, *Modern Dance*, 47.

123 Ibid., 40–41.

124 Ibid.

125 Ibid.,74.

126 Making an argument based on the influence of climate, Laban argued that soil shaped "animal nature", resulting in the fact that Negroes were less developed than whites, and in fact, closer to animals. In a subsequent

text, he identified rhythm and posture and two racially inflected features of dance. Lilian Karina and Marion Kant, *Hitler's Dancers: German Modern Dance and the Third Reich* (New York: Berghahn Books, 2003), 253–54.

127 Quoted in Susan Manning, *Modern Dance, Negro Dance: Race in Motion* (Minneapolis: University of Minnesota Press, 2004), 167.

128 Martin, *Introduction to the Dance*, 256.

129 John Joseph Martin, *The Dance* (New York: Tudor Publishing, 1946), 10.

130 Yvonne Rainer, *Work 1960–73* (Halifax: Press of the Nova Scotia College of Design and New York University Press, 1974), 180. I was made aware of this passage by dance scholar Ananya Chatterjea who encourages an interrogation of these kinds of descriptions in her intercultural history. See Ananya Chatterjea, *Butting Out: Reading Resistive Choreographies through Works by Jawole Willa Jo Zollar and Chandralekha*, 1st ed. (Middletown, Conn.: Wesleyan University Press, 2004).

131 Freud's first use of Einfühlung was in explaining the status of the prank and how, by placing oneself in the other's shoes, one could sense the meaning and motivation of the joke. Subsequently, he developed the idea of empathy as the process of identification between patient and analyst. See G. W. Prigman, "Freud and the History of Empathy," *International Journal of Psychoanalysis* 76 (1995).

132 For a succinct overview of empathy in social psychology, Mark H. Davis, *Empathy: A Social Psychological Approach*, Social Psychology Series (Boulder, Colo.: Westview Press, 1996), 1–12.

133 Carl Rogers, for example, described empathy as a process in which one is "entering the private perceptual world of the other and becoming thoroughly at home in it. It involves being sensitive, moment to moment, to the changing felt meanings which flow in this other person, to the fear or rage or tenderness or confusion of whatever, that he/she is experiencing. It means temporarily living in his/her life, moving about in it delicately without making judgments, sensing meaning of which he/she is scarcely aware." Carl Rogers, "Empathic: An Unappreciated Way of Being," *Counseling Psychologist* 5 (1975): 4.

134 Rosalind Dymond was one of the first to formulate empathy in this way and her work was followed by a vast number of experiments set up along similar lines. See Rosalind F. Dymond, "A Scale for the Measurement of Emphatic Ability," *Journal of Consulting Psychologist* 13 (1940). See also R. F. Dymond, A. S. Hughes, V. L. Raabe, "Measurable Changes in Empathy with Age," *Journal of Consulting Psychology* 16 (1952).

135 Edith Stein, *On the Problem of Empathy*, trans. Waltraut Stein (The Hague: M. Nijhoff, 1964). Maurice Merleau-Ponty, *Phenomenology of Perception* (London: Routledge, 1962).

136 Edith Stein, *On the Problem of Empathy*, trans. Waltraut Stein, 2d ed. (The Hague: M. Nijhoff, [1917] 1970), 16.

137 Ibid.,17.

138 Merleau-Ponty, *Phenomenology of Perception*, 185.

139 Gallese cites Herbert Mead, who at the beginning of the twentieth century argued that precisely through the use of gesture the individual determines the boundaries of self. Similarly, he looks to the work of phenomenologists Edith Stein, Edmund Husserl, and Maurice Merleau-Ponty. See Vittorio

Gallese, "The Shared Manifold Hypothesis," *Journal of Consciousness Studies* 8 (2001): 43–44.

140 Vittorio Gallese, "Empathy, Embodied Simulation, and the Brain: Commentary on Aragno and Zepf/Hartmann," *Journal of the American Psychoanalytic Association* 56 (2008): 773.

141 See Giocomo Rizzolatti et al., "From Mirror Neurons to Imitation: Facts and Speculations," in *The Imitative Mind: Development, Evolution, and Brain Bases*, ed. Andrew N. Meltzoff and Wolfgang Prinz, *Cambridge Studies in Cognitive Perceptual Development* (Cambridge, England: Cambridge University Press, 2002), 253.

142 Gallese, "Shared Manifold Hypothesis," 39.

143 Vittorio Gallese, "The Roots of Empathy: The Shared Manifold Hypothesis and the Neural Basis of Intersubjectivity," *Psychopathology* 36 (2003): 174.

144 Gallese, "Shared Manifold Hypothesis,"41–42. Gallese is not alone is speculating along these lines about human development and the foundation of social and individual identities. See also Andrew N. Meltzoff, "Elements of a Development Theory of Imitation," in Meltzoff and Prinz *Imitative Mind*, 19–42.

145 See Ivar Hagendoorn, "Some Speculative Hypothesis About the Nature and Perception of Dance and Choreography," *Journal of Consciousness Studies* 11, nos. 3–4 (2004).

146 Rizzolatti et al., "From Mirror Neurons to Imitation," 256.

147 Gallese, "Empathy, Embodied Simulation," 774.

148 Here I am referencing theories of performativity, such as those proposed by Judith Butler in her application of speech act theory in the 1990s. See Judith Butler, *Gender Trouble: Feminism and the Subversion of Identity* (New York: Routledge, 1990).

149 See B. Calvo-Merino et al., "Action Observation and Acquired Motor Skills: An Mri Study with Expert Dancers," *Cerebral Cortex* 15 (August 2005).

150 N. Katherine Hayles, "Virtual Bodies and Flickering Signifiers," *October* 66 (1993).

4 Choreographing Empathy

1 For an exposition of this relationship focused on British exploration of America, see Louis Montrose, "The Work of Gender in the Discourse of Discovery," *Representations* 33 Special Issue: *The New World* (1991).

2 For a comprehensive overview of Native American dance artists' relationship to the concert dance tradition, see Jacqueline Shea Murphy, *The People Have Never Stopped Dancing: Native American Modern Dance Histories* (Minneapolis: University of Minnesota Press, 2007). I have been guided in the analysis that follows by her arguments concerning the central role that land plays in forging Native aesthetics.

3 *Woman and Water* premiered at Visualeyez: Latitude 53's Festival of Performance Art, a festival on the theme of domesticity curated by Todd Janes in 2006 in Edmonton, Alberta, Canada. I witnessed it when it was presented at UCLA as part of the Actions of Transfer Conference sponsored by the Center for Performance Studies in November 2008.

4 Jacqueline Shea Murphy argues that *Woman and Water* explores and emphasizes subsistence, noting that when the piece first premiered Lukin Linklater actually brought food and fed the audience as part of the piece. See Jacqueline Shea Murphy, "'Gathering from Within: Indigenous Nationhood' and Tanya Lukin Linklater's 'Woman and Water,'" *Theatre Research International* 35, no. 2 (2010): 165–71.

5 Lukin Linklater studied with dance technique with Alejandro Ronceria, Penny Couchie, Georgina Martinez, and Muriel Miguel, each of whom brought together their studies in western techniques with indigenous movement systems. Her current daily practice focuses on vinyasa yoga in combination with an altered Alaska Native movement form inspired by bird movement and clowning. Personal communication, January 25, 2010.

6 Interview by Jacqueline Shea Murphy with the artist. Actions of Transfer Conference, sponsored by UCLA Center for Performance Studies, November 16, 2008.

7 Jacqueline Shea Murphy, "Mobilizing (in) the Archive: Santee Smith's Kaha:Wi," in *Worlding Dance*, ed. Susan Leigh Foster (Basingstoke: Palgrave Macmillan, 2009), 32–52.

8 For an excellent overview of these interfaces, see Harmony Bench, "Choreographing Bodies in Dance-Media" (PhD dissertation, University of California at Los Angeles, 2009).

9 Rimini Protokoll includes artists Helgard Haug, Daniel Wetzel, and Stefan Kaegi. *Call Cutta* grew out of a Goethe Institute sponsored trip to the city of Calcutta, where the artists viewed a call center first-hand and began to speculate about how they could interact with it. I participated in *Call Cutta* when it was presented by the Hebbel Theater in Berlin in Spring 2005.

10 *Cell* premiered and was performed across the city of Philadelphia in spring 2006. My discussion of it is based on video viewings of the work, and also extensive interviews with Andrew Simonet, member of Headlong Dance theater and the principle director or the piece.

11 *Call Cutta* was created, in part, to advertise and critique the working conditions of South Asian laborers who man banks of phones daily to answer questions concerning financial and commercial transactions of multinational corporations. These corporations have outsourced voice communication with their customers to highly articulate and well-mannered assistants who will work for a fraction of the salary required in the first-world. The work is quite hard on the body, as it sits for many hours conversing without respite, and it also produces a distinctive anxiety, in that the assistant must pass as a member of the economy she or he is serving while remaining solicitous of all the customers needs. Typically, this involves soothing, pacifying, and jollying the customer while following the rules of corporate exchange. Neither party ever witnesses the other or enjoys the opportunity to get to know them. The system offers no way to acquire a history of familiarity, reliability, or favor, since each phone call routes to a different worker. These workers are interchangeable and completely anonymous within the social economy. In an interview with Florian Melzacher, the artists comment: "Yes, two completely different markets are connected over the phone. And through employees who are constantly acting as though they were part of the Western market but are actually part of the Indian market." Florian

Melzacher, "Do You Find That Interesting, Too?" http://www.goethe.de/
kue/the/prj/cak/int/enindex.htm.

12 Even *Call Cutta*'s choice to use a standard cellphone issued by the theater,
and *Cell*'s use of the viewer's own cellphone reinforces this difference
between someone who is being well treated by a corporation and someone
who is working hard to uphold his or her part of a larger operation.

13 For an overview of this culture of surveillance, see Stephen Graham,
"Geographies of Surveillant Simulation," in *Virtual Geographies: Bodies,
Space and Relations,* ed. Phil Crang Mike Crang, and Jon May (London:
Routledge, 1999), 131–48.

14 Thus, in the opening section where the viewer is told to follow a pedestrian,
the dispatcher selects this person at whim, and depending upon the
willingness and vigor of the viewer, may chose to switch pedestrians
abruptly, or even channel the viewer onto a bus or subway. The dispatcher
must then deliver the viewer to the park bench in time for the next
improvised interaction. Because each viewer's trajectory intersects with
those who come before and after, the dispatcher must cannily assess the
viewer's progress, motivating them to speed up or slow down in order to
intersect with the other dispatcher-viewer duos at the right moments.

15 According to Andrew Simonet, the vast majority of viewers presumed
that they were being surveilled using the equipment in the tiny office
where they eventually encounter their dispatcher. Rather than imagine a
live body tracking them, they assume, like the viewers in *Call Cutta*, that
they are being tracked electronically. Whereas in *Call Cutta* it might be
possible to implant each phone with a tracking device, in *Cell* the only
plausible means of surveillance would be hidden cameras placed around
the city. The synthesizing of the information provided by the cameras
would require far more machinery than that witnessed by the viewers
when they meet the dispatcher face to face. Nonetheless, the culture of
surveillance in which we, in first-world urban centers, now live, implants
Cell with a comparable technological orientation. Susan Leigh Foster,
October 13, 2006. Interview with Andrew Simonet.

16 In 2004 Singaporean producer Tang Fu Kuen invited French artist Jérôme
Bel to Bangkok to collaborate with Thai dancer Pichet Klunchun. As Bel
recounts in the program notes: "Jet lag, the fascination that the city of
Bankok and its inhabitants exerted on me, the monstrous traffic jams that
did not make it possible to do all the rehearsals, the context of the
Bangkok Fringe Festival where the piece was to be premiered, led us to
represent to the audience a kind of theatrical report of our experience."
These are Bel's words, written in Seoul, Korea, June 1, 2005, and printed
in the program for the New York premiere of the piece at Dance Theater
Workshop, November 7–10, 2007. My analysis is based on a viewing of
the piece there and also in Los Angeles at the Disney-Redcat Theater,
February 27–28 and March 1, 2009.

17 My analysis of these two works is based on video viewings of performances:
I am a Demon, performed at Tanz im Auguste, August, 2006; and *About
Khon*, performed in Hong Kong in 2008.

18 For an overview of Anderson's earlier work, see Sherril Dodds, "Breaking
the Boundaries of High Art," *Dancing Times* 91 (2001); V. Briginshaw,
"Getting the Glamour on Our Own Terms," *Dance Theatre Journal* 12,

no. 3 (1995–96). And for a lucid analysis of her choreographic strategies, see Martin Hargreaves, "The Cut-up Pleasures and Politics of Lea Anderson's Choreography," *Theater Journal* 18, no. 3 (2002). KATHY is a collective of three classically trained dancers who perform primarily in visual arts venues. They never appear in public unmasked, and they circulate information about their projects and their history in the form of rumors via the internet. For an English language analysis of KATHY, see Carol Martin, "Lingering Heat and Local Global J Stuff," *Drama Review* 50, no. 1 (2006). My analysis of both works is based on video viewings and also on interviews with the artists.

19 This is Anderson's title for the character.

20 Nobuko Anan, "Reconsideration of Japanese Women's Bodies: Kathy's Parody of Singin' in the Rain," in *Portrayals of Americans on the World Stage: Critical Essays*, ed. Jr. Kevin J. Wetmore, Jr. (Jefferson, N.C.: McFarland, 2009), 134–54.

21 As Shu-Mei Shih has shown convincingly in her study of Sinophone cultures, constructions of the feminine can purvey distinctive sets of meanings within local, regional, and national contexts. Shih untangles the many layers of significance embedded in visual images, paintings and films, as they travel across borders and are received by viewers who continue to affiliate with China while also identifying with their diverse local communities. She also demonstrates how multiple gazes – patriarchal, ethnic, post-Communist, and Orientalist – operate to influence a work's reception, but also how some of those gazes can be shown to be anticipated and rebuffed within a given artist's work. See Shu-mei Shih, *Visuality and Identity: Sinophone Articulations across the Pacific* (Berkeley: University of California Press, 2007).

22 For an expanded analysis of post-Thatcher theater in Great Britain, see Amelia Howe Kritzer, *Political Theatre in Post-Thatcher Britain: New Writing: 1995-2005* (Basingstoke, England: Palgrave Macmillan, 2008).

23 For an insightful analysis of the effects of late capitalism on women's bodies, see Susan Bordo, *Unbearable Weight: Feminism, Western Culture, and the Body* (Berkeley: University of California Press, 1993).

Bibliography

Ackerknecht, Erwin. H. "The History of the Discovery of the Vegetative (Autonomic) Nervous System." *Medical History* 18, no. 1 (January 1974): 1–8.

Addison, Joseph, Richard Steele, and others. *The Spectator.* Edited with notes by Donald F. Bond ed. Oxford: Clarendon Press, [1711–12] 1965.

An Account of the Late Terrible Earthquake in Sicily; with Most of Its Particulars. London: Printed for Richard Baldwin, 1693.

Anan, Nobuko. "Reconsideration of Japanese Women's Bodies: Kathy's Parody of Singin' in the Rain." In *Portrayals of Americans on the World Stage: Critical Essays,* edited by Kevin J. Wetmore, Jr. 134–54. Jefferson, N.C.: McFarland, 2009.

Andry de Bois-Regard, Nicolas. *Orthopædia or, the Art of Correcting and Preventing Deformities in Children: . . . To Which Is Added, a Defence of the Orthopædia, by Way of Supplement, by the Author. Translated from the French of M. Andry, . . . In Two Volumes. Illustrated with Cuts.* London: Printed for A. Millar, 1743.

Anon. "No, 88." In *The Tatler,* edited with an introduction and notes by Donald F. Bond, 55–58. Oxford: Clarendon Press, [1709] 1987.

Arbeau, Thoinot. *Orchesography.* Translated by Mary Stewart Evans. New York: Dover Publications, [1589] 1967.

Armstrong, Nancy, and Leonard Tennenhouse. *The Ideology of Conduct: Essays on Literature and the History of Sexuality,* Essays in Literature and Society. New York: Methuen, 1987.

Armstrong, Nancy. "The Rise of the Domestic Woman." In *The Ideology of Conduct: Essays on Literature and the History of Sexuality,* edited by Nancy Armstrong and Leonard Tennenhouse, 96–141. New York: Methuen, 1987.

Arnold, David. "Hunger in the Garden of Plenty: The Bengal Famine of 1770." In *Dreadful Visitations: Confronting Natural Catastrophe in the Age of Enlightenment,* edited by Alessa Johns, 81–100. New York: Routledge, 1999.

Banes, Sally. *Democracy's Body: Judson Dance Theater, 1962–1964.* Ann Arbor, Mich.: UMI Research Press, 1983.

Barker-Benfield, G. J. *The Culture of Sensibility: Sex and Society in Eighteenth-Century Britain*. Chicago: University of Chicago Press, 1996.

Barthes, Roland. *The Responsibility of Forms: Critical Essays on Music, Art, and Representation*. 1st ed. New York: Hill and Wang, 1985.

Battersby, Christine. "An Enquiry Concerning the Humean Woman." *Philosophy* 56, no. 217 (1981): 303–12.

Bejamin, Walter. "The Return of the Flaneur." In *Walter Bejamin: Selected Writings, 1927–1934*, edited by Michael William Jennings Marcus Paul Bullock, Howard Eiland, and Gary Smith, 262–67. Cambridge, Mass.: Harvard University Press, 1999.

Bench, Harmony. "Choreographing Bodies in Dance-Media." PhD dissertation, University of California at Los Angeles, 2009.

Berthoz, Alain. *The Brain's Sense of Movement*, Perspectives in Cognitive Neuroscience. Cambridge, Mass.: Harvard University Press, 2000.

Blasis, Carlo. *The Code of Terpsichore: A Practical and Historical Treatise, on the Ballet, Dancing, and Pantomime: With a Complete Theory of the Art of Dancing: Intended as Well for the Instruction of Amateurs as the Use of Professional Persons*. Translated by R. Barton. London: James Bulcock, 1828.

———. *Traité Élémentaire Théorique Et Pratique De L'art De La Danse Contenant Les Développmens, Et Les Démonstrations Des Principes Généraux Et Particuliers, Qui Doivent Guider Le Danseur*. Milan: Chez Beati et Antonie Tenenti, 1820.

Bordo, Susan. *Unbearable Weight: Feminism, Western Culture, and the Body*. Berkeley: University of California Press, 1993.

Boring, Edward G. *Sensation and Perception in the History of Experimental Psychology*. New York: D. Appleton-Century, 1942.

Brandstetter, Gabriele. "The Code of Terpsichore: The Dance Theory of Carlo Blasis, Mechanics as the Matrix of Grace." *Topoi* 24 (2005): 67–79.

Briginshaw, V. "Getting the Glamour on Our Own Terms." *Dance Theatre Journal* 12, no. 3 (1995–96): 36–39.

Brown, Laura. *Fables of Modernity: Literature and Culture in the English Eighteenth Century*. Ithaca, N.Y.: Cornell University Press, 2001.

Brown, Theodore M. "From Mechanism to Vitalism in Eighteenth-Century English Physiology." *Journal of the History of Biology* 7, no. 2 (1974): 179–216.

Buisseret, David, ed. *Monarchs, Ministers, and Maps: The Emergence of Cartography as a Tool of Government in Early Modern Europe*. Chicago: University of Chicago Press, 1992.

Bulwer, John. *Chirologia: Or, the Natural Language of the Hand, and Chironomia: Or, the Art of Manual Rhetoric*, Landmarks in Rhetoric and Public Address. Carbondale: Southern Illinois University Press, [1654] 1974.

Butchart, Alexander. *The Anatomy of Power: European Constructions of the African Body*. London, England: Zed Books, 1998.

Butler, Judith. *Gender Trouble: Feminism and the Subversion of Identity.* New York: Routledge, 1990.

Calvo-Merino, B., D. E. Glaser, J. Grèzes, R. E. Passingham, and P. Haggard. "Action Observation and Acquired Motor Skills: An Mri Study with Expert Dancers." *Cerebral Cortex* 15 (August 2005): 1243–49.

Caps, Steve. "How Long Will It Be before You Come out of the Subway and You Hold up Your Screen to Get a Better View of What You're Looking at in the Physical World?" *New York Times,* February 17, 2009, D1 and D4.

Caroso, Fabritio. *Nobiltà Di Dame.* Edited with an introduction by Julia Sutton; music transcribed and edited by F. Marian Walker. Oxford: Oxford University Press, [1600] 1986.

Carter, Alexandra. *Dance and Dancers in the Victorian and Edwarian Music Hall Ballet.* Aldershot, England: Ashgate, 2005.

Carter, Paul. *The Road to Botany Bay: An Exploration of Landscape and History.* 1st American ed. New York: Knopf: Distributed by Random House, 1988.

Certeau, Michel de. *The Practice of Everyday Life.* Berkeley: University of California Press, 1984.

Chaplin, Joyce E. "Natural Philosophy and an Early Racial Idiom in North America: Comparing English and Indian Bodies." *William and Mary Quarterly* 54, no. 1 (1997): 229–52.

Chase, Thomas. "An Account of What Happened to Mr. Thomas Chase, at Lisbon, in the Great Earthquake: Written by Himself, in a Letter to His Mother, Dated the 31st of December, 1755." In *The Lisbon Earthquake of 1755: Some British Eye-Witness Accounts,* edited by Judite Nozes, 40–60. Lisbon: British Historical Society of Portugal, 1987.

Chatterjea, Ananya. *Butting Out: Reading Resistive Choreographies through Works by Jawole Willa Jo Zollar and Chandralekha.* 1st ed. Middletown, Conn.: Wesleyan University Press, 2004.

Coleman, Francis X. J. *The Aesthetic Thought of the French Enlightenment.* Pittsburgh: University of Pittsburgh Press, 1971.

Colley, Linda. *Britons: Forging the Nation, 1707–1837.* New Haven: Yale University Press, 1992.

Condillac, Etienne Bonnot de. *Condillac's Treatise on the Sensations.* Translated by Margaret Geraldine Spooner Carr. London: Favil Press, [1754] 1930.

Cosgrove, Denis E. *Apollo's Eye: A Cartographic Genealogy of the Earth in the Western Imagination.* Baltimore: Johns Hopkins University Press, 2001.

———. *Geography and Vision: Seeing, Imagining and Representing the World.* London: Palgrave Macmillan, 2008.

Crary, Jonathan. *Techniques of the Observer: On Vision and Modernity in the Nineteenth Century.* Cambridge, Mass.: MIT Press, 1990.

Craske, Matthew. *Art in Europe, 1700–1830: A History of the Visual Arts in an Era of Unprecedented Urban Economic Growth.* Oxford, England: Oxford University Press, 1997.

Cross, Stephen J. "John Hunter, the Animal Oeconomy, and Late Eighteenth Century Physiological Discourse." In *Studies in the History of Biology*, 1–110. Baltimore: Johns Hopkins Press, 1981.

Cvetkovich, Ann. *Mixed Feelings: Feminism, Mass Culture, and Victorian Sensationalism*. New Brunswick, N.J.: Rutgers University Press, 1992.

Damasio, Antonio, and Mary Helen Immordino-Yang. "Tweet This: Rapid-Fire Media May Confuse Our Moral Compass," http://www.physorg.com/ news158864256.html.

Dana, Peter H. "The Geographer's Craft Project," http://www.colorado.edu/ geography/gcraft/notes/gps/gps.html.

Darwin, Erasmus. *A Plan for the Conduct of Female Education in Boarding Schools*. New York: S. R. Publishers, [1797] 1968.

Davis, Mark H. *Empathy: A Social Psychological Approach*, Social Psychology Series. Boulder, Colo.: Westview Press, 1996.

DeFrantz, Thomas. *Dancing Revelations: Alvin Ailey's Embodiment of African American Culture*. Oxford ; New York: Oxford University Press, 2004.

Deloria, Philip Joseph. *Playing Indian*. New Haven, Conn.: Yale University Press, 1998.

Derrida, Jacques. *The Archeology of the Frivolous: Reading Condillac*. Pittsburgh: Duquesne University Press, 1980.

Diem, Carl. "Per Henrik Ling; on the Occasion of the One Hundredth Anniversary of His Death," http://www.la84foundation.org/ OlympicInformationCenter/OlympicReview/1939/ORUE5/ORUE5b.pdf.

Digby, Kenelm. *A Late Discourse Made in a Solemne Assembly of Nobles and Learned Men at Montpellier in France Touching the Cure of Wounds by the Powder of Sympathy: With Instructions How to Make the Said Powder: Whereby Many Other Secrets of Nature Are Unfolded*. Translated by R. White. London: Printed for R. Lownes and T. Davies, 1658.

Dodds, Sherril. "Breaking the Boundaries of High Art." *Dancing Times* 91 (2001): 433–39.

Doiron, Normand, and Gillian Lane-Mercier. "Travel Essays." In *Literature of Travel and Exploration, an Encyclopedia*, edited by Jennifer Speake, 1192–94. New York and London: Taylor and Francis, 2003.

Doolittle, Thomas. *Earthquakes Explained and Practically Improved*. London: John Salusbury, 1693.

Dougherty, M. Frances. "Theater Forms." In *Encyclopedia of Physical Education, Fitness, and Sports*, edited by Rueben B. Frost, 578–597. Reading, Mass.: Addison-Wesley Publishing, 1977.

Douglas, Bronwen. "Climate to Crania: Science and the Racialization of Human Difference." In *Foreign Bodies: Oceania and the Science of Race 1750–1940*, edited by Chris Ballard and Bronwen Douglas, 33–99. Canberra, Australia: ANU E Press, 2008.

DuBos, Abbé. *Critical Reflections on Poetry, Painting and Music with an Inquiry into the Rise and Progress of the Theatrical Entertainments of the Ancients. Translated into English by Thomas Nugent, Gent. From the Fifth*

Edition Revised, Corrected, and Inlarged by the Author. London: Printed for John Nourse, 1748.

"A Dull Season in Paris." *New York Times*, March 17, 1878.

Dymond, R. F. "A Scale for the Measurement of Emphatic Ability." *Journal of Consulting Psychologist* 13 (1940): 127–33.

Dymond, R. F., A. S. Hughes, and V. L. Raabe. "Measurable Changes in Empathy with Age." *Journal of Consulting Psychology* 16 (1952): 202–6.

Edney, Matthew H. "Bringing India to Hand." In *The Global Eighteenth Century*, edited by Felicity A. Nussbaum, 65–78. Baltimore: Johns Hopkins University Press, 2003.

——. *Mapping an Empire: The Geographical Construction of British India, 1765–1843*. Delhi: Oxford University Press, 1999.

Elyot, Thomas. *The Book Named the Governor*. Edited by S. E. Lehmberg. 2d ed. New York: Dutton, [1531] 1962.

Engelhardt, Molly. "Seed of Discontent: Dancing Manias and Medical Inquiry in Nineteenth-Century British Literature and Culture." *Victorian Literature and Culture* 35 (2007): 135–56.

Engelhardt, Molly. *Dancing out of Line: Ballrooms, Ballets, and Mobility in Victorian Fiction and Culture*. Athens, Ohio: Ohio University Press, 2009.

Essex, John. *For the Furthur Improvement of Dancing, a Treatis of Chorography . . . Translated from the French of Monsr Feuillet*. London: Sold by I. Walsh and P. Randall, I. Hare, I. Culen, and by ye author, 1710.

Fairfax, Edmund. *The Styles of Eighteenth Century Ballet*. Lanham, Md.: Scarecrow Press, 2003.

Fontaine, Philippe. "Identification and Economic Behavior: Sympathy and Empathy in Historical Perspective." *Economics and Philosophy* 13 (1997): 261–80.

Forget, Evelyn. "Evocations of Sympathy: Sympathetic Imagery in Eighteenth-Century Social Theory and Physiology." In *Oeconomies in the Age of Newton*, edited by Margaret Schabas and Neil De Marchi, 282–307. Durham, N.C.: Duke University Press, 2003.

Foster, Susan Leigh. "Choreographies of Gender." *Signs* 24, no. 1 (1998): 1–33.

——. "Choreographies of Protest." *Theatre Journal* 55, no. 3 (2003): 395–412.

——. Interview with Andrew Simonet. October 13, 2006.

Fournier, Marian. *The Fabric of Life: Microscopy in the Seventeenth Century*. Baltimore: Johns Hopkins University Press, 1996.

Franko, Mark. *The Dancing Body in Renaissance Choreography (C. 1416–1589)*. Birmingham, Ala.: Summa Publications, 1986.

Franko, Mark. *The Work of Dance : Labor, Movement, and Identity in the 1930s*. Middletown, Conn.: Wesleyan University Press, 2002.

Fuller, Buckminster. *Synergetics Dictionary*. Vol. 2. New York: Garland Publishing, 1986.

"The Fusion of Music and Dancing." *The Times*, July 26, 1913, 11.

Gallese, Vittorio. "Empathy, Embodied Simulation, and the Brain: Commentary on Aragno and Zepf/Hartmann." *Journal of the American Psychoanalytic Association* 56 (2008): 769–81.

——. "The Roots of Empathy: The Shared Manifold Hypothesis and the Neural Basis of Intersubjectivity." *Psychopathology* 36 (2003): 171–80.

——. "The Shared Manifold Hypothesis." *Journal of Consciousness Studies* 8 (2001): 33–50.

Gallini, Giovanni-Andrea. *A Treatise on the Art of Dancing.* London: R. and J. Dodsley, in Pall Mall; T. Becket, in the Strand; and W. Nicoll, in St. Paul's Church-Yard, 1762.

Garnett, James Mercer. *Seven Lectures on Female Education, Inscribed to Mrs. Garnett's Pupils, at Elm-Wood, Essex County.* Richmond: T. W. White, 1824.

Garnham, Neal. "Both Praying and Playing: 'Muscular Christianity' And the YMCA in North-East County Durham." *Journal of Social History* 35, no. 2 (2001): 397–407.

Gautier, Théophile. *Gautier on Dance: Théophile Gautier.* Translated and edited by Ivor Forbes Guest. London: Dance Books, 1986.

"Gay Parisian Topics." *New York Times*, April 2, 1882.

Gere, David, and Dance Critics Association (US). *Looking Out: Perspectives on Dance and Criticism in a Multicultural World.* New York: Schirmer Books, 1995.

Gibson, James Jerome. *The Ecological Approach to Visual Perception.* Boston: Houghton Mifflin, 1979.

——. *The Senses Considered as Perceptual Systems.* Boston: Houghton Mifflin, 1966.

Giersdorf, Jens Richard. "Dance Studies in the International Academy: Genealogy of a Disciplinary Formation." *Dance Research Journal* 41, no. 1 (2009): 23–44.

Goff, Moira. "Dancing-Masters in Early Eighteenth-Century London." *Early Music* 26, no. 2 (May 1998): 213–28.

Goring, Paul. *The Rhetoric of Sensibility in Eighteenth-Century Culture.* Cambridge, England: Cambridge University Press, 2005.

Goss, John. *The Mapmaker's Art: A History of Cartography.* London: Studio Editions, 1993.

Graham, Martha. *Blood Memory.* 1st ed. New York: Doubleday, 1991.

Graham, Stephen. "Geographies of Surveillant Simulation." In *Virtual Geographies: Bodies, Space and Relations*, edited by Phil Crang, Mike Crang, and Jon May, 131–48. London: Routledge, 1999.

Greenfield Boyce, Nell. "Moo North: Cows Sense Earth's Magnetism," http://www.npr.org/templates/story/story.php?storyId=93956323.

Guazzo, Stefano. *The Civile Conversation of M. Steffan Guazzo Written First in Italian . . .* Translated by George Pettie. Imprinted at London: By Richard Watkins, 1581.

Guest, Ivor. *Ballet in Leicester Square: The Alhambra and the Empire, 1860–1915*. London: Dance Books, 1992.

H'Doubler, Margaret Newell. *The Dance and Its Place in Education*. New York: Harcourt, Brace and Company, 1925.

———. *The Dance*. New York: Harcourt, Brace, 1925.

———. *Rhythmic Form and Analysis*. Madison, Wis.: J. M. Rider, 1932.

Haasum, James Douglas. *Ling's System. Swedish Gymnastics*. London: Librairie Hachette, 1885.

Hagendoorn, Ivar. "Some Speculative Hypothesis About the Nature and Perception of Dance and Choreography." *Journal of Consciousness Studies* 11, no. 3–4 (2004): 79–100.

Hall, Donald E. *Muscular Christianity: Embodying the Victorian Age*. Cambridge, England: Cambridge University Press, 1994.

Halpern, Alice J. *The Technique of Martha Graham*. Pennington, N.J.: Society of Dance History Scholars at Princeton Periodicals, 1991.

Hammergren, Lena. "The Re-Turn of the Flâneuse." In *Corporealities*, edited by Susan Leigh Foster, 53-69. London: Routledge, 1996.

Hammond, Sandra Noll. "International Elements of Dance Training in the Late Eigtheenth Century." In *The Grotesque Dancer on the Eighteenth-Century Stage*, edited by Rebecca Harris-Warrick and Bruce Alan Brown, 109–50. Madison, Wis.: University of Wisconsin Press, 2005.

Hargreaves, Jennifer. *Sporting Females: Critical Issues in the History and Sociology of Women's Sports*. London: Routledge, 1994.

Hargreaves, Martin. "The Cut-up Pleasures and Politics of Lea Anderson's Choreography." *Theater Journal* 18, no. 3 (2002): 16–19.

Harris-Warrick, Rebecca, and Carol G. Marsh. *Musical Theatre at the Court of Louis Xiv: Le Mariage De La Grosse Cathos*, Cambridge Musical Texts and Monographs. Cambridge, England: Cambridge University Press, 1994.

Hayles, N. Katherine. "Virtual Bodies and Flickering Signifiers." *October* 66 (1993): 69–91.

Headley, John M. "Geography and Empire in the Late Renaissance: Botero's Assignment, Western Universalism, and the Civilizing Process." *Renaissance Quarterly* 53, no. 4 (2000): 1119–55.

Hedrick, Elizabeth. "Romancing the Salve: Sir Kenelm Digby and the Powder of Sympathy." *British Journal for the History of Science* 41, no. 2 (2008): 161–85.

Hewitt, Andrew. *Social Choreography: Ideology as Performance in Dance and Everyday Movement*. Durham and London: Duke University Press, 2005.

"High Court of Justice." *The Times*, August 6, 1890, 2–3.

Hill, John. *The Actor: A Treatise on the Art of Playing*. London: R. Griffiths, 1750.

Hinton, Laura. *The Perverse Gaze of Sympathy: Sadomasochistic Sentiments from Clarissa to Rescue 911*, Suny Series in Feminist Criticism and Theory. Albany: State University of New York Press, 1999.

Hobson, Marian. *The Object of Art: The Theory of Illusion in Eighteenth-Century France*, Cambridge Studies in French. Cambridge, England: Cambridge University Press, 1982.

Horst, Louis, and Carroll Russell. *Modern Dance Forms in Relation to the Other Modern Arts*. Brooklyn, N.Y.: Dance Horizons, 1977.

Howard, Ian P., and William B. Templeton. *Human Spatial Orientation*. London: Wiley, 1966.

Howard, Skiles. *The Politics of Courtly Dancing in Early Modern England*. Amherst: University of Massachusetts Press, 1998.

Hughes, Russell Meriwether. *Dance Composition, the Basic Elements*. Lee, Mass.: Jacob's Pillow Dance Festival, 1965.

———. *Total Education in Ethnic Dance*. New York: M. Dekker, 1977.

Hume, David. *A Treatise of Human Nature Being an Attempt to Introduce the Experimental Method of Reasoning into Moral Subjects*. Vol. 2. London: Printed for John Noon, 1739.

Humphrey, Doris. *The Art of Making Dances*. New York: Rinehart, 1959.

J. D. R., French Minister. *The Earth Twice Shaken Wonderfully*. Translated by Edward Locke. London: Sion's College, 1693/1694.

Jaffe, Audrey. *Scenes of Sympathy: Identity and Representation in Victorian Fiction*. Ithaca, N.Y.: Cornell University Press, 2000.

Jaucourt, Chevalier de. "Entry on Sympathy." In *Encyclopédie, Ou Dictionnaire Raisonné Dessciences, Des Arts Et Des Métiers*, 220–28. Paris: Briasson, 1762–72.

Jenyns, Soame. *The Art of Dancing: A Poem in Three Cantos*. Edited by Anne Cottis. London: Dance Books, [1729] 1978.

Jeyasingh, Shobana. "Getting Off the Orient Express." *Dance Theatre Journal* 8, no. 2 (1990): 34–37.

Jones, E. G. "The Development of the 'Muscular Sense' Concept During the Nineteenth Century and the Work of H. Charlton Bastian." *Journal of the History of Medicine and Allied Sciences* 27, no. 3 (July 1972): 289–311.

Jordan, Stephanie. *Striding Out: Aspects of Contemporary and New Dance in Britain*. London: Dance Books, 1992.

Jordanova, Ludmilla J. *Nature Displayed: Gender, Science, and Medicine, 1760–1820: Essays*. London: Longman, 1999.

Karina, Lilian, and Marion Kant. *Hitler's Dancers: German Modern Dance and the Third Reich*. New York: Berghahn Books, 2003.

Kennedy, John F. "The Soft American." *Sports Illustrated* (December 26, 1960): 14–17.

"The King of Siam." *The Times*, September 17, 1897, 19.

Knight, Isabel. *The Geometric Spirit: The Abbé De Condillac and the French Enlightenment*. New Haven: Yale University Press, 1968.

Koerner, Lisbet. "Carl Linnaeus in His Time and Place." In *Cultures of Natural History*, edited by Nicholas Jardine, James A. Second, and Emma Spary, 145–62. Cambridge, England: Cambridge University Press, 1996.

Krasner, David. "Empathy and Theater." In *Staging Philosophy: Intersections of Theater, Performance, and Philosophy*, edited by David Krasner and David Z. Saltz, 255–77. Ann Arbor, Mich.: University of Michigan Press, 2006.

Kraut, Anthea. "Race-Ing Choreographic Copyright." In *Worlding Dance*, edited by Susan Leigh Foster. London: Palgrave-McMillan, 2009, 76–97.

Kriegsman, Sali Ann. *Modern Dance in America – the Bennington Years*. Boston, Mass.: G. K. Hall, 1981.

Kritzer, Amelia Howe. *Political Theatre in Post-Thatcher Britain: New Writing: 1995–2005*. Basingstoke, England: Palgrave Macmillan, 2008.

Kupperman, Karen Ordahl. *Indians and English: Facing Off in Early America*. Ithaca, N.Y.: Cornell University Press, 2000.

Lamy, Bernard, and Pierre Nicole. *The Art of Speaking: Written in French by Messieurs Du Port Royal: In Persuance of a Former Treatise, Intituled, the Art of Thinking. Rendred into English*. The second , corrected ed. London: Printed for W. Taylor; and H. Clements, 1708.

Laqueur, Thomas Walter. *Making Sex: Body and Gender from the Greeks to Freud*. Cambridge, Mass.: Harvard University Press, 1992.

Laurenti, Jean Noël. "Feuillet's Thinking." In *Traces of the Dance*, edited by Laurence Louppe, 81–103. Paris: Editions Dis Voir, 1994.

Law, John. *Money and Trade Considered with a Proposal for Supplying the Nation with Money*. Edinburgh: Printed by the heirs and successors of Andrew Anderson, 1705.

Lee, Vernon. *The Beautiful; an Introduction to Psychological Aesthetics*. Cambridge, England: Cambridge University Press, 1913.

Lepecki, André. "Choreograpy as Apparatus of Capture." *TDR: The Drama Review* 51, no. 2 (T 194) (2007): 119-23.

Lepore, Jill. *The Name of War: King Philip's War and the Origins of American Identity*. New York: Vintage Books, 1999.

Lisby, M., J. Barlow, R. Brugess, and R. Rothstein. "Choreography of the DNA Damage Response Spatiotemporal Relationships among Checkpoint and Repair Proteins." *Cell* 118, no. 6 (2004): 699-713.

Lithwick, Dahlia. "Once More, without Feeling: The GOP's Misguided and Confused Campaign against Judicial Empathy," http://www.slate.com/id/2218103/pagenum/all/.

Locke, John. *The Educational Writings of John Locke. A Critical Edition with Introduction and Notes by James Axtell*. Cambridge, England: Cambridge University Press, 1968.

Macaulay, Catharine. *Letters on Education*, Revolution and Romanticism, 1789–1834. Oxford, England: Woodstock Books, [1790] 1994.

Macaulay, Rose. *They Went to Portugal*. London: Jonathan Cape, 1946.

Magalhaens, l'Abbé de. *Lettre Écrite Aux Auteurs Du Journal Étranger Du Moi D'avril*: n.p., 1760.

Maguire, Jennifer Smith. *Fit for Consumption: Sociology and the Business of Fitness*. London: Routledge, 2008.

Manning, Susan. "Danced Spirituals." In *Of the Presence of the Body: Essays on Dance and Performance Theory*, edited by André Lepecki, 82–96. Middletown, Conn.: Wesleyan University Press, 2004.

———. *Ecstasy and the Demon : Feminism and Nationalism in the Dances of Mary Wigman*. Berkeley: University of California Press, 1993.

———. *Modern Dance, Negro Dance: Race in Motion*. Minneapolis: University of Minnesota Press, 2004.

Marshall, David. *The Figure of Theater: Shaftesbury, Defoe, Adam Smith, and George Eliot*. New York: Columbia University Press, 1986.

Martin, Carol. "Lingering Heat and Local Global J Stuff." *TDR: The Drama Review 50*, no. 1 (2006): 46–56.

Martin, John Joseph. *America Dancing; the Background and Personalities of the Modern Dance*. New York,: Dodge publishing company, 1936.

———. *Introduction to the Dance*. New York: W. W. Norton, 1939.

———. *The Dance*. New York: Tudor Publishing Company, 1946.

———. *The Modern Dance*. New York: A. S. Barnes, 1933.

Martin, Randy. *Critical Moves : Dance Studies in Theory and Politics*. Durham N.C. ; London: Duke University Press, 1998.

———. "Dance's Diversity: A U.S. Perspective." In *Dance: Transcending Borders*, edited by Urmimala Sarkar Munsi. New Delhi: Tulika Books, 2008.

———. "Overreading the Promise Land: Toward a Narrative Context in Dance." In *Corporealities : Dancing, Knowledge, Culture, and Power*, edited by Susan Leigh Foster, xvii, 263. London ; New York: Routledge, 1996.

Marx, Robert F. *Pirate Port: The Story of the Sunken City of Port Royal*. Cleveland: World Publishing, 1967.

Mayhew, Robert J. *Enlightenment Geography: The Political Languages of British Geography, 1650–1850*. New York: St. Martin's Press, 2000.

McIntosh, Peter C. *Sport in Society*. London: C. A. Watts, 1963.

Mead, George Herbert, and Charles W. Morris. *Mind, Self & Society from the Standpoint of a Social Behaviorist*. Chicago: University of Chicago Press, 1934.

Meltzoff, Andrew N. "Elements of a Development Theory of Imitation." In *The Imitative Mind*, edited by Andrew N. Meltzoff and Wolfgang Prinz, 19–42. Cambridge, England: Cambridge University Press, 2002.

Melzacher, Florian. "Do You Find That Interesting, Too?" http://www.goethe.de/kue/the/prj/cak/int/enindex.htm.

Menestrier, Claude-François. *Des Ballets Anciens Et Modernes Selon Les Regles Du Theatre*. A Paris: Chez R. Guignard, 1682.

Merleau-Ponty, Maurice. *Phenomenology of Perception*. London: Routledge, 1962.

Meurs, Johannes van. *Ioannis Mevrsi Orchestra. Sive, De Saltationibvs Vetervm, Liber Singularis*. Lvgdvni Batavorvm: ex officinâ Godefridi Basson, 1618.

"Modern Dances Held to Mean a Modern Renaissance." *New York Times*, May 3, 1914.

Monro, Alexander. *Observations on the Structure and Functions of the Nervous System Illustrated with Tables. By Alexander Monro.* Edinburgh: Printed for, and sold by, William Creech; and Joseph Johnson, London, 1783.

Montrose, Louis. "The Work of Gender in the Discourse of Discovery." *Representations* 33 Special Issue: *The New World* (1991): 1–41.

Moore, F. B. "Glorified Ballet Art." *New York Times*, December 24, 1916.

More, Hannah. *Strictures on Female Education*, Revolution and Romanticism, 1789–1834. Oxford: Woodstock Books, [1799] 1995.

Morris, Gay. *A Game for Dancers: Performing Modernism in the Postwar Years, 1945–1960.* Middletown, Conn.: Wesleyan University Press, 2006.

Mulcaster, Richard. *Positions Concerning the Training up of Children.* William Barker ed. Toronto, Ont.: University of Toronto Press, [1581] 1994.

Müller-Wille, Staffan. "Nature as Marketplace: The Political Economy of Linnaean Botany." In *Oeconomies in the Age of Newton*, edited by Margaret Schabas and Neil De Marchi, 154–72. Durham, N.C.: Duke University Press, 2003.

Nevile, Jennifer. *The Eloquent Body: Dance and Humanist Culture in Fifteenth-Century Italy.* Bloomington: Indiana University Press, 2004.

"New Ballet Puzzles." *New York Times*, July 12, 1913.

Norton, David Fate. *The Cambridge Companion to Hume.* Cambridge, England: Cambridge University Press, 1993.

Novack, Cynthia Jean. *Sharing the Dance : Contact Improvisation and American Culture.* Madison, Wis.: University of Wisconsin Press, 1990.

Noverre, Jean Georges. *Letters on Dancing and Ballets.* Translated by Cyril W. Beaumont from the rev. and enl. edition published in St. Petersburg. Brooklyn, N.Y.: Dance Horizons, [1803] 1966.

Nozes, Judite, ed. *The Lisbon Earthquake of 1755: Some British Eye-Witness Accounts.* London: British Historical Society of Portugal, 1987.

Obama, Barack. *The Audacity of Hope: Thoughts on Reclaiming the American Dream.* New York: Random House, 2008.

Olwig, Kenneth. *Landscape, Nature, and the Body Politic: From Britain's Renaissance to America's New World.* Madison, Wis.: University of Wisconsin Press, 2002.

Osler, Sir William. *Sir Kenelm Digby's Powder of Sympathy.* Los Angeles: Plantin Press, 1972.

Peltier, Leonard F. *Orthopedics: A History and Iconography*, Norman Orthopedic Series, no. 3. San Francisco: Norman Publishing, 1993.

Pemberton, E. *An Essay for the Further Improvement of Dancing.* London: Printed, and sold by J. Walsh, J. Hare, and at the author's, 1711.

Piaget, Jean. *The Moral Judgement of the Child.* London: Kegan Paul, 1932.

Playford, John. *The English Dancing Master or, Plaine and Easie Rules for the Dancing of Country Dances, with the Tune to Each Dance.* Hugh Mellor and Leslie Bridgewater ed. London: Dance Books, 1984 [1651].

"A Play to Run Six Months." *New York Times*, October 30, 1882.

Pocock, J. G. A. *Virtue, Commerce, and History: Essays on Political Thought and History, Chiefly in the Eighteenth Century*. Cambridge, England: Cambridge University Press, 1985.

Pond, Irving. *The Meaning of Architecture*. Boston: Marshall Jones, 1918.

Poovey, Mary. *Making a Social Body: British Cultural Formation, 1830–1864*. Chicago: University of Chicago Press, 1995.

Porter, Roy. *Flesh in the Age of Reason*. London: Allen Lane, 2003.

Pred, Allan. "The Choreography of Existence: Comments on Hagerstrand's Time-Geography and Its Usefulness." *Economic Geography* 53, no. 2 (1977): 207–21.

Prigman, G. W. "Freud and the History of Empathy." *International Journal of Psychoanalysis* 76 (1995): 237–52.

Prinz, Wolfgang. "Experimental Approaches to Imitation." In *The Imitative Mind: Development, Evolution, and Brain Bases*, edited by Andrew N. Meltzoff and Wolfgang Prinz, 143–62. Cambridge, England: Cambridge University Press, 2002.

Rainer, Yvonne. *Work 1960–73*. Halifax: Press of the Nova Scotia College of Design and New York University Press, 1974.

Ralph, Richard. *The Life and Works of John Weaver: An Account of His Life, Writings and Theatrical Productions, with an Annotated Reprint of His Complete Publications*. New York: Dance Horizons, 1985.

Ravelhofer, Barbara. *The Early Stuart Masque: Dance, Costume, and Music*. Oxford: Oxford University Press, 2006.

Reed, Edward S. *James J. Gibson and the Psychology of Perception* New Haven: Yale University Press, 1988.

Reynolds, Dee. *Rhythmic Subjects*. Alton, Hampshire England: Dance Books, 2007.

Risse, G. B. "Cullen, the Seasoned Clinician: Organization and Strategies of a Successful Medical Practice in the Eighteenth Century." In *William Cullen and the Eighteenth-Century Medical World*, edited by J. P. S. Ferguson, A. Doig, I. A. Milne, and R. Passmore, 133–51. Edinburgh: Edinburgh University Press, 1993.

Rizzolatti, Giocomo, Luciano Fadiga, Leonardo Fogassi, and Vittorio Gallese. "From Mirror Neurons to Imitation: Facts and Speculations." In *The Imitative Mind: Development, Evolution, and Brain Bases*, edited by Andrew N. Meltzoff and Wolfgang Prinz, 247–66. Cambridge, England: Cambridge University Press, 2002.

Roach, Joseph R. *The Player's Passion: Studies in the Science of Acting*. Newark: University of Delaware Press, 1985.

——. "The Artificial Eye: Augustan Theater and the Empire of the Visible." In *The Performance of Power: Theatrical Discourse and Politics*, edited by Sue-Ellen Case and Janelle Reinelt, 131–45. Iowa City: University of Iowa, 1991.

Rogers, Carl. "Empathic: An Unappreciated Way of Being." *Counseling Psychologist* 5 (1975): 2–10.

Ross, Janice. *Moving Lessons: Margaret H'doubler and the Beginning of Dance in American Education*. Madison, Wis.: University of Wisconsin Press, 2000.

"The Russian Ballet." *The Times*, June 24, 1911, 6–7.

Ruyter, Nancy Lee Chalfa. "The Intellectual World of Genevieve Stebbins." *Dance Chronicle* 11, no. 3 (1988): 381–97.

——. *Reformers and Visionaries: The Americanization of the Art of Dance*. New York: Dance Horizons, 1979.

Sachs, Curt. *World History of the Dance*. Translated by Bessie Schönberg. New York: W. W. Norton, 1937.

Saint-Léon, Arthur, and Flavia Pappacena. *La Sténochorégraphie 1852*. Facsimile reprint ed. Lucca: Libreria Musicale Italiana, 2006.

Sargent, Dudley Allen. *Handbook of Developing Exercises*. Cambridge: n.p., 1897.

Savigliano, Marta. "Worlding Dance and Dancing out There in the World." In *Worlding Dance*, edited by Susan Leigh Foster, 163-90. London: Palgreave, 2009.

Sawday, Jonathan. *The Body Emblazoned: Dissection and the Human Body in Renaissance Culture*. London: Routledge, 1995.

"Scenes from Paris Life." *New York Times*, March 7, 1882.

Scheibinger, Londa L. *Plants and Empire: Colonial Bioprospecting in the Atlantic World*. Cambridge, Mass.: Harvard University Press, 2004.

——. "Skeletons in the Closet: The First Illustrations of the Female Skeleton in Eighteenth Century Anatomy." *Representations* 14 (1986): 42–82.

Schlundt, Christena L. *Daniel Nagrin: A Chronicle of His Professional Career*. Berkeley: University of California Press, 1997.

Schoenfeldt, Michael Carl. *Bodies and Selves in Early Modern England: Physiology and Inwardness in Spenser, Shakespeare, Herbert, and Milton*, Cambridge Studies in Renaissance Literature and Culture. Cambridge, England: Cambridge University Press, 1999.

Schwartz, Hillel. "Torque: The New Kinaesthetic of the Twentieth Century." In *Incorporations*, edited by Jonathan Crary and Sanford Kwinter, 70–127. Cambridge, Mass.: MIT Press, 1992.

Shea Murphy, Jacqueline. "'Gathering from Within…': Indigenous Nationhood' and Tanya Lukin Linklater's 'Woman and Water.'" *Theatre Research International* 35, no. 2 (2010): 165–71.

——. "Mobilizing (in) the Archive: Santee Smith's Kaha:Wi." In *Worlding Dance*, edited by Susan Leigh Foster, 32–52. Basingstoke: Palgrave Macmillan, 2009.

——. *The People Have Never Stopped Dancing: Native American Modern Dance Histories*. Minneapolis: University of Minnesota Press, 2007.

Sherrington, Charles Scott. *The Integrative Action of the Nervous System*. New Haven: Yale University Press, 1906.

Shih, Shu-mei. *Visuality and Identity: Sinophone Articulations across the Pacific*. Berkeley: University of California Press, 2007.

Shoemaker, J. W. *Delsartean Pantomimes, with Recital and Musical Accompaniment: Designed for Home, School, and Church Entertainments.* Philadelphia: Penn Publishing, 1919.

Shower, John. *Practical Reflections on the Earthquakes That Have Happened in Europe and America, but Chiefly in the Islands of Jamaica, England, Sicily, Malta, &C. With a Particular and Historical Account of Them, and Divers Other Earthquakes.* London: Printed and sold at the following pamphlet shops, Cook, James, and Kingman; Cooper; Robinson, 1750.

Sims, Laura S. *The Politics of Fat: Food and Nutrition Policy in America.* Armonk, N.Y.: M. E. Sharpe, 1998.

Siris, P. *The Art of Dancing, Demonstrated by Characters and Figures; . . . Done From the French of Monsieur Feuillet.* London: printed for the author, 1706.

Sklar, Deidre. "Can Bodylore Be Brought to Its Senses?" *The Journal of American Folklore* 107, no. 423 (1994): 9–22.

Smith, Adam. *The Theory of Moral Sentiments,* Great Books in Philosophy. Amherst, N.Y.: Prometheus Books, [1759] 2000.

Soares, Janet Mansfield. *Martha Hill and the Making of American Dance.* Middletown, CT: Wesleyan University Press, 2009.

Sparshott, Francis Edward. *Off the Ground: First Steps to a Philosophical Consideration of the Dance.* Princeton, N.J.: Princeton University Press, 1988.

Spencer, Herbert. "The Dynamics of Exclusion." In *Education: Intellectual, Moral, and Physical,* 252–58. London: Appleton, 1882.

Stebbins, Genevieve. *Delsarte System of Dramatic Expression.* New York: E. S. Werner, 1886.

——. *The Genevieve Stebbins System of Physical Training.* New York: E. S. Werner, 1898.

Stein, Edith. *On the Problem of Empathy.* Translated by Waltraut Stein. The Hague: Nijhoff, [1917] 1964. 2d ed. 1970.

Stocking, George. "From Chronology to Ethnology: James Cowles Prichard and British Anthropology, 1800–1850." In *Researches into the Physical History of Man,* edited by James Cowles Prichard, ix–cx. Chicago: University of Chicago Press, 1973.

Stott, Rosalie. "Health and Virtue: Or, How to Keep out of Harm's Way: Lectures on Pathology and Therapeutics by William Cullen Circa 1770." *Medical History* 31 (1987): 123–42.

Straub, Kristina. *Sexual Suspects Eighteenth-Century Players and Sexual Ideology.* Princeton, N.J.: Princeton University Press, 1992.

Taylor, Diana. *The Archive and the Repertoire : Performing Cultural Memory in the Americas.* Durham: Duke University Press, 2003.

Temkin, Owsei. *Galenism; Rise and Decline of a Medical Philosophy,* Cornell Publications in the History of Science. Ithaca, N.Y.: Cornell University Press, 1973.

Temple, Kathryn. "'Manly Composition:' Hume and the History of England." In *Feminist Interpretations of David Hume*, edited by Anne Jaap Jacobson, 263–82. University Park, Pa.: Pennsylvania State University Press, 2000.

The Compleat Geographer or, the Chorography and Topography of All the Known Parts of the Earth. To Which Is Premis'd an Introduction to Geography, and a Natural History of the Earth and the Elements. . . . To Which Are Added Maps of Every Country. Wherein the descriptions of Asia, Africa and America are compos'd anew. Third edition London: Awnsham and John Churchill. And Timothy Childe, 1709.

The Tatler, Tuesday, November 1 1709.

Thompson, Charis. *Making Parents : The Ontological Choreography of Reproductive Technologies.* Cambridge, Mass. ; London: MIT Press, 2005.

Thorpe, Jennifer. "Dance in the London Theaters C. 1700–1750." In *Dance, Spectacle, and the Body Politic, 1250–1750*, edited by Jennifer Nevile, 136–52. Bloomington: Indiana University Press, 2008.

Titchener, Edward Bradford. *Lectures on the Experimental Psychology of the Thought-Processes.* New York: Macmillan, 1909.

———. *A Text-Book of Psychology.* New York: Macmillan, 1909.

———. *A Textbook of Psychology (1910)*, History of Psychology Series. Delmar, N.Y.: Scholars' Facsimiles & Reprints, 1980.

Tomko, Linda J. "Mr. Isaac's *the Pastorall* and Issues Of 'Party.'" In *Dance, Spectacle, and the Body Politic, 1250–1750*, edited by Jennifer Nevile, 241–64. Bloomington: Indiana University Press, 2008.

Tournefort, Joseph Pitton de. *Eléments De Botanique, Ou, Méthode Pour Connoître Les Plantes.* Paris: De l'Imprimerie royale, 1694.

Traub, Valerie. "Mapping the Global Body." In *Early Modern Visual Culture*, edited by Peter Erickson and Clark Hulse, 44–97. Philadelphia: University of Pennsylvania Press, 2000.

Vigarello, Georges. "The Upward Training of the Body from the Age of Chivalry to Courtly Civility." In *Fragments for a History of the Human Body, Part Two*, edited by Michel Feher Jonathan Crary, Hal Foster, and Sanford Kwinter, 148–99. Cambridge, Mass.: MIT Press, 1989.

Vischer, Robert, Harry Francis Mallgrave, and Eleftherios Ikonomou. "On the Optical Sense of Form: A Contribution to Aesthetics." In *Empathy, Form, and Space: Problems in German Aesthetics, 1873–1893*, 89–124. Santa Monica, Calif.: Getty Center for the History of Art and the Humanities; distributed by the University of Chicago Press, 1994.

Walker, Alexander. *Woman Physiologically Considered as to Mind, Morals, Marriage, Matrimonial Slavery, Infidelity and Divorce.* 2d ed. London: A. H. Baily, 1840.

Walker, Donald, and John William Carleton. *Walker's Manly Exercises; Containing Rowing, Sailing, Riding, Driving, Racing, Hunting, Shooting, and Other Manly Sports.* 10th ed, Bohn's Illustrated Library. London: H. G. Bohn, 1857.

Walker, Donald. *Exercises for Ladies Calculated to Preserve and Improve Beauty, and to Prevent and Correct Personal Defect, Inseparable from Constrained or Careless Habits: Founded on Physiological Principles.* London: T. Hurst, 1836.

Wear, Andrew. "Explorations in Renaissance Writings on the Practice of Medicine." In *The Medical Renaissance of the Sixteenth Century,* edited by A. Wear, R. K. French and I. M. Lonie, 118–45. Cambridge, England: Cambridge University Press, 1985.

——. "Making Sense of Health and the Environment in Early Modern England." In *Medicine in Society: Historical Essays* edited by Andrew Wear, 119–48. Cambridge, England: Cambridge University Press, 1992.

Weaver, John. *An Essay Towards an History of Dancing in Which the Whole Art and Its Various Excellencies Are in Some Measure Explain'd.* London: printed for Jacob Tonson, 1712.

——. *The Loves of Mars and Venus.* London: W. Mears, 1717.

——. *Orchesography; or, the Art of Dancing, by Characters and Demostrative Figures. Wherein the Whole Art Is Explain'd; with Compleat Tables of All Steps Us'd in Dancing, and Rules for the Motions of the Arms, &C. Whereby Any Person (Who Understands Dancing) May of Himself Learn All Manner of Dances.* London: Printed by H. Meere at the Black Fryar in Black Fryar for the author and are to be sold by P. Valliant French bookseller near Catherine Street in the Strand, 1706.

Wheeler, Roxann. *The Complexion of Race: Categories of Difference in Eighteenth-Century British Culture.* Philadelphia: University of Pennsylvania Press, 2000.

Whorton, James C. *Crusaders for Fitness: The History of American Health Reformers.* Princeton, N.J.: Princeton University Press, 1982.

Wong, Yutian. *Choreographing Asian America.* Middletown, CT: Wesleyan University Press, 2010.

Index